A GRAVER
DANGER

WHITE CHALK CRIME™
The Stunning First-Ever Explanation for School Shootings
& How We End Them

KAREN HORWITZ, M.Ed.

Amazon.com & other booksellers

Paperback: 979-8-89079-208-2
Ebook: 979-8-89079-209-9
Audiobook: 979-8-89079-210-5

Independently Published*

*If you are reading this book years from 2024 and are shocked to hear about White Chalk Crime,™ this book will still be relevant. You must read this book if you do not know about teacher abuse and the crime it hides. If you are perplexed as to why this nation elected a dangerous, mentally ill, con artist for president, read this book.

I dedicate this book to the hero educators blowing the whistle on White Chalk Crime™ for almost three decades. Caring deeply about children and our democracy, they refuse to give up despite the costs, which have included teaching careers for most. They are too many to introduce, but not enough to be heard given the power of White Chalk Crime.™

I dedicate this book to Laura, my friend and one of the few teachers who taught me new skills in the counterfeit school where we met. She was one of the best teachers I ever knew. Despite being my friend for years, she never joined my whistleblowing group because she needed to work. Unlike me, she chose the silent path. The abuse she encountered due to her magnificent skills led to an early death. May she rest in the peace she never had as one dedicated to teaching.

I dedicate this book to NAPTA's angel, Frankie Bailey, who has been our volunteer webmaster for 22 years and made this all possible. The website has been crucial for locating silenced and whistleblowing teachers. Since new members kept sharing their stories of abuse, giving up was impossible.

Last but not least, I dedicate this book to my husband and partner, Jeff, who has had to hear about the crime in our schools for three decades. He has generously supported my work in every way, while others had no idea that our schools were about to implode our democracy.

I make these dedications with the hope that this book will produce the noise needed to pierce the privileged protection of the all-powerful democracy thieves in our schools and shine a light on the public officials, the media, and our courts, who have failed to do anything about harmful wrongdoing. Their time needs to be up, so our democracy's time isn't up!

As a thank you for buying this book and joining our grassroots movement to end school shootings at EndSchoolShootings.com, you can request a free PDF of the Enhanced Ebook version of this book, which includes this book as well as an abridged version of my 2008 book, *White Chalk Crime: The REAL Reason Schools Fail.*

CONTENTS

ABOUT THE AUTHOR vii

HOW TO READ THIS BOOK xi

PREFACE. xv

PROLOGUE xix

INTRODUCTION xxix

Chapter 1: Adrift in a Bipartisan Swamp. 1

Chapter 2: The End of Normal. 16

Chapter 3: The Take Down of Teacher Influencers. 29

Chapter 4: Democracy's Bones 40

Chapter 5: You Don't Have to Just Take it From Me 55

Chapter 6: Counterfeit Schools 74

Chapter 7: The Essence of Teacher Abuse 96

Chapter 8: Why WCCrime is So Hard to Grasp 108

Chapter 9: Democracy - A Closer Look 132

Chapter 10: FINALLY, the Why Behind School Shootings -
            WCCrime's Miserable Curse 150

Chapter 11: Why a Book? 168

Chapter 12: Media Illiteracy. 182

Chapter 13: What I Do: My 1995 Manifesto 193

Chapter 14: I Knew We'd Lose It Back Then. 237

Chapter 15: Visions - for Visionary Schools 248

Chapter 16: Meet the Future - After WCCrime. 283

Chapter 17: Deep State or Dumb State? 292

Chapter 18: Make Schools Right to Make our
             Nation Right 306

AN ADDITIONAL DOSE OF INSIGHT. 311

EPILOGUE: COURT-ASSISTED,
END OF A TEACHER STORY 319

A POEM: Trying Everything to be Heard 339

CONCLUSION. 343

TAKE ACTION FOR DEMOCRACY
& THANK YOU 349

ENDNOTES 353

When I included segments from my 2008 book, I kept the links to the no longer available online reference sources for you to see that I had sourced all the data in my prior book.

In the "References" section available at https://www.whitechalk-crime.com/references/, I included a page with online links to White Chalk Crime™ that has occurred since the 2008 book was published. They validate that White Chalk Crime™ has not stopped and will not stop unless we, the people, demand that it does. This will never happen if you do not educate yourself about it.

ABOUT THE AUTHOR

Karen Horwitz graduated with honors from Oak Park River Forest High School in Oak Park, Illinois, and earned a BA with honors in elementary education from the University of Illinois, Champaign, Illinois. She felt a calling to share her gifts for preparing children to become successful students and citizens.

In 1975, teaching jobs were scarce. She became a marketing director for an educational film company. Since teaching was her passion, she earned an M.Ed. in Reading at National Louis University in 1992 and returned to teaching. She soon discovered White Chalk Crime™ and blew the whistle on it. Thus, a talented kid whisperer became a pariah in the world of White Chalk Criminals. Her district concocted charges against her and terminated her. Tenure did not matter.

She raised three children. Her four grandchildren and her new great-grandson inspire her to expose education's nasty secret. She believes all children deserve better—much better. As long as we live in a democracy, she will not stop blowing the whistle on White Chalk Crime.™ Hence, this is her third book on it.

Her school board admitted she was an excellent teacher. They hatched the following charges to justify terminating her:

1. Refusal to give them all copies of her audio tape of a meeting that proved the principal of her school was harming children. She refused with pride. The tape, still in her possession, exists in a vacuum where no one with power has bothered to do their job to protect this nation, thus

allowing toxic leaders to hijack our democracy and erase the former democracy influencers and supporters—our teachers.

2. Refusal to undergo psychological testing. The Board ordered her to see the school's psychiatrist, and he found that if she kept "imagining" harassment, she would need psychological testing. She filed federal lawsuits—including age discrimination and First Amendment—against the district. The Board deemed these lawsuits as her "imagining harassment" and thus ordered psychological testing. State law mandated that only a physician could order psychological testing. Since a school board, not a physician, ordered the testing, she refused to obey the unlawful order. Nevertheless, the courts found their unlawful order grounds for termination despite the law saying otherwise.

She thought the courts would protect our children. She was wrong. She remains determined to teach the public the truth about education, not available elsewhere, which explains why our democracy is imploding.

The principal lied, falsely telling Mrs. Horwitz's students that she was sick. Unaware that the district had ordered her teacher to stay home, one of her anxious 5th-grade students wrote a piece for the class newspaper (see below). Since children should not be pawns in a reprehensible game, she became a whistleblower.

What's Wrong?

by ▮▮▮▮▮▮▮▮

Everybody has been worried, frantic, and scared that the 5th grade teacher, Mrs. Horwitz, has been sick for the past 4 weeks, or is just waiting for the school doctors to okay her to come back to school. I hope that she is all right and that she will come back very soon. I think that the whole class and school has been worried for her, and wants her to come back, but I think that I am the most worried. The reason is that she has taught me the best because she has gotten deep down to my thoughts to teach me the best (meaning that she taught everyone by their own personal needs, and not by her needs, like other teachers do). I think that she tries to get to everyone that way. That is why I think that she is a very good teacher. From all of the classes that I have been to, I know that Mrs. Horwitz has taught me the most. Since I have had her for two years, she started teaching 5th grade this year, I feel that I am very attached to her. She doesn't really feel like a teacher anymore; she feels more like a friend, because she has gotten me through tough times, and I am very thankful for that. I bet that you think I'm just saying this because she's gone, huh? Well, I have proof that I am telling the truth. Do you think that I would request and go out of my way to write a note saying that I wanted to stay in her class for the 5th grade also, just to write this article? I think not. So now you know what happened, and you're not totally clueless. I think that I have done my job here, so, see you next time around.

Day After Day

by ▮▮▮▮▮▮▮▮

This week has to be the most busy week since Mrs. Horwitz's unknown sickness. It is Tuesday, May 12th, 1998. Yesterday, the whole 5th grade went to Marie Murphy for the 5th grade orientation, because this 5th grade will be going to Marie Murphy next year. We got assigned a 6th grade partner to show us around. Some of the teachers talked to us before we met our buddies, though, telling us what we'd be doing. So, when we got our partners, we went and got our lunch. After lunch, we had recess. After recess, the sixth graders showed us around the school, and every room in the 6th grade wing.

HOW TO READ THIS BOOK

I wrote this book in a way that addresses different learning styles and accommodates busy lives. Below is how this paperback book differs from the enhanced ebook version.

The paperback book is the same as Part One of the enhanced ebook. It is a memoir of a devoted, once-shattered teacher and a bridge connecting you to why this topic is essential. It is new. It compellingly connects education and democracy, explaining so much, from school shootings and social influencers' disproportionate effect on our children to how Trump happened and what we need to do to bring back normalcy.

Soon to be available as an audiobook, it speaks to all and needs to be read by all. It contains my thoughts and experiences as a teacher who didn't fit in the system called to maintain our democracy.

Part Two, in the enhanced ebook only, is a quick way to learn what White Chalk Crime™ is and has done to our society I call QuickNotes. It is a new, fast, straightforward explanation.

Part Three, in the enhanced ebook only, are the lessons from my past book. The history of my books helps explain:

My 2008 book, an exposé on the lawlessness in our schools that spoke to reporters and public officials, was monstrously long so it could also contain the voices of 140 other called-to-teach educators. It had the receipts—other teachers' and mine. I wrote it for Oprah and investigative reporters, not the mass market. It reads like a college textbook/legal brief. It's dense and scholarly. It was a weighty tome. I hoped an investigative reporter would take over my job. No one did.

I then published an abridged version of my 2008 book in 2019, designed for parents and citizens, knowing reporters could access the 2008 book to hear more voices. Part Three of the enhanced ebook is the lesson section of the 2019 book. It's an abridged version of the lessons written in 2008, so you'll know this has been happening for decades, and those in power could have stopped this crime.

Part Four, in the enhanced ebook, contains my 2008 memoir, *Court-Assisted, End of a Teacher Story*, about my journey starting with discovering what I was up against through my teacher's termination hearing to dealing with our highest court. The enhanced ebook includes the entire 2008 memoir; a portion of it is the Epilogue in the paperback book.

In the enhanced ebook, Part Five is my poem expressing the loss of real schools for those to whom poetry speaks. Although not denoted as Part Five in the paperback, it is found after the Epilogue and before the Conclusion.

In my commitment to make this book work for busy lives, I included the REFERENCES online at WhiteChalkCrime.com—endnotes, appendices, current links to crime in our schools, and the bibliography.

Some documents are also online. For instance, there is a meaningful, long document showing what the union knew and did nothing about while conspiring with the state to keep my record from me. I hope investigative reporters will contact me for whatever they need to prove that this crime is alive and well while democracy isn't. I have safeguarded the receipts!

I am reaching out to others via words that work for them. Some will read it all. Most will get what they need to do by reading the paperback book or listening to the audiobook, which is also Part One of the enhanced ebook. Investigative reporters will need the documentation in Part Three of the enhanced ebook. I offer choices so citizens will learn about this crime and join a movement to end it.

Read to the extent you love democracy while there's still time to protect it. If Trump is elected, he will follow the autocratic playbook and dismantle democracy. If you value democracy, secure a copy of this book before it's too late. An autocrat can and will control what you read and access online. He will mold our schools to breed obedient followers. He will cement the injustice that led many to support him. And if so, I will end my mission to expose our schools since missions like mine are part of a democracy. I will stop my democratic work when I, along with you, no longer live in a democracy and no longer have a voice.

You may support Trump while I do not, but the state of our schools is a matter on which we can agree. I am one of the few never-Trump people who understand why some very good people like him. He can out-bully the bullies running our schools, whereas someone like me has spent twenty-nine years and made little progress.

I plan for this book to eliminate the need for a grenade-like human for president. We need authentic schools in order to live with different values and opinions in a mutually beneficial community. Once called-to-teach teachers become powerful, America can be a sanctuary rather than a powder keg—my goal. I do this work, so we don't need to elect a bully.

(If you have also purchased my 2008 or 2019 book, please get in touch with me at WhiteChalkCrime.com for a free PDF of *A Graver Danger* Enhanced Ebook.)

PREFACE

"The truth will set you free, but first it will make you miserable."

James A. Garfield

In 1993, a school district with accolades that attracted the upper echelons of society hired me, Karen Horwitz, a called-to-teach teacher, to teach fourth grade. Many parents told me I was the best teacher their child ever had. But because our schools had lost their way, I was a square peg in a round hole. My success with children was proportional to my failure with the leadership in place. Six years later, they terminated me using trumped-up charges but failed to terminate my calling.

They didn't know I was born Karen Graver. They didn't know that a calling has a reverse side, which, in my case, came alive as a never-going-to-give-up activist and is taking you on an eye-opening journey inside our schools never before available for reasons you'll learn.

People have it all wrong when it comes to our schools. An assumed-to-be outstanding school ended my career for speaking out. They terminated a person who knows this: what's going on in our schools is a graver danger to democracy than anything, and that anything includes Trump, a force our lousy schools put into motion.

Our fraud-filled schools brought us Trump, what you will learn by reading this book. They made too many people shallow thinkers rather than critical thinkers and too many people narcissists rather than citizens. These cynical opportunists exchanged our once all-American aspiration for expertise with a drive for personal ambition. Celebrity replaced substance; self-service replaced public service.

When I retired, my goal was to have helped several hundred children realize their potential. When they terminated me, my goal became to alert several million people about our schools. The MAGA followers are right. There is a deep state. I know. I worked for it. I intend to be the gravest possible danger to the white-collar crime mixed with mind-boggling incompetence that I call White Chalk Crime™—a way of life in our schools.

You've heard of teachers ranging from Mary Kay Letourneau, who married her preteen student, to Catholic nuns, who never married. No one has ever met a teacher like me, and those running our schools did everything they could, so you never would. This book is your chance to spend time with a teacher who knows how we can protect our children from school shootings and save our democracy. It offers you an insider's view from the passenger seat of my car.

In addition to the why behind our school shooting epidemic, you will learn what really goes on in our schools and why you don't know what really goes on in our schools. You will understand why our nation is so polarized, why we elected Trump, and how we lost the truth. You will meet the kind of teaching we could have but mostly don't have. And why education reform never worked and how we can absolutely make it work.

Along with offering a visionary plan to fix our schools, this book will teach you who we can't rely on to make transformation happen while giving you a massive dose of hope for our schools and democracy.

You will learn why no other book—no other person—gives you the truth about our schools as I do. It took an insider, which means someone willing to be fired. It required activating my inner warrior and some uncommon tenacity that must be part of my born-to-teach birth package, given its over-the-top, never-give-up on a student level. No ordinary person could take on this power-house. You will see that it demanded legal, journalistic, writing, technology skills, and, most of all, good old American guts, democracy's precious resource.

It took courage to be the first to do what no one else wanted to do. Like the actress who caused Harvey Weinstein's demise, there is always a first. It takes a combination of intestinal forti-tude and spiritual urging. The former helps you do it, while the latter makes you do it.

Do you feel frightened and guilty when your child comes home from school telling you about their active shooter drill. Do you wonder why children no longer can expect better lives than their parents? Are you worried about America? Are you thinking of moving to another country? Do you feel called to teach but not in the schools we have? Does everything feel unstable, and would you like to understand why?

This book will answer all those questions plus give you hope that we can bring back children achieving more than their parents again. It offers a path for our nation to find the civility it once had and an opportunity for you to play a role in making that happen.

I knew what needed to be done in 1995. Still, I cofounded an organization to locate others to verify that I was right. After "meeting" over 2,200 others who ranged from thrilled to find my organization to not committing suicide since they discovered it, I began this journey that will only stop when our president knows what I know—or if Trump wins.

This book tells you what really happened to America while carving a glorious path back to the country we once loved. It encourages you to join a movement to make this happen, which you can do at: http://www.endteacherabuse.org/MemForm/MembershipForm.html

PROLOGUE

"The truth will set you free, but first it will make you miserable."

James A. Garfield

Whenever a forlorn pundit asks what happened to our country—a more than daily event—I feel like screaming the answer through the television. Because I can't, I wrote a book. Our overrun-with-fraud dysfunctional schools are what happened to our country!

This book is a never-before-offered odyssey through our schools, where you'll discover things you could never have imagined, unknown to you for reasons you also could never have imagined.

I was a teacher. Without a doubt, being a teacher is an under-the-bus career. Many, if not most, running our schools, the media, and the courts keep teachers under the bus for reasons you will soon learn. Since I'm more of a Rosa Parks type regarding buses, you will finally learn the truth about our schools.

School massacres are the tip of an iceberg that's been slowly destroying our democracy. Ponder this: Women's liberation opened the floodgates about fifty years ago. Women could finally choose professions once only available to men. Education lost. Since then, it has become like sports teams with only a few great athletes—not the same.

Up to that point, most brilliant women automatically became teachers since it was the only choice for all but a handful of women. Yet, no one in education leadership thought to do a thing about how education was careening downhill due to that loss then or now. The lingering inability to recognize the need to compensate for a monumental sociological change proves that no one leading education can be trusted.

Hence, the persistent absence of effective educational leadership due to the sparse batch of available talent, diminished regard for education, and a clandestine takeover rife with mafia-like tactics about which you'll soon learn subverted the very purpose of education.

The institution, which was intended to serve as the bedrock and defender of democracy, reduced our children to pawns of a dangerous system and almost half of our voters into wanting a reality show rather than a presidency. Our schools' war against expertise and ethics started when limited, selfish minds took them over. It will only end when brilliant, generous minds take our schools back. The latter will not happen without you!

When discussing Trump less than six months before the 2024 election, a reporter who had extensively interviewed Trump for his book about the Celebrity Apprentice spectacle found Trump forgetful and shallow, not presidency material; Nicole Wallace, a former Republican, now television host, who expresses daily angst about the state of our union, and Donny Deutsch, a marketing expert who usually has it all figured out, were all stumped as to why half this country would want to elect an empty shell of a person as their president. Deutsch said: What's wrong with us? How did we get here? What the hell happened to us? All three wore a silent look of terror.

This book answers his questions. My question is: How do I get this book to Donny Deutsch? I need him to help me market what we need to do to reawaken American brains.

For sure, you won't hear this elsewhere. Those presently in charge of our schools choose to subject children to the trauma of active shooter drills rather than forfeit the power and perks they now enjoy. And those subjected to these power mongers' wrath, should they speak out, do what most powerless people do—nothing. This book, a whistleblowing teacher's memoir, explains and documents the hollowing out of our schools and answers: What happened to America?

This book doesn't just tell you why we have an epidemic of children being massacred at our schools, even though that explanation is worthy of a book. Our schools are corrupt. It's not ordinary corruption. It's compounded corruption. It's a unique, devastating corruption you must learn about. Every day, corruption brings down businesses and organizations. The corruption that has taken over our schools, which I call White Chalk Crime™ [WCCrime], is taxpayer-supported. Thus, it erases natural consequences and allows this institution to stand firm despite utter failure. It has metastasized into our daily lives and produced a hopelessly polarized culture.

Once you understand WCCrime, you'll understand why our presidents may have been clueless about it and, thus, failed to stop it. It's fraud with equal parts of ignorance. It is the beneficiary of an entirely unknown cover-up of a magnitude never before seen. Although it feels like democracy let us down, our schools took democracy down by becoming a breeding ground for divisiveness and superficiality rather than citizenship and intelligence. This book shows what happens in our schools, so you'll understand why democracy is crumbling. Soon, you'll wonder how these inept, lawless schools held society together as long as they did.

Many people are outraged. They think our past administrations have been corrupt. Thus, they're agreeing to hand over our democracy to one man, Hitler-style. They're so irate and so convinced both political parties are corrupt that they're ignoring the following unsigned poem aimlessly wandering on the internet, filled with undeniable wisdom:

It's so simple. I don't know why people don't get it.
A man with a pattern of cheating his customers, vendors, and
business partners is going to cheat you.
A man who's casually betrayed his wives,
Again and again, will casually betray you.
A man who lies all the time is lying to you.
A man who has spent his entire life screwing people
is going to do the exact same thing to you.

Our schools obscured the obvious. Were these administrations
corrupt? No one knows for sure, but I know for sure that our
education system has been corrupt for decades, and all of our
administrations have done nothing about it. A solid education
is a lifeline. Denying it has left many people without one—lost
and resentful. Our schools are the real reason so many people
are hostile. Since what's going on in our schools is unknowable,
they're following anyone who says there's something very wrong
since there IS something very wrong.

Our schools are in a deep state of corruption and, thus, fatally
deficient. They ARE the hidden deep state that so many want to
end! The act and the outcome of letting us down in education
is the source of an unsettling suspicion that conjures up a deep
state since it lies deep within. That's why the exact words of one
of the concerned pundits who must read this book: "We have no
calm and agreed-upon truth to unite our fragile country," made
me want to yell the following even louder: We do—our schools.

We must unravel the answer to what happened to this country
from the tangled mess our government allowed in our schools—
the purpose of this book. It must become a counter-vision against
Project 2025, the authoritarian playbook for ending our democracy and taking away our freedom.

One of Project 2025's stated goals is to back state education
leaders. After you read this book and see what my state education
leaders did to me, an award-winning teacher, you'll know what a
horror that will be. Another is to institutionalize Christian nation-
alism, which includes having our government control women's

bodies and other soon-to-come surprises despite a vast majority against that. Undeniable proof our schools failed us—stole our ability to think critically—is the following: Project 2025, with its sinister agenda, has been able to see the light of day!

Even those with conservative values must question the integrity of a plan that denies freedoms that over half of our citizens value and expands the power to our president when they're planning to hand over that power to a cognitively impaired, mentally ill, dangerous, convicted felon and sexual assaulter of women who called for the execution of disloyal staffers.

If Project 2025 had merit, it would have been shelved until a conservative person of integrity took office. The fact that he is neither ethical nor conservative exposes Project 2025 as neither. Only vicious, greedy souls would give a person like Trump all that power. Therefore, all ethical citizens, whether conservative or liberal, must think critically and counter Project 2025; this book provides a blueprint. Ending democracy is Project 2025's vision; reviving democracy must be ours.

Democracy is the only path to compromise. Decent people with divergent values want to compromise. Indecent people want to take away freedom from those with different values. We need to fix our democracy, not end it and make half this country miserable. Only evil-minded people would want that! The MAGA vision would not have widespread support if Americans understood why democracy fell apart and that there was a solution to restore it.

When we find our answer to why our presidents from both parties have allowed education to become entirely dysfunctional, we'll know who's to blame for leaving so many people ill-prepared for life and why we became open to electing Trump, an icon for a lost democracy. Sticking with the status quo and its deep state of inferior education is not a counterforce to Project 2025! Instead, it will help dig its foundation.

This book has the answer as to who and what stole education and left our country a mess. It shows how we lost our way. Once known, the facts about education, a most unstudied but essential discipline, help explain why so many presidents may have missed this. The only way we'll know if our leaders are evil or whether their ignorance allowed evil is if the truths in this book become public.

I'm a human bridge. I'm 100% against electing a person like Trump as president, but I'm 100% on the same page that there's a deep state of corruption that needs a disrupter. This book describes that deep state in detail, and although I believe this deep state of corruption exists due to ignorance, once this book goes viral, based on how our leaders respond, we will all know whether it's an intentionally corrupted deep state or an unintentional, lamentable mistake. Even if you see Trump as the solution for this country, please read this book written by a person who understands why you do, a rare soul, and see if you still do once you meet the actual deep state of corruption.

Democracy means compromise, which is what our schools used to teach. Citizens learn the value of accepting a combination of happiness and unhappiness. The over 900-page chilling transition plan, Project 2025, which says abortion is not healthcare even when doctors find it necessary, big oil and gas interests will regain center stage as it ends the transition to clean energy and the climate initiative that was to roll back protections against climate change, will definitely make over half of our citizens miserable.

And the price that less than half of this country will pay to suppress liberal views—some views that over 60% of this nation favor—will be far higher than they can imagine. Ask anyone from an authoritarian country about that cost, which includes disconnection from family members who disagree.

At the same time, even if we protect democracy from the candidate who wants to see it end, democracy will continue to implode if we don't address WCCrime. The existence of Project 2025 confirms that! To save our democracy, read this book and become part of a movement to get our leaders to read it. Both sides need to read this book. That's the only way to return to a democracy that works for all.

And for those willing to give up freedom to squelch liberal ideas, which is Project 2025's agenda, they will not only miss their freedom. In time, they will tire of living in a hostile country that rewards almost half and depresses the other half, mainly when all the peasants, including them, don't count. A despotic government only allows some powerful, wealthy leaders; many powerful wealthy types end up dead. Once we give up democracy, we won't be citizens; we will be pawns for the powerful and wealthy. It was our schools, not political parties, not our leaders, that stopped making us more. This book will help redirect your anger to the actual deep state.

A democracy means compromise. Our democracy stopped working because of our corrupted schools. We need to fix our schools to make our country great again. It's uncertain why our leaders let it happen. Still, their failure to act on a demoralized education system is their fault. This book allows them to rectify their massive error. Please read it before you decide what to do about how America is falling apart.

More significantly, ALL presidents have failed us when it comes to education, including the presidential candidate who wants to erase democracy and handle this country himself. During his four years, he was either oblivious to or participated in WCCrime; thus, he's no better than any of our prior leaders regarding the deep state!

Since our education system is the root cause of corruption, we must have a leader who knows how to repair education. That has yet to happen because our education leaders, the people our presidents depend on for advice, have turned education into an incubator for stupidity and incivility, causing too many people to want to get even rather than to get along. I have the answer to how we can make America great again. We must bring back authentic schools.

We have one-half of America thinking we need a man lacking values and mental health to save this nation, and another half thinking we can go on with leadership that has caused our lifelines to keep shrinking. Both are wrong, but the one trying to save democracy has my vote but not my confidence. We won't save democracy until the truth about education needing significant systemic changes drives our government's decision-making, with the exposure and elimination of WCCrime at the top of that list.

Even though being a teacher is an under-the-bus career, you won't regret spending time hearing what this teacher has to say since this teacher has a solution for the chaos stealing our joy and the hollowing out of our schools and answers the question: What happened to America?

When more people understand WCCrime—particularly our public servants—we can save democracy. Once citizens discover that gifted teachers, those who promote growth, are pariahs to the incompetents and WCCriminals running our schools, who promote groveling, they'll understand how school shootings blossomed and democracy broke down. Rather than producing citizens, this toxic brew given free run of our schools has created distrust of government so deep that most have lost their way. Learning about our schools will help Americans find their way back.

Trust is democracy's glue. Low trust is its undoing. Since the institution that was to engender trust pulled a bait-and-switch on us, we've become unglued. This book will help a chunk of people who lined up behind a polarizing figure because they've had enough begin to understand what they've had enough of, so they can line up behind a group of dedicated teachers who know how hollow our schools are but have been powerless to do anything about them. This powerlessness kept teachers from doing democracy's job.

This book explains why so many people are right to be mad. I understand why many support Trump despite angering their friends and family, who they think should also be angry. Since they know they're right that our leaders have let us down, they are following anyone who'll take them elsewhere. However, operating from anger about an unknown problem opens the door for a dictator.

Our leaders have allowed evil people to take away our most precious commodity—our schools. This book will explain how this happened and help everyone understand why. It will mend families and friendships because people who chose Trump are right on one level. There's something very wrong in this country. However, picking a person lacking civility and morality to solve it is a terrible choice. It makes the other half equally mad.

Once the people who despise Trump learn that this battle over Trump is partially between people who know something is wrong but don't know what but insist on doing something about it versus people willing to stick with the leaders who let it happen, we can solve this problem together. This book will educate both sides.

MAGA haters must learn that not all MAGA followers are racists. I know because so many people dedicated to teaching voted for Trump due to what our government has allowed in our schools. Unlike Charlottesville, there are good people on both sides. However, MAGA followers must learn that Trump was one of the presidents who did nothing about our corrupt schools, so he is not the solution for a verified reason well beyond the valid points that anti-Trump people hold.

This book identifies the problem so we can solve it together. It's a call to action. It starts with: I won't judge your solution because I understand why WCCrime alienated us. WCCrime's hidden nature scattered us rather than helped us work together to solve it.

Some sinister people stole our schools from us, and our leaders let it happen. You will learn how this happened and how to solve it. You will discover that it's partly understandable and partly evil. It's been entirely bipartisan. Even though the Democrats' tie with the union seems to put all the blame on Democrats, both parties lost their way when it comes to our schools

Please educate yourself about WCCrime so we can stand together with the good people whose votes are for anyone but the individuals who allowed our schools to deteriorate to this extent. Let's work together toward restoring schools that foster democracy rather than schools that divide us.

INTRODUCTION

"The truth will set you free, but first it will make you miserable."

James A. Garfield

"The price good men pay for indifference to public affairs is to be ruled by evil men."

Plato

"Education is not the filling of a pail, but the lighting of a fire."

William Butler Yeats

You may have noticed that I used the exact quote several times: the truth makes you miserable. It was intentional. I was preparing you for the sad truth about our schools—that they have been cheating all of us for decades now. It will set you free from feeling hopeless about our schools.

I want this to be my last book. After many people lost a lot of money due to Bernie Madoff's sinister actions, a whistleblower, who no one listened to, wrote the book *No One Listened*. This whistleblower, yours truly, is authoring a book to inspire action and awareness that will end school massacres and help to not end democracy, while praying that a book like he wrote will not be necessary.

Most people think it's impossible to reform our schools. I know differently. The truth is there are people intentionally making reform impossible. I'll introduce you to them so you can help exile them and watch reform begin. However, those introductions will come later.

You might be surprised that insight about reforming our schools starts with the Kardashians. Their overwhelming success is a red flag that our schools are failing us. In reality, they aren't society's first social influencers. Their accomplishment is that they have shifted "influencing" from expanding our minds, what teachers used to do, to expanding our desire for status and material objects. By making admirers feel inferior, they get them to buy and watch more. They did this by becoming celebrities, the most powerful influencers in society since the beginning of time.

They are hugely successful. But all, including the master marketer, Mom K, are unaware of the unknown force that left the influencing field wide open for the moral teardown that began with the meteoric inertia of her daughter's sex tape. And as far as I, a non-reality TV person, know, the jury is out whether Mom K used the pornographic tape by design or whether it was a grenade thrown at her. I know that a scandal that altered our nation's moral compass triumphed because schools had lost their way.

Outstanding teachers used to engage our children's minds—get them to love learning, use their talents, and feel good about themselves. They stirred their passion to make this a better world. They were our influencers. My fourth-grade teacher, Mrs. Rakove—yes, decades later, I remember her name—used a contest to turn us on to ancient history. She got me reading nonfiction, my penchant to this day!

When we shifted from democracy influencers to social media influencers and switched focus to breast size, glitzy makeup, and nail glue, society became unglued. Social influencers make billions on things that make women not feel less than others while pulling the curtain on moral, practical, and traditional community ideals.

Most have given the birth of social media too much credit for this societal swing because they don't know what I know. As a replaced influencer, I recognize the force that altered who would reign supreme in the world of influencers.

It was a very organized white-collar crime fused with rampant incompetence in our schools, what I call WCCrime, committed by WCCriminals who hijacked our schools, turning many, if not most, into criminal enterprises. They forged fertile grounds for school shootings and muzzled those who influenced for the sake of democracy. The WCCriminals' agenda is as incompatible with public service as gangsters are with the Girl Scouts.

The Kardashian way uses branding to replace substance. In Donald Trump's 2022 legal deposition, he said branding got him the presidency. It did. Branding is taking over, using popularity and manipulation rather than natural talent and quality. It wins over people with words and influence rather than substance.

Branding has replaced the authentic skills and talents that schools were supposed to instill in people. It creates unearned celebrity status. Elizabeth Taylor was beautiful. Social influencers get you to see them as beautiful, and branders get you to view their mediocre minds as brilliant.

A teacher's job is to help you not be conned—to help you think critically. It outlaws fantastical thinking—what's common-place of late. Critical thinking is the kiss of death to branding. It means thinking for yourself, deeming you a much more chal-lenging sales target. You won't find critical thinkers in a cult or most schools today. Mediocre minds now run the education show, and a show it is.

The replacement of teacher influencers is more apparent when you accept that the school's job of getting children to learn what they do not want to know is formidable. Children may like their teachers, but most have little to no interest in the subjects taught. Most dislike them. Nevertheless, great teachers get children to learn, helping them achieve balance.

Schools serve vegetables, the healthy disciplines of life, while television and social media serve desserts. If it were up to children, you know what they'd take a pass on. Once, spinster teachers pounded the multiplication table into our heads, paving the way for an easier life. Then, teachers added that spoonful of sugar to make the lessons go down.

Unlike candy and cake, vegetables are not fun to eat the first time, but they keep us healthy and alive. Schools help develop a taste for healthy subjects and thoughts, keeping our minds fit and well-functioning.

Television and the internet are the dessert table of life; few will reject the delicious goodies and eat only the fruit, akin to staying off the internet and only watching public television. So, our schools need to be where we get our mental vegetables that foster stability.

Instead, those leading schools, with profiles ranging from shallow to criminal, serve up something worse than dessert. We have over-processed, high-fructose creations without the institution used to maintain our mental fitness.

We know the feeling of overeating dessert. Imagine that sensation guiding your brain's decision-making. That describes how so many people make decisions these days. When we had real schools, we educated enough citizens to keep a democracy functioning.

Our phony schools, staffed with WCCriminals and their puppets—too many zombielike, battered teachers—have ended our democracy's sane balance. We've always had bad guys in government, but we've also had good guys to cope and correct. Because of corrupted schools, we've lost equilibrium.

Making matters worse, social media's rise coupled with our schools not properly preparing our children, has led to other pressing issues. An article NPR published in June 2024 entitled "'An Unfair Fight' The U.S. Surgeon General Declares War on Social Media"[1] said:

> Vivek Murthy, U.S. surgeon general has taken action on the problem of suicides due to social media in an op ed he published in *The New York Times* calling for warning labels on

social media similar to those on cigarettes and alcohol. His goal is to alert young people of the danger social media poses to their mental well-being and development. He cites the success of the tobacco and alcohol labels, which have discouraged consumption…Part of Murthy's guidance includes keeping children off of social media platforms until their critical thinking skills have had more time to grow and strengthen against what the algorithms might be showing them.

He's not the only expert warning of this danger. There are dozens of books talking about this anxious generation and the increase in suicides. With the schools we have, the learning of critical thinking is no guarantee. It is likely to be insufficient if it occurs at all. Thus, self-inflicted death also hovers over our children as they participate in active school shooter drills in our inept schools. This makes reading this book even more miserable but also more urgent.

The surgeon general is calling for these written warnings, unaware of WCCrime. If he knew the extent of dysfunction WCCrime is causing in our schools, he'd want those labels on our school doors! Instead, this book is the only warning that parents must take proper action.

Whereas parents can regulate their children's exposure to social media—okay, I admit that's impossible as a former parent, so I take that back. However, they can join a movement to end WCCrime—the hidden force incompatible with child safety and proper learning—to ensure their children learn to think critically. Teachers and other caring educators, and even our surgeon general, are powerless to combat it as long as WCCrime prevails, which is what this book aims to prove. Shortly thereafter, he announced a similar campaign against guns' effects on health, emphasizing children's exposure to them at schools.

What WCCrime has done to our children is enough for most to become part of a movement to end it. What it has done to our country takes that to a place that questions why anyone with a working brain would decide they are too busy to read this book.

Our education system is the root cause of most of what's wrong with our country. And there's a lot! So, for many, Trump is the path to soothe this discomforting imbalance. They are correct. He will change the balance. They will stop feeling like they are up in the air on a symbolic scale of justice. But the price for electing him rather than figuring out how to get our footing back will end democracy. And anyone who's studied history cannot come up with one worthy dictator.

I've read that many adored Saddam Hussein before he became brutal—a typical autocrat trajectory. History shows democracy as flawed but our best bet. A chunk of society that has not eaten its history vegetables in years is choosing a dictator. Choosing him as the solution, coupled with many government officials in power for their own sake, is an end-of-life state of affairs for democracy.

Many well-educated people have also decided that an authoritarian is better than what we have. They lost faith in democracy. A May 2024 opinion piece in *The New York Times*, "Trump Embraces Lawlessness, but in the Name of a Higher Law," by Matthew Schmitz, corroborates this. This author says, "When the authorities are regarded as corrupt and malevolent, people will celebrate those who defy them."

Respect for a failing education system is another component of the democracy equation that suggests corruption to many. Doing nothing to compensate for the loss of bright women after women's liberation sent women in any direction other than education indicates either ignorance about the need for intelligent teachers or an intention to dumb down our schools.

Schools broke their trust in our system long before the rigged election lie did. That lie was the straw that broke the camel's back. There is no better path for restoring their faith than figuring out what went wrong in our schools.

Up until now, it's been in no one's financial or political interest to admit they failed with our schools. That's why it's taken me so long to expose the crime that has devoured education and, thus, democracy. The fact that influential people avoid these truths screams to Trump's followers that democracy is the problem.

I get that. But I see things differently. This lesson is too big, too unbelievable, and too challenging to grasp. Thomas A. Edison said, "Opportunity is missed by most people because it is dressed in overalls and looks like work."

I can mention it to a stellar public figure, and he'll not take the time to absorb it. He'll work hard to save our democracy in ways he thinks will help. It's not greed that misguides him. It is the work it takes to learn what has happened to our schools. The number of people participating in WCCrime out of greed is small, but their effect is catastrophic.

In my 2008 book, I warned that WCCrime could end democracy. I all but warned of a Trump-like figure filling democracy's secret gap. The real genius of those running our schools, whom I called EducRAT$, no explanation needed, is their skill at getting people like you not to listen to people like me.

In 2010, Dr. Jill Biden responded to my emails but has yet to follow up. Oprah's researcher called me and has yet to follow up. Union leader Randi Weingarten ignored my work and my emails. Hundreds of other public figures, officials, and reporters have ignored me. Dealing with this is just too hard for most. It's easier to look the other way for those whose only advantage in maintaining the status quo is that exposing this is too hard.

A reporter caught my state violating the law and, with one short call, forced them to render a decision on my improper termination—a decision that they were scheming to deny me. She never followed up. If she had, she could have blown open WCCrime in 2001. Since she and others didn't, regardless of their motive for ignoring WCCrime, our democracy's downward spiral took flight. We're at the edge of a cliff.

I want to remember the context since education is a forever-go-nowhere topic. Nevertheless, ABC reporter Jonathan Karl recently said about education, "It suggests something's wrong with the system." He became one more person who realizes education needs a deep investigation and one more who won't do it.

Trump is a giant flashlight that has shown democracy's cracks by breaking its laws and getting away with it. He's shown us the power of shamelessness when combined with celebrity and money. It takes you to a place outside the law, which has been available to many shameless educators for decades now that celebrity has replaced substance.

Our biggest, most dangerous to democracy crack has been in education. You don't know about it for reasons this book explains. Trump's flashlight has become a torch. We need to come together and fix education's fracture. Read this book like our democracy depends on it because it does. It's worth your time. It will not just help save democracy. It will help end school shootings and make Trumpism and all those awful family and social conflicts over politics go away.

1

ADRIFT IN A BIPARTISAN SWAMP

"Kids don't remember what you try to teach them. They remember what you are."

Jim Henson

"Teaching kids to count is fine, but teaching them what counts is best."

Bob Talbert

"If the child is not learning the way you are teaching, then you must teach in the way the child learns"

Rita Dunn

I will explain later how they do what I am about to say. Still, I promise they do this: administrators curate a mesmerizing reality by turning teachers into three-dimensional mannequins that keep parents from even considering that something terrible is going on.

That's why exposing WCCrime has taken so long. It's not like having nothing else to do kept me on this activist path. I have a tower of books to read. My list of hobbies is extensive.

Since I was six years old, I've been making things, from sewing purses to jewelry, knitting sweaters, and crocheting afghans. I've made curtains, drapes, and pillows for every home I've lived in—twelve of them.

I've even made two stained glass windows. I've done acrylic painting and recently learned watercolor at the same age as Grandma Moses. I sold a watercolor painting—my first creation I sold other than when I was a little kid and sold my jewelry at lemonade stands. So, I'm eager to get back to painting. Then there are the baby gifts I need to knit as our first great-grandchild was just born.

Yet, I've put almost everything aside to get this book done.

I read to figure out why I'm so obsessed with exposing WCCrime when so many interests call me. I sought the answer to why I could follow a belief for three decades when most would have given up years ago.

Biographies have helped me the most. When I got to the inventors, the Geiger counter went off. An impelling idea forced each not to give up. Every inventor struggled with knowing something no one else knew.

I've experienced the dark belly of education. So I know how we can put it back together. And like most people who know something important that no one else knows, I need to get this known. I read about Marie Curie and realized I'm not crazy unless she was crazy.

After reading about her, it was clear. We each had a hunch that drove us to do the work so that our hunches made a difference. I know WCCrime is the missing link for saving democracy the way Marie Curie knew there was a substance that could cure cancer awaiting discovery. She knew: no one else knew what she had figured out. She had to birth her invention. So do I. I have to get around the doubts that will abort it.

The knowing is what won't let me quit. Knowing drove Curie to spend too much time with radium, which killed her. My knowing won't kill me. Not sticking with it will kill democracy.

I'm not saying no one else knew about corruption in our schools or no one knew about teacher abuse and education's low esteem. No one has figured out how to expose what this lethal combination has taken from our nation so we can end it and move education forward. Education must progress from its anyone could do it status to an honored profession, the way law and medicine once did so many years ago that we assume they were always sophisticated professions.

At one time, people read books and became lawyers, mothers treated illnesses, and there were no medical schools. The Industrial Revolution turned antiquated medical practices into much different practices in the eighteenth century. Medicine and law advanced. Education remained an underdeveloped, disrespected, top-down institution. No one revamped its original model: the exploitation of women. Chauvinism blocks intellectualism. It keeps universities from wanting any connection with it. WCCriminals, a perfect fit, invaded.

This book is not just about corruption. It's an idea invention. I'm putting forth an easy way to save democracy. It's essential to read it and get this save-our-democracy invention working before we find ourselves under the rule of a dictator. It crystallizes the story of teacher abuse, the calculated use of psychological terror to squelch resistance used on me and many others, into what it is about and what it accomplished.

It's about WCCrime or uninvestigated acts that insecure, incompetent, sadistic, and greedy imposters inflict upon our children and our country via our schools. There's no good WCCrime. It ranges from bad to worse. Predators posing as caring leaders raid our schools and rob us of teacher influencers.

To understand the essence of WCCrime, picture Donald J. Trump in charge of an extensive school system. He would hire "yes" people rather than competent people. He would focus on arranging kickbacks and embezzling. He would pretend to care about the children's education and safety while being not the least bit interested—as he handled COVID-19, which resulted in hundreds of thousands of tragic, unnecessary deaths. Everything from the textbooks to the lunches would be financial opportunities.

I remember the "horse meat substituted for beef scandal" as a kid. He might take lunches there or even go beyond to a cheaper mammal—bats, non-mammals—something unthinkable to most. He would bully out of the organization those trying to put children first.

While everyone would wear *Children First* pins, children would be last. He would make you think he cares while taking advantage of you in every way that advantages him. Maybe the beef was beef where I taught. Still, they donned their phony pins and spoke about ethics over the loudspeaker at every opportunity, showing they knew putting children first and ethics were good things to pretend to do.

Nothing about schools with WCCrime is democratic. Tyrants run them for their pleasure, money, power, or both. It's no coincidence that I described our current schools using the Trump governing method. Abraham Lincoln prophetically warned, "The philosophy of the school room in one generation, will be the philosophy of government in the next."

Recently, Noah Schachtman co-wrote a Rolling Stones article that exposed how, under Trump's watch, therapists shared federal workers' confidential information with inquiring bosses. He said, "Immediately after counseling sessions, therapists were pressed for information about what they were told." This journalist expressed shock. I'm not at all shocked. Many teachers discovered our administrators knew things only our therapists knew. Abraham Lincoln got a lot of stuff right!

There is a spectrum of WCCriminals. Some break more laws than others, but all fail to educate, protect, and support democracy. Authentic schools are not on their agenda. And they are far less talented con artists. They happened upon an opportunistic niche, an institution missing intellectual thought, loaded with powerless females, so beloved that reporters and judges trust them on autopilot. It's theirs for the taking. The people of moral character around them are the only thing stopping them.

Since experiencing Trump's power grab, you know people with moral character as guardrails against wrongdoing is not a thing. So indulging in WCCrime like a pig in excrement became the way in many, if not most, of our schools. They kept their evil deeds under the radar, using ruthless teacher abuse to cover up their lawlessness. They left a vacuum for the Kardashians and their ilk.

If you watched *Leave It to Beaver*, a popular mid-century TV show, you remember Eddie Haskell. He ingratiated himself with the parents but tormented and bullied "the Beaver" when the parents weren't around. *The Eddie Haskell* effect can be insidious in a workplace because these two-faced bullies can mistreat subordinates without consequences. When the boss is looking, they are always on their best behavior. Regarding our schools, you, the citizens, are the boss. Teachers are like "the Beaver," relentlessly bullied without an escape hatch.

And fame is a currency that is out of reach for teachers. Yet, teacher influencers can have more power over children than parents. I know, having done both. An episode during my early years of teaching proves this.

I led a productive classroom from day one. With each new class, I sold the idea that we were together on a voyage. It was going to make learning both fun and worthwhile. I found the perfect book to teach democracy, a source for my effective discipline. It was called *Just Me*, a book filled with stick figures that taught getting along. Maintaining a democratic classroom was central to how I helped students find their gifts. That book was my bible. No one told me to seek anything like that out. I knew I needed to create unity, having been called to teach, i.e., called to be an influencer.

In my first year of teaching, my second-grade students wholly bought in. One day, they were at their desks working on a writing assignment. A child vomited on her extra absorbent, manilla-lined writing paper. All kept working, including the child with the soiled paper, which wafted the familiar noxious odor soon to envelop our classroom. She only stopped working when I rushed to her desk with a towel and asked another student to take her to the nurse.

Everyone hates vomit, and children do even more. Yet I had so influenced my students that even what was vile to them was no obstacle to the goal I had taught them to adopt: their work is serious. We were working hard to be the best, visualizing our classroom as a boat that needed everyone aboard to do their share.

Meanwhile, there was no chance my children at home would let me parent them if there was a way out. Influencing them was impossible. I rarely could. I know that I never did when it came to big life decisions. Children come programmed to wear parents down. Influencing happens in a place where parents are rarely allowed. Thus, influencing is powerful and consequential and must be in the hands of role models with democratic goals. I know this is true based on my wild success at influencing my students compared to my narrow ability to influence my children.

As WCCriminal masterminds took over and replaced confident, role-model-worthy teachers with controllable puppets, children looked elsewhere for influencers. Instead of filling that void with democratic influencers—an impossibility since they became intentionally rare—social media influencers took over.

Granted, even great schools would face a battle of influencers since the advent of social media. However, I'd put my money on great teachers maintaining balance and having the upper hand at character formation. Without competition, social media influencers teach children to worship celebrities like them. They push materialism to keep them prosperous. Whereas teachers used to teach that one should avoid superficial values, the replacement influencers teach the exact opposite. As gold took center place, the Golden Rule lost.

Trump became timber because he was a celebrity. As fewer teacher role models crossed their paths, what Trump was selling took hold. I saw Trump speaking to the Boy Scouts in 2016 and despaired over how low society had fallen. He bragged to his audience of starry-eyed boys about his material existence and pursuit of wild times.

He penetrated society, while few teachers of substance survived our schools. His values took over like a toxin released into an unsuspecting water system. While some thought it was cute, and others thought it wasn't bad enough not to vote for him, his undemocratic values ate away at democracy.

As one born to teach democracy, it bothered me more than most. I knew that WCCriminals had hollowed out our schools with their landslide of inappropriate and unlawful deeds. They had eliminated the counterforce blocking his horrific values. Each time I heard another offensive act he spewed on democracy, the need for this book grew. I knew if I could help others make the connection to WCCrime, we could turn this boat headed to hell around.

Look at how Republicans are behaving due to a powerful authoritarian political agitator who breaks down institutions with no ability and, worse, no desire to fix them. Operating as a soul cannibal, he devours flawed souls, turning them into loyal, grateful liars as democracy spirals downward.

It parallels how teachers are behaving in our schools due to influential administrators. Before Trump snatched power, many politicians told the truth, calling him everything from a mob boss to the person most likely to ruin this country. Once mighty, due to his cult of people who made him powerful, fear made these once-haters pretend to like Trump, who could end careers using his worshippers. He can sic his gun-toting, violent-loving troops on anyone who goes against him. He threatens his opponents and their families, turning truth-tellers into puppets. Candor ended.

Administrators also create a cult of powerful others desiring to keep the status quo they enjoy. Do they all like this fraudulent world that captured them? Perhaps some feel guilty, and others feel scared, but fear takes precedence. Senator Mitt Romney, the only senator with the courage to vote twice to impeach Trump, commented that his party allowed the rot from the extremists to fester and that most calculate that doing the politically ambitious thing is more intelligent than telling the truth. He admitted that most of his party doesn't believe in the Constitution.

There are two significant takeaways from this. Had all these politicians been educated about democracy, as in the past, less would have slid down the slippery slope of immorality, violating their oath to the Constitution. And they're doing precisely what they're doing in education: political acrobatics. They've replaced truth and justice with loyalty and power.

Elise Stefanik and Lindsey Graham are two of many who denounced the January 6 violent insurrection when it occurred, later pretending it was no big deal. Both cannot be true. One is a lie. This not well-educated culture, filling the seats of power, missed the lessons that would have encouraged them to be solid citizens. They also missed history lessons about what happened to people who worshipped power. They gave up on democracy, pressuring others to follow them.

I know. There's a flaw in my argument. Stefanik attended Harvard; older politicians had a proper education. In response, I say that some politicians never cared about others and welcomed this shift. Ambition, which has replaced values for many, may have been part of their birth package. There is big money and power for those who capitalize on fame and connections.

Since politics attracts the greedy, for whom good schooling has less effect, we need educated, solid citizens to balance them. Stefanik is an example of why losing that balance was a disaster. Good schools are protection against people like her or Trump. Authentic education fills the void that they slipped into.

The parallels between the WCCrime-infiltrated education world and Washington are stunning yet expected since human nature is what it is. Political agendas replaced educating in the world of education, the way political agendas replaced governing in the world of government. We know that our dysfunctional government neglects its duties, yet most believe administrators do their best when it's so untrue.

People who believe in democracy do not fit with those who value power in government and schools. Republican officials like Mitt Romney, Liz Cheney, and Adam Kissinger spoke out, knowing it would end their careers, as I did. Most teachers and administrators look the other way to avoid an end to their careers, as most politicians do.

Knowing this is true about politicians but not considering this could be true about our educators is foolish. Whether public servants are in Washington or education, most capitulate when subject to political muscle. In the past, we had enough who would not abandon their values and who stood up to power. We need more in Washington and have even less in education.

The solution for a secure democracy is to raise children who understand why they need to stand up to power-mongers and tyrants. They must learn to see Hitler as a grave mistake rather than as a person to idolize as Trump does. Historically, schools used role models to teach history to attach children's brains to reality. Brains unattached to reality cannot think clearly. Our schools have put our brains to sleep. Recently, Liz Cheney said, "We're sleepwalking into a dictatorship." She's right.

Bullies will always exist. We need the anti-tyrants our schools created when critical thinking was king. Now that schools have kings, they have abolished teachers capable of critical thinking or teaching critical thinking. Our schools carved a path for a demagogue when they stopped producing citizens who put values over the pursuit of power and others who would maintain a healthy balance between values and control.

The Republicans may be taking the hatchet to our democracy now, but the Democrats did their share, too. Schools are a swamp in which both parties add alligators and crocodiles. Both know they're complicit. Neither party will admit their misdeeds, details of which appear in my books. They both paved the way for many to give up on democracy when they allowed democracy to die in our schools, both in terms of our schools' top-down structure and in terms of their ending the teaching of democracy.

Both parties looked the other way when told about WCCrime. The ACLU blew off countless teacher requests as if our issues weren't weighty. Our problems are about everyone's civil rights, not just ours. Lovers of education, responding to my pleas and promising to follow up, have yet to do so. Others likely encouraged them not to upset the apple cart. Each apple typifies a world of insane fraud within our schools that no one wants to touch. They know no person can reveal these truths and stay powerful, much less employed. They dodge this issue while forgetting that schools and democracy are inseparable.

The Democrats support unions that back WCCriminals instead of teachers. This support shows that they are either naive or complicit, guaranteeing that nothing will change. Additionally, their support of charter schools contributes to the decline of public schools, revealing their lack of understanding of their needs.

In short, neither political party has taken the time to examine the situation and ensure our schools are genuine. Taking this on is political suicide. Not taking this on is the end of democracy.

Trump supporters feel lawlessness is a given, so they choose his lawlessness, not the establishment's WCCrime lawlessness. We need public officials to behave in a way that puts others first and become leaders for democracy. When enough officials overcome their fear of losing their jobs and start doing what is right for our nation, not doing so will bring back shame, the currency of democracy now being trashed.

When we lose shame, we lose our tool to protect democracy. We began losing it when many permitted themselves to punish our disappointing government, leading to choosing someone to do the punishing for us. People forgot the Golden Rule: two wrongs don't make a right. They were not wrong that our nation was disappointing or even deceiving us. To me, WCCrime is a swamp and deep state. Those in power let us down. But the solution is exposure, accountability, and change, not retribution.

We, the people, must redirect those in power. They must look at what happened to schools under their watch. We need to investigate and restore them as democracy's guardrails. To do that, we need more citizens to understand what went wrong and what we can do.

Cynicism isn't an excuse. Only if you don't think of yourself as a citizen and part of the solution can you justify cynicism about our government. Instead of hating our presidential choices, do what you can to make the candidates address education. A democracy is a large family. If your parents lost their way, would you turn your back on them? Our democracy needs you. Not finding time to learn about our schools or resorting to Trump are both ways of turning your back on democracy.

Some people are born connected to spirituality. They feel a strong bond with others and have no desire to harm them or seek power. Some people require teachers to help them develop critical thinking skills and form connections with others. We lost the latter group when we lost called-to-teach teachers.

I recently saw Julie Chen Moonves, a TV celebrity from *Big Brother* and *The Talk*. She spoke about her total transformation. She used to be preoccupied with material things. But having found born-again Christianity, she became focused on others. I found it fascinating. I needed to be born once to know what she had to learn as a mature adult. It was part of my birth package, yet not in hers. We're all different.

I know we're all different because, as a child, I often heard my mother say that I had an inferiority complex. When I learned what that meant, I knew she was wrong. She didn't understand me. She thought my way of putting others first meant I found myself unworthy. Despite being my mother, her birth package limited her thinking about me.

Looking at society in terms of a bell curve helps us understand why some people take risks to speak out while others only think of themselves. We are born with a tentative placement on the bell curve regarding our values. Life changes us in both directions; some think more, others believe less, but we have a range that reflects each of us. Google "bell curve" if you're unfamiliar with what it looks like. It shows the middle of the bell as the largest group, rapidly decreasing to small numbers at each end.

At one end, there are selfless people like Mother Teresa, dedicated to helping others. There's been criticism of her. No one is perfect. Since she is the name most associated with extreme selflessness, she works as an example for that far end of the bell curve. On the other far end, there are selfish people like Charles Manson. One could argue mental illness caused his actions. Nevertheless, the source of his selfishness is irrelevant to this exercise. We can agree his acts were not helpful to others.

The rest own varying levels of otherness and selfishness as you approach the opposite ends. People in the otherness category find fulfillment by helping others and following ideals instead of craving material objects. People in the selfish category compete with others for those objects. At the far end of the selfish category, they don't care if they hurt others to get what they want. One end feels connected to an eternal life, and the other lives for now.

George Monbiot's article "To beat Trump, we need to know why Americans keep voting for him. Psychologists may have the answer" says the same thing differently. It describes the variance of people's values as gravitating toward either an intrinsic pole, my Mother Teresa domain, or an extrinsic pole, my Charles Manson domain.

We're both saying that almost everyone has some selfishness, with half or more having enough to vote selfishly. He's describing how psychologists think about this. I look at it spiritually.

I'm sure being called to teach is spiritual because it makes no earthly sense to work in what's become a psychological hell hole for low pay. There may not be enough teachers now that WCCrime has reduced a once challenging job to an intolerable nightmare. Still, there are way too many teachers, considering how they treat them. The attraction must be spiritual when earthly rewards are so lacking.

Monbiot also said, "Ever since Ronald Reagan came to power, on a platform that ensured society became sharply divided into 'winners' and 'losers', and ever more people, lacking public provision, were allowed to fall through the cracks, US politics has become fertile soil for extrinsic values."

Monbiot attributes this shift of our values toward selfishness, which also matches the rise of WCCrime, to the Reagan years.

In Chapter 11, I mention Kurt Andersen's book *Evil Geniuses*, which describes a selfish takeover in business due to trickle-down economics that clones what happened in education. His book educates citizens about the lead-up to Project 2025 in the business world; this book educates citizens about the lead-up to Project 2025 in the education world. (There's more on this topic and all topics in this book in the enhanced ebook version with the same name. The ebook version includes documented, detailed information that was in my 2019 book.)

Montbiot, Andersen, and I agree that the Reagan swing was closer to mourning sadness in America than waking up to a nice morning in America—no, there are four of us who agree. Later in the book, I mention a letter that my father, concerned about lowering tax on the rich, wrote to Reagan. (Just in case my sarcasm isn't apparent, I do know that millions agree, including my daughter. I don't want her to read this book and then put me in a run-down nursing home!)

What Monbiot doesn't mention, unaware of WCCrime, is that before their decline, good schools kept this a somewhat caring, far more balanced world. To the extent teachers help students find their purpose at an early age, they learn to value the community as a place to share it. Thus, even those with values leaning toward selfishness or who are extrinsic—his label for selfishness—cooperate with the community because they need it to fulfill their purpose. Of course, that's if they've learned that from a democracy influencer. Since I've scientifically proven the ineffectiveness of parents influencing their children, I'm saying learned it from a teacher!

It's indisputable that leaders' values sway the bell curve in their direction. Explaining why so many people support Trump Monbiot said, "But there is one I have seen mentioned nowhere, which could, I believe, be the most important: Trump is king of the extrinsics."

I add that he's clueless about intrinsics. In this book, I mention Trump's use of the word "sucker" from the article "Exclusive: John Kelly goes on the record to confirm several disturbing stories about Trump." The article relayed that Trump expressed an inability to understand why anyone would give their life for our country, proving Trump is closer to Manson's place on this curve. However you label it, he was born with a soul so far from people who sacrifice for others that their opposing purpose for being on earth was incomprehensible to him.

When Trump removed decency, our human guardrail, he created a never-before opening for everyone to dig up whatever selfishness they owned to rush into life like it was Black Friday at Walmart. This included those smack dab in the middle of the bell curve. Meanwhile, the third section of the bell curve, closer to Mother Teresa, recoiled in horror. It's just not in them to be indecent to others. And they probably avoid shopping on Black Friday, too.

Teaching is a spiritual endeavor. Two months before Horace Mann, the father of public education, died in 1859, he gave a commencement speech asking students to embrace his influential worldview. He said, "I beseech you to treasure up in your hearts these my parting words: Be ashamed to die until you have won some victory for humanity."

I found his words powerful. Shame is the variable. It ranges from smothering to non-existent as you go from selfless to self-ish. Shame isn't a thing at the Manson end since it's what you owe others. It's democracy's lubricant. A democracy on solid footing, one standing on good schools, keeps the shameless in check. The Moonves example shows that individuals can move toward Mother Teresa. To maintain a democracy, schools must teach critical thinking to those in the vicinity of selfishness, those extrinsic types.

Pundit PJ O'Rourke was a person oblivious to the bell curve. His statement in my 2008 book, "Altruistics [sic] give us the wil-lies because we don't know what they are in it for," has haunted me. Rather than "willies," it made me depressed that he thinks everyone is selfish and one must be wary of those who pretend to be altruistic and concerned for the welfare of others. If he were correct, why would anyone become a teacher or a social worker, helping others for a low salary?

I know he's wrong because I know myself. I choose to help others because that makes me happy. To O'Rourke, religious teachings such as "love thy neighbor" are mere dialogue. I know why. He was too close to Manson on the curve. People project their values on others. Those on the selfish side of the curve hesitate to trust others, whereas people on the other-centered side are too trusting. People who think like O'Rourke shouldn't be anywhere near teaching.

With their limited spirituality, "extrinsics" can't help children find their way. Education reform needs leaders who comprehend that the qualities essential for leading for profit and those for leading for principle are opposites. Someone like Jack Welch, a renowned CEO of General Electric, would be as unable to lead a principle-driven organization as someone like me would be unable to lead a business. I worked as a teacher for less than $40,000 a year. I wonder if he would have worked for less than $40,000,000 per year. I have worked at exposing WCCrime for decades with material loss rather than gain, an act that someone like him could not fathom.

The profile needed to educate children is opposite from the profile required to excel in business. Education is not about "taking" profits but about "giving away" our wisdom to a new generation. There are only spiritual profits in education. Welch has chosen an entirely different road in life, and whether a genius or a scoundrel, people like him have no place in education reform. (Part Three of the enhanced ebook details how the business sector chose him to reform education, which proves they were not after education reform.)

2

THE END OF NORMAL

"Remember: everyone in the classroom has a story that leads to misbehavior or defiance. 9 times out of 10, the story behind the misbehavior won't make you angry. It will break your heart."

Annette Breaux

"What a man can be, he must be."

Abraham Maslow

"Our greatest weakness lies in giving up. The most certain way to succeed is always to try just one more time."

Thomas A. Edison

One's place on the bell curve, combined with one's upbringing, determines one's best fit in society. When you know it, you make better career choices. My parents were strict. Good values topped their list of demands, so I need help determining what came with my overwhelmingly other-centered life package and what was an add-on.

One rule they had: I was not to lie about going to college when I sought a summer job. Honesty was not negotiable in our family. Yet, everyone lied about that. Everyone I knew did. Summer jobs were hard to get, so you had to make your boss think they weren't wasting their time training you. Telling the truth was such an impossible limitation that I decided to start college during the summer right after my high school graduation and graduate at the end of the fourth summer—in three years.

I wrote my senior thesis on how this creative plan solved having to live with sky-high standards. There was something that paid less than a teacher's pay—four summer jobs. It was financially advantageous to graduate in three years. Most of all, it cemented my birth package on that curve, giving me limited wiggle room toward self-centeredness. It made teaching perfect for me, and it seemed as if women's limited choices in those days did not matter a bit for a person like me.

I knew teaching was my purpose. When the lack of teaching jobs forced me to forge a business career, I eventually resorted to sales. I hoped my relationship skills would provide a slot in the business world. As a teacher, I excelled at selling my students the desire to learn, so I figured that it might.

I began selling advertising space for a local phone book publisher. On my first day out, I hit the jackpot. I sold the back cover. The owner was thrilled. I felt relief that an idealist like me had a place in business.

About three days into the job, a fellow salesperson told me the owner lies about how many phone books he circulates. My career fizzled like a ballon that met a razor. I could only sell a product that benefited the buyer. Misrepresenting a product to make a sale was intolerable. As a person filled with otherness, I quit. What made me a bad fit for business made me an excellent fit for public service. Our life experiences help us find our place on the bell curve, which, when known, brings fulfillment.

Is there selfishness in being called to teach? When I saw how messed up our schools were, I envisioned a chaotic democracy that would make us miserable. I worried a dictator would take over. My work is my selfish desire to protect my grandchildren from an ugly, divisive world and also so I won't have to live in it. Regardless, callings cannot be considered selfish since they don't belong to us.

People stay mostly the same from where they landed on this curve at birth. A glaring example is my notorious principal, who oozed cruelty. She made it known that her mother had deserted her and her siblings when she was young. She may have shared this to justify all the nasty things she did, but it did help me understand how she became a master of teacher abuse.

One day, I spoke with Darlene. She was my partner in starting our group to educate and expose teacher abuse. I mentioned how my principal's childhood made her selfish. Darlene told me that her mother also abandoned her family when she was young. Their opposite reactions showed that we are born with different abilities to care about others. The bell curve of our humanity describes this. Darlene used her unfair teaching experience to help change things. She was a public servant, whereas my principal was and is an opportunist.

Darlene passed away right after the Washington, DC, insurrection. Knowing her as I did, I believe that day was too much for her heart. We both started trying to expose WCCrime decades ago. Year by year, our country grew more hateful and less open to solving its problems. This culminated in that dreadful day. Our work couldn't stop it. We failed. It was hopeless and heart-wrenching.

I didn't use to believe in the devil until Trump. It now seems like a maybe. Perhaps if I had lived in Germany during Hitler and watched that madman take over my country, I might have. But studying Hitler wasn't enough to get there. Living through Trump taking over so many other once decent souls on almost a daily basis brought me to a maybe. He is so good at getting people to sell their souls it feels otherworldly, not normal.

I have known many bad people. But his badness is unique. I see him as a soul cannibal. He controls others and absorbs them into who he is as if he eats their souls. We keep hearing "unprecedented" when speaking of his antics because they are unprecedented. I want to use the word "spiritual" to describe how he feels to me, but that word is too associated with good. I can't. But he's taking over people's spirits. What he's done to the evangelicals makes that a fact. How can he not be the devil?

I doubt any of us have ever met anyone so able to hollow out people. Even the Mafia has limits on that. They maintain family loyalties and aspects of honor that don't get in their way of doing a crime. And frankly, despite fearing them since my childhood, Trump has taken us to new lows. It feels worse.

The other aspect that has me pondering "devil" is what being called to teach means. It is also otherworldly. It's being on earth too focused on helping others fulfill their soul's purpose—kind of like those soldiers Trump calls suckers. It seems like the other side of a coin featuring Trump, a person on this earth, focused on making people not care about others. We turned over that coin.

Looking at this spiritually helps us understand how our nation lost its balance. We've locked up the angels that came to release other souls' purposes and allowed a lot of souls to waste their lives. Did a higher power send him to teach us a lesson? It sure feels like that to me.

I cannot think of a way I'm not opposite from Trump. I've never cared about money or fame. I've often felt sorry for celebrities. They can't know if their friends are real friends. I listened to Barbra Streisand's book describing her friendships, thinking, would they have been friends like my friends? It's almost impossible to trust others when you're famous. I have loved having a good friend since I was ten and one since I was thirty, amongst other good friends. To me, fame is an albatross that makes your fame, not your soul, flourish.

Watching Trump line up souls like a hunter lines up the skins of animals he's killed when my life's purpose has been the exact opposite of his makes me think maybe he's the devil to counter the angels sent to teach. He has no real friends. His success at badness is outstanding. It rises to groundbreaking levels. It does feel like the devil. Even if those called to teach aren't angels and he isn't the devil, they are at opposite extremes on the bell curve. Definitely!

Rationally, it makes sense that we can't throw away the great teachers and have nothing in place to counter those who choose badness. Since we did that, badness is winning. There will always be people that great teachers cannot help. But if most souls learn to find their purpose in authentic schools, they wouldn't elect a person like him.

Most people have some otherness and some selfishness within. How hard doing wrong feels to people determines how other-centered they live. Many blame Trump for shifting our nation to two tribes rather than operating as a community. We cannot blame him. We are born two tribes. We became a society that chose him. Something that was leading our society shifted us toward selfishness.

That something is not our former leaders either, although their disappointing choices helped slide us toward Charles Manson. Our schools propelled us down the selfish slope, like a slow-motioned landslide, as we stopped producing citizens who knew what to do about disappointing leaders. Reactive cynicism replaced the proactive acts needed to maintain a healthy democracy and brought us to where we are now. We lost our balance and began a slow decline from holding our own on caring about others' side to reaching the quicksand-laden selfish side.

A higher power furnished the souls we need for all to share life. It's up to us to make it work. That's what teacher influencers used to do. Other-centered teachers called to teach, handled challenges, and created harmony. Once WCCrime hijacked schools, these gifted teachers became square pegs in WCCriminals' sketchy round holes. They needed these "threatening" teachers gone. They returned the gift that made democracy work. An avalanche of social poison ensued.

As nature's harmony works, a variety of souls, good and bad, work as long as leadership uses the gifts within. Decent leaders lost their way, opening the door for indecent power seekers.

Democracy is slipping away because we lost our connection to the souls intended to make a peaceful nation work—great teacher influencers. We replaced them with souls who lack otherness or souls restrained from using their otherness. Our bell curve didn't change. Our leaders have changed how they're tapping into it. And nothing will cure this spiritually unsound state of affairs, with selfishness leading, more than empowering great teachers.

This slant toward selfishness makes caring about others hard. Many deserted democracy, seeking power instead. Others lost faith in it and are tossing the baby—democracy—with the bath water. Not me.

Trump is a far-right authoritarian, a fascist. Google fascism and you'll see a picture of Adolph Hitler. Think about the fact that there hasn't been a baby named Adolph since we got to know him, as everyone hated him. Does it make sense to throw out the baby you can't name Adolph so you can bring back an Adolph? Let's bring the name back before we let another Adolph take over. That gives time for Jews and—who else did he kill?—to leave the country.

Hitler humor is sick. Our democracy is sick. It's like a baby in putrid water because our officials and media neglect, ignore, or corrupt it.

Plenty of stand-up public servants can and will change the water, and many more citizens will rejoice if they do. We will always have the people we need to nurture humanity if nurturing is our goal. The bell curve spread doesn't change. Leadership is what changes whether we have more or less selfishness.

It's time to study what went wrong and care for that baby. Doing it the MAGA way is like a Hitler revival plus a tenth-month abortion. (By the way, the mentioning of the Hitler boycott must end now that so many admire and imitate him.)

The democratic way is to deal with the sludge-filled water flowing from our education system. And although it will take time to relaunch a solid citizenry, changing it will please all but those at the far dark end of the bell curve. They will not be happy with any efforts to improve the system. We have always kept those types in the toxic, dark corner at bay while benefitting from those in the light-filled corner. That is democracy's foremost job!

Trump dwells near that dark corner with his supporters void of otherness. He counts on his clan. He manipulates disgruntled people who have lost other-centeredness due to disappointment. Using crisis, chaos, and pretense that he cares about them, he gets them to help him accumulate the wealth he covets. If we give the discontents reason to believe in democracy again, some will move on from their crutch—Trump.

Our problem is there's no light-filled place to beckon them We can create it by ending WCCrime. We need a movement to defeat the authoritarian, many would say fascist, Project 2025, the only American movement at this time. It must answer people's deep questions, including why our schools are so dysfunctional.

This book can start that long-needed movement for democracy. Once the veiled shift from moral leaders to power seekers becomes known, it should be easy to accept that WCCrime hijacked our schools.

Accept this truth. Then, understanding how our country imploded will be easy. You will understand what happened to us once you grasp how corrupt our schools are and divorce the myth that good guys are trying their best to run our schools.

Without a WCCrime intervention, our country will "fix" democracy as it "fixed" our schools—not at all. This book explains why school reform has been a colossal debacle and democracy has fallen apart. We can fix both. We need to fix both. It must start with our schools.

Schools and our democracy are more than connected at the hip. They are a stream that must flow, or neither survives. Schools create faithful public servants; they determine the type of government we will have. Schools are the parents. Our public officials reveal their parenting. Look at our government. It tells you how bad our schools are.

When I returned to teaching in 1992, I found education teetering as the place where children discovered their purpose.

Yet my classroom was a bastion for children developing into well-functioning citizens. Soon, the administrators let our staff know, the way Mafia bosses let their people know, that we were not there for the children. We were there for them.

The principal openly said she did not want older teachers and disposed of a few despite federal law prohibiting that. I knew I was next.

Keep in mind that older meant those annoying, competent pre-women's lib teachers. "So what if it's illegal," my principal thought, acted upon, and succeeded as she destroyed my career and some of the remaining fibers of democracy. She operated as she pleased with the help of bowled-over enablers.

If we fail to rid our schools of WCCrime, losing our democracy is inevitable. Our nation will be an autocracy, just like our schools. You will live in a nation that is as unfair as the school that falsely accused and fired me.

Schools, like autocracies, can break laws without consequences. Join me and thousands of teachers and parents in a grassroots movement to expose the truth about our schools. Let's repair democracy and stop this menacing move toward autocracy. You are reading this because we are still a democracy. We may be crippled and tangled, but we're a democracy where a person like me can publish a book like this.

There will always be outsiders influencing our children. It's up to us who they will be. As long as we do the work to maintain authentic schools, great teachers and critical-thinking influencers will protect democracy.

Society's moral formation was pervasive until WCCrime stomped it out. Moral education became less prevalent in the '60s. Still, it remained embedded in the teaching of democracy and first of mind in those called to teach.

Democracy is government through elected representatives. It relies on everyone sharing their skills and needs to create a more ideal society. To the extent each person is more developed, democracy flourishes. Teachers uncover students' innate talents and help them build character and the desire to contribute to society. Solid teaching props up democracy.

WCCrime, a mob-like racket that benefits school leaders, transformed education. It changed everything. Teaching good character and morals didn't fit with the selfish desires of lawless criminals. Those who value good character and morals threatened their existence. Everyone in the orbit of WCCrime was either stripped of their right to think differently about right and wrong or removed from the profession. WCCriminals disposed of conscientious people. A tightly wrapped profession slipped into a cult of silence.

This book explains how they exiled the dedicated teachers gifted to us, erasing their role in character formation integrated into their teaching. As I write, I am climbing the slippery walls of unbelievability to expose our schools and disempower the criminals. Forgive me if I repeat as I slip on those walls.

This vast, mind-blowing issue is not just a hot potato; it's a giant barrel of fear mixed with confusion. It is as shocking as priest abuse and too complex for reporters to dissect. We have a democracy with education swept under the rug rather than its intended, steadfast foundation. Telling about it is vexing.

WCCriminals used bullying to take over our schools for a long time. Trump identically prevails over our democracy. He has bullied our nation into a disinformation cloud, a feat not easily accomplished with properly educated citizens. It would have been difficult to trick a critical-thinking society into accepting criminals.

If public officials and the media, aware that Trump is a scam, use their influence to expose the flaws in our education system, honesty will open the way for meaningful change. If they choose to continue to cover up their failure to deal with WCCrime, they will remain stuck in the quicksand of lies where Trump's skill with evil wrongdoing far surpasses theirs.

He's successful because he engenders either love or hate. Both promise to weaken democracy. Love will do that by electing him and hate by preoccupying his enemies so they won't solve the democracy problem.

Democracy and its laws are like the vampire's silver cross or the witch's bucket of water. They're the con man's curtain pull. Trump is skilled at keeping our emotions preoccupied and far from the curtain that the *Wizard of Oz* taught us to pull when up against too much power.

Dealing with Trump is not easy since he's become heroin for many. Some say that Trump is the new heroin. Heroin is potent, so I've heard. And it's not good for you. I wouldn't know about heroin if I hadn't taught school.

While teaching fourth grade, a policeman gave weekly drug avoidance lectures to our students. Due to state law, the teacher needed to remain in the classroom. They told us to stay, do our work, and let the policeman take over.

It was hard not to listen, especially the day the policeman told my class the problem with heroin. He said it gave you such a great feeling the first time you tried it that you couldn't stop trying to recreate that feeling. It's just soooooooo good you get hooked. He stretched out that so in a way that hooked me on finding out more about heroin.

I knew heroin was a bad idea. I never thought about it. I'd never heard it was so great. I won't comment on the wisdom of making that statement to children. Still, the concept that a great feeling can hook you to something horrible and cause your demise stayed with me. I see that exact formula taking place with Trump.

Trump is a master salesman. He could sell anything for a while. He has set fire to our democracy. It's up to us to learn how our democracy let this fire in and put it out. Our problem is having a hollowed out foundation rather than a vibrant education system. To those so disgusted with our off-track democracy that they became hooked on Trump, I offer a chance to detox and solve our democracy problem.

We can change our schools. Our schools are to be the source of democracy based on the people they attract and mold. Yet, teaching isn't a profession. It's a trap. Teachers are primarily good-intentioned citizens who want to make this a better world. However, administrators psychologically strip them of their power and force them to accept the crumbs offered to them, making them ineffective.

Education became a mental concentration camp with walls of fear holding its residents powerless and silent. Educrats wear teachers down by getting parents mad at them and keeping students out of control. They use teacher abuse, so there's no escape. As the battered wife stripped of dignity, teachers stay, blaming themselves. Fraudulent public servants gaslight teachers into worthlessness to hide them from history.

I'm one of the few it didn't work on. If you learn about what's going on in our schools and help me build a counterforce to the brutes holding the power, we will get democracy back. I will help you either fall in love with education or give it the respect it deserves as you learn our society's mistake of undervaluing one of the most sacred disciplines.

You cannot trust anyone defending our schools. If they're not complaining, they live on the surface and are not worthy of teaching or are paralyzed with fear. Teachers who look the other way and allow colleagues to be trashed are modeling greed. Their ability to teach your children is compromised.

Even if they land in a few well-functioning districts, they are professional hermits if they do not know about their colleagues' suffering or the nationwide intellectual disrespect in which education is drowning.

It takes little time for WCCriminals and their bluster to invade a district of faithful public servants, forcing them to compromise their teaching and expend their loving energy coping with WCCrime. Given its privileged status, this is an ominous feat.

We must keep those from the business world and those seeking power far from education's leadership. We need a team of people who understand the significance of education and how children learn to protect and guide democracy. Only they will keep it from becoming the behemoth of self-interest it has become.

In the twisted forest WCCrime created, our nation lost its way. My goal is to inspire you to value education enough to help those of us who would have led it as intended but who WCCriminals terminated, so we couldn't. We need to make this country normal again.

Ordinary thinking is what solid teachers use to teach. If you can't join the military with a felony on your record, allowing a felon to become commander-in-chief makes no sense. It's not normal thinking for people to want to do that to our troops. Nominating a rapist and convicted felon for president is not normal thinking.

It went missing along with the solid teachers driven from the profession, and we will get normal thinking back once we build solid schools, society's missing balancer. It won't happen under the leadership of anyone who has surrendered to WCCrime, including everyone who has yet to report it, from union leadership to government officials.

Education leaders must rise from those who put children's and society's needs above their self-interest. We will find most of our future education leaders on the outside, banished for rejecting WCCrime.

Just as Trump became president due to branding rather than competence, our nation has branded our schools as trustworthy when they operate like a mafia. The establishment has fallen for its branding and continues to choose leaders who support WCCrime. You must demand authentic schools.

As you read, remember that you are not just saving democracy and individual freedom by becoming educated about the covert, wicked world of education. Bringing back authentic education will reinvigorate the American dream and lessen income disparity. It will repair racial injustice. Last but not least, it will end school shootings, a direct consequence of WCCrime, explained in Chapter 10. Education, a medieval fiefdom fortified against change, needs a disrupter.

I am doing my best to be that. On the cover of my 2008 book, a teacher is writing, "Please do not erase" on a blackboard.

I wonder if many people knew why I included that. Teachers often wrote tomorrow's lesson on the blackboard. "Please do not erase" was a note to the custodian not to erase that lesson when cleaning the boards at night. I wrote that many times years ago, not realizing its prophetic nature. I was to be erased.

Since the powerful have had their way with me, and other educators like me, and others have refused to take this on, we must unite to replace sham educators with authentic educators.

Democracy lost its home in our schools. I'm defining the problem. I'm sharing my unshakable vision. I need your help. WCCrime affects your children's lives. They disrespect you for allowing this. Help shift that scorn to its proper owners—WCCriminals. Let the Kardashians do their thing, but help me be an antidote for what they do. Help me balance this country.

Please help me make America normal again. I know I can do that with your help. Otherwise, the only kind of influencer I will be is a Nordstrom influencer, something they remind me I am each month when I get my bill.

3

THE TAKE DOWN OF TEACHER INFLUENCERS

"It is the supreme art of the teacher to awaken joy in creative expression and knowledge."

Albert Einstein

"It is easier to build strong children than to repair broken adults."

Frederick Douglas

"If a child is acting disruptive within the school system, don't be too quick to assume there is something wrong with her. She simply may be doing her best to say that the system is not large enough to house the fullness of her creative spirit."

Vince Gowmon

The truth about our education system is far more sinister than you could ever imagine. Administrators who value loyalty over authentic teaching have reduced dedicated teachers, once the backbone of our schools, to mere foot soldiers.

They swiftly purge those who dare to speak out about their wrong-doing, which I'll be discussing throughout this book.

This loyalty-first practice, reminiscent of the Trump regime, has flourished for decades, pushing authentic teaching to the brink of extinction. It's a complex and unbelievable situation that, if left unaddressed, threatens the very fabric of our democracy. If you truly understood the state of our schools, you'd know this. But you will only get the genuine picture if you hear from whistleblowers like me. Welcome to the truth, which begins with WCCrime's effect in the classroom.

We must hold sacred the need to value and honor called-to-teach teachers. Here's a story that explains what these teachers can do if permitted and illustrates how WCCriminals cancel them. This story makes clear what our nation has lost and needs to bring back.

There are children charged with the moniker the "learning dead." They find learning so hard they give up. Some act out. Others go through school as if they aren't there. Unlike the rage-filled children that become timber for school shootings, these types often live a life of not finding their gifts.

Called-to-teach teachers, don't let that happen. Jack was one of the "learning dead." Schools always write up children like him to ask a team to serve their special needs. That occurs even at WCCrime schools that offer children a lot of talk and little action.

The year they put Jack in my class, the special education director seemed confident, even smug, that they had saddled me with him. The frustration that a lack of success unloads on teachers, especially on more skilled teachers, accompanied this boy. I'm sure he thought Jack would be my comeuppance.

Our first meeting about Jack was a chorus of "no one has ever figured him out." From the special education director to the others on the team who had worked with him, there was solid agreement that no one could unmask this boy's needs.

I had to try, no matter what I heard. When you're called to teach, that is the only option. So I did my usual. I started analyzing the facts. I put my gift for understanding children on high mode and took off.

The first thought that surfaced was that the special education teacher, whom they had assigned to be by his side in the classroom much of the day, was a person who would make me a non-learner. Mrs. O was a loud, know-it-all New Yorker who would make even wanting to live hard if it meant doing it with her. Someone coined the word "obnoxious" just for her. The entire staff rolled their eyes at the mention of her name.

I recall a lunchroom conversation about our ten-year-old daughters and wildly expensive designer jeans. I said that I wouldn't buy them for my daughter. She'd have to earn the money if she wanted them. Mrs. O said *that's all my daughter wears* as if it was only about money and she had more.

I got the message that our values were as different as our abilities to reach children and saw that as a clue to why, after many years with him, she hadn't reached Jack, a fifth grader.

I knew this boy would not grow as a learner with the burden of someone like her. Of course, I couldn't disparage her to anyone. The universe solved that problem since my first instinct was that this boy needed space to start believing in himself, and even a loving person who felt like an appendage was a mistake for him. A person hovering over him as if he were a dummy reinforced the worthlessness in which he was drowning.

Suggesting we not have a person helping him in the classroom meant I'd have more work. Since I was there to help children succeed, I welcomed it if that was the solution. I was determined to figure out this boy's needs like I always did.

I consulted with his mom about my idea to switch this helping setup without sharing my thoughts about Mrs O. She was okay with trying something else. I then asked Jack how he felt about eliminating Mrs. O's several hours a day in-class assistance versus staying after school an hour once a week so I could help him instead. He seemed to light up, but just a little. I couldn't be sure that I was digging the tunnel to his gifts, but the light meant maybe. I designated every Wednesday after school as my extra time for Jack.

Even if Mrs. O was lovely, I knew it was insanity to keep doing what wasn't working. My ability to get deep inside my students allowed me to feel their feelings. Being singled out for help was embarrassing. It was like putting decorative plastic over a bush that wasn't growing, thinking you were doing something to help that bush survive.

In addition to erasing some humiliation from his life, what had turned him into the "learning dead" surfaced during the extra time with him. When I figured it out, my decision to remove Mrs. O from the classroom turned out to be spot on.

During a Wednesday session, he said he wished he had flunked kindergarten to be smarter than his classmates. Voila. I knew I was right to eliminate embarrassment. A need for a helper was a never-ending red flag waving a visual of, "I'm stupid."

Once he shared his feelings, I dove in with learning techniques I knew would work. I explained that his problem was not about "smarts." It was about not having decided to be a student. I explained how kids who choose to succeed in school succeed often, not because they're smart. They do the work, unlike him who doesn't. That's why they seem intelligent. I made sure he understood that not being a student makes you look like you're dumb.

Most would think what I taught him was obvious. Most don't understand children like I do. I teach a child what that child needs; sometimes, needs are odd. A good teacher doesn't judge. She figures out and opens blocked doors regardless of how strange, understanding that differences are part of what makes each of us unique.

I knew learning requires an unblocked path partly from my own experience. My parents forced my two sisters and me to take piano lessons for nine years, and we all hated it. Our teacher did his best, so he taught me guitar chords so I could read and play popular music.

I became proficient but avoided the piano. Then, while earning my bachelor's degree in elementary education, I had to take a course to learn to play piano in a classroom. They devised a method so teachers could learn to play quickly.

I was 19 years old, but I was a lot like Jack about learning, but for different reasons. I resented having to learn this new, simple way when I knew chords and could play fairly well. I met with my professor and unloaded how much I despised the piano after so many years of forced learning. He agreed to let me play music and show him what I could do, and if I could do enough, he'd excuse me from learning their method.

His decision freed me from the convoluted barrier I had erected between me and the piano. During my fourth year of teaching, I had my fifth graders perform a musical play, and I played the piano! Some years later, I bought a piano.

Children need teachers who understand the unique pitfalls that block learning. They are often strange, but when you're called to teach, you figure them out. Teachers who connect with students make magic happen. Never going near a piano would not have been a tragedy for me, but never figuring out how to learn would have been a tragedy for Jack.

From that day, I knew what he needed. I researched gifted special education students and found an outstanding article that confirmed my thinking that having this challenging combination was his dilemma. His idea that flunking would have helped him told me he was a bright thinker, seeking solutions to becoming smart at school despite how hard school was for him due to his disabilities.

Whereas weekly spelling tests for the first few months meant a word or two correct, he started studying and got a few B's and even one A. This boy had grown.

I came up with an idea to help him understand himself as a learner. I folded a piece of paper into four squares and made one column "bad things learned" and the other "good things learned." Then I made one-row fourth grade—last year, and one-row fifth grade—this year. I asked him to fill in the squares.

He wrote, "Teacher did all my work" in both rows for fourth grade and "I didn't do much work" in the "bad" row for fifth grade. Part of my strategy was to prioritize his need to develop self-understanding over getting work done. Real-life consequences are the best way to learn. Also, by doing it this way, I relayed to him that I believed in him. I was confident he would eventually do his work. And he did.

I liked teaching intermediate grades because that's when you teach children how to be students. When you teach a subject like history, you're teaching how to learn history more than the facts about history. Other than reading and math, subjects they need to learn starting in first grade, most teaching is about helping them become learners when learning the facts matters. My style proved to be successful. A couple of the junior high teachers told me that of the four fifth-grade classes, mine was the only one ready to do sixth-grade work.

Because Jack had such a hard time with reading, and no one had figured out how gifted he was, he fell off the self-esteem cliff and needed someone to help put him on solid ground. As I helped put the ground under his feet, I focused even harder on my turning-him-into-a-student job, which children of this age need.

He seemed thrilled to discover a role he could do well. He was filling in his ideas on the four-square paper with zest, which had no place in his prior life. He wrote something I could only remember on the fifth-grade good square on the concept level. I need to paraphrase what he communicated instead of his exact words.

It included an expression like, "I realize that I need a teacher who understands me." On the other hand, I definitely remember what his words ignited when the team saw that chart. His realization that he needed a teacher like me rather than one like her became atomic evidence to use against me.

The fact I got this boy doing work for the first time; the fact that his dad found him typing on the computer past bedtime for the first time in his life and was unable to admonish him; and the fact that I made this impossible-to-figure-out boy into a student didn't matter. What mattered was hiding me as quickly as possible so parents wouldn't expect teachers like me. My success meant they needed to terminate my career.

One would think that the team would be elated that some-one finally cracked the code for a boy who had puzzled all. One would think his fourth-grade teacher, who hadn't figured him out, would feel the joy that someone did. He changed from pathetic to vibrant. Sadly, it was victorious for only a few.

I don't know what his fourth-grade teacher thought, but I know she became a witness against me at my termination based on the written exercise that I used to free this boy from his demons. The exercise became all about her teaching skills rather than about a student's long, baffling needs surfacing.

He didn't say she was a lousy teacher. He did say he needed a teacher more like me in the good row for fifth grade. He needed to understand that some teachers have depth and some are shal-low. I bet, looking back as a grown-up, he understands. He was bright. That's why seeming stupid was so hard for him. I bet that teacher still doesn't understand.

Try to absorb this. This district, which also accused me of vio-lating special education law for sharing issues about this boy with board members, had his fourth-grade teacher, no longer at our district, become involved in this issue so she could testify against me. They shared all the information with her, a non-employee, yet I was wrong to share it with board members, whose job is to protect the community.

He was a boy who had failed and who everyone agreed no one could figure out. He wasn't judging his teachers. He was feeling his needs. Fifth grade was better for him, but he didn't say it was better for everyone. The principal had an agenda, and it wasn't helping children grow. If this were a success-oriented school, the principal would have helped her and the team understand what I did right.

Putting aside which teacher succeeded with Jack, consider the facts. She was in her early twenties, a few years out of college, and married for a year with no children. I was twice her age. I had taught for many years and had much more life experience. Some of my children were out of college. I was a grandmother, too.

And wouldn't helping her learn from this incredible success make sense? What's more. The teacher was no longer at our school. They didn't need to tell her what he said if the goal was not to hurt her feelings. Or it could have been said to help her grow as a teacher. The principal could have shared the article on gifted, special education students with her and the team. Instead, she used that growth sheet to gain an enemy against me. The principal's focus was on bullying me and not at all helping this child or the team that had failed this boy.

There was so much wrong here. The principal's lack of respect for experience goes against logic. Her lack of respect for success goes against the goals of education. Her lack of respect for me, a seasoned, successful teacher, makes her wrong for education.

Please remember this story about Jack when you read Chapter 15, where I share my vision for the kind of principals we need. His story exemplifies that not all teachers are skilled, deep thinkers. Thus, we need principals who are professional, deep thinkers so they can nurture what children need rather than stomping it out due to their ignorance or pettiness. Principals need to have taught long enough to show they have the depth and the intellect to choose and lead others who can.

The lowering of teacher quality is no accident. WCCrime makes teachers like me a problem to incompetent administrators. And the way my Board ignored my plea to investigate this principal was not mere stupidity; the lawless acts they used to eliminate me suggested she was what they wanted.

My point throughout this book is an institution that has strayed so far from its purpose is no longer doing its job. And when the straying includes lawless acts, our government must address the criminality. To do otherwise asks democracy to survive without the institution it depends on.

If Jack were your son, you'd want the teacher who could figure him out and help him, not the inept team that had worked with him since kindergarten and agreed he was a puzzle beyond their scope.

Schools are not social clubs where popularity assigns rank, especially when what's popular is sketchy. Yet that's closer to what they've become. People know to choose doctors based on their competence rather than on their social status. Since the public does not get to select teachers, we must have great minds doing that instead of inept opportunists.

When it comes to teachers, those running our schools have the public confused, so you'll think they're doing the best they can. They have stolen your odds of finding the best teachers for your children. Teachers with excellent skills suppress their talent to stay employed. My goal is to help you learn that so you'll insist on the teachers who could change the world if their built-in power still belonged to them.

They didn't leave Jack's parents unscathed either. The Board accused them of supporting me so they didn't have to help their child with his work as they had over the years. Before, the teacher, the special education teacher, and the parents worked with or for him. Now, Jack was operating like a typical, struggling fifth-grade student. As was the case for many others, he only finished some of his work. But he felt good about himself for the first time ever—my goal, which thwarted the Board's need for powerless teachers.

WCCrime twisted everything about this incident. Special education law, the boy's success, and what the parents wanted were meaningless to my administrators. Their goal was getting rid of teaching that showed how unsuccessful they were—one of the worst aspects of WCCrime. Their shameful mission to sabotage my attempt to help this boy shows exactly how WCCrime has ended teacher influencing. Based on testimony from thousands of teachers, this is happening nationwide. You need to know this.

Get this. I was a dues-paying member of the NEA, my union, the entire time I taught. Mrs. O was the only teacher I knew who had never joined the union. When it came time for my termination, our union president protected this nonmember from my alleged disparagement of her. I am trying to remember what they concocted. But I know the union president took her under her wing and made dinner out of me, which included making a statement to the press after I filed my federal lawsuit. She said, "If Horwitz is so unhappy, she should leave."

The next day, a parent called and asked, "What's going on? I've dealt with unions all my life, and unions don't talk like that." I didn't tell him how the union was representing a nonmember to go after me. Things were so perverse, so corrupted. My second job was to stay out of their tornado of hate and remain professional.

Later in this book, I explain that WCCrime forces teacher unions to oblige. As a result, they're corrupt. Please remember this event where my local union took me down so the team could continue not to know what to do with students.

And when you read Chapter 10 about how WCCrime causes school shootings, you can substitute a raged-filled student for sweet Jack with the same inept team trying to help and a random caring teacher like me. Then, think about why that teacher would not try to use her insight to help that potential shooter.

The story of Jack has all the lessons teachers have learned that make them avoid problem-solving. You don't let an inept team know they're incapable. You don't help a child at that team's expense. If you do, the union will help them go after you. You keep your mouth shut and your talents locked in a personal safety vault when you teach at a WCCrime school

Kappa Delta Pi

An Honor Society in Education

WHEN life seems without hope, and when the forces of evil seem to rule the world, I will maintain faith in the improvability of human nature. Contact with humanity will be intimate, and I will remain loyal to the ideal that young and old of every race and creed shall, through continuous education based on equal opportunity for all, enjoy the right to physical health, social intelligence, and economic justice. All this I pledge as an ideal of Fidelity to Humanity.

EDUCATION builds not alone for the present but for the future; not merely for self, but for society as well. Service, incentive of the world's great teachers, means that I will so live that others are empowered and enriched thereby. It means that as a teacher I will lose myself and so find myself in ceaseless effort to advance justice and peace for all people. All this I pledge as an ideal of Service.

SCIENCE it means that I will be faithful to the cause of free inquiry, and will accept truth where I find it, no matter how reluctlessly it may tear out the roots of prejudice and superstition. I will not be blinded by the new or the spectacular, condemning the old and tried simply because it is old and tried. I will not distort or weigh evidence to support a favored theory, suspending judgment for more nearly adequate evidence. This I pledge as an ideal of Science.

TOIL and the will to do the task my hands find are necessarily involved in the other ideals listed here; let them be consciously involved. I believe in the social necessity of my profession. Through this faith I will gain power to work and live. If, through my work, one life is given larger freedom and nobler vision, I will not have lived in vain. All this I pledge as an ideal of Toil.

SO TO teach that my words inspire childhood and youth with a will to learn; so to serve that each day may enhance the growth of exploring minds; so to live that I may guide young and old to know the truth and love the right. To the fulfillment of these ideals as a member of Kappa Delta Pi I pledge my efforts and my faith, and, subscribing to these ideals, I affix my signature below.

May 18, 1966
Date

_____
Chapter

_____
Institution

_____
President

_____
Signature

_____
Counselor

Some of us took our jobs seriously.

4

DEMOCRACY'S BONES

"Education is our only political safety. Outside of this ark, all is deluge."

Horace Mann

"A child without education is like a bird without wings."

Tibetan Proverb

"Democracy cannot succeed unless those who express their choices are prepared to choose wisely. The real safeguard of our democracy, therefore, is education."

Franklin Delano Roosevelt

Others outside of education, including some of our most outstanding journalists, are doing their best to look inside. They try, but when up against WCCrime, they look through blackened windows. I'm taking you past those windows to show why whistleblowing teachers are our democracy's and children's only hope.

In his 2023 heartfelt article, "How America Got Mean,"[2] David Brooks recognized our schools' lack of moral training. He said, "We live in a society that's terrible at moral formation…in which people are no longer trained in how to treat others with kindness and consideration. Our society has become one in which people feel licensed to give their selfishness free rein."

He mentioned Notre Dame sociologist Christian Smith's 2008 research that said, "One of their findings was that the interviewees had not given the subject of morality much thought. 'I've never had to make a decision about what's right and what's wrong,' one young adult told the researchers. 'My teachers avoid controversies like that like the plague,' many teenagers said." These comments validate my central premise—teachers live in fear of upsetting their WCCrime administrators.

Like every public figure, Brooks speaks about education with a lack of depth. He couldn't explain the why behind this decline. This stepchild institution and the scorned discipline that guides it live on a deserted island. It escapes scrutiny. Since the 1859 death of Horace Mann, it has blown in the wind. Whether a curse over the world of education or a sloppy omission, there has yet to be an effective education leader since him. In fact, there's been no acknowledged leader since him.

Education has been vulnerable to the forces of the day rather than awarded adequate status by the great universities. It has built-in susceptibility to crime, as does an ignored, vacant building. And no group of people is more lassoed and branded than the gentle souls who become teachers.

WCCrime survives outside the radar. People let it be as if they have no right to judge education, the wayward son they never chose to parent. Gifted writers give only a surface nod as they mention education's failings.

Famous biographers like Ron Chernow or Walter Isaacson have not written a best-selling biography of Horace Mann, who built the pillars that upheld our democracy for almost two hundred years. Education's inability to attract intellectual status is at the core of its failure.

I have worked to expose our education crime problem for almost three decades. Education's belittled nature is its downfall.

It is a neglected island rather than an illuminating lighthouse. Noted writers and officials' superficial connections leave a desire to rescue it absent.

As I read Brooks' article, the unmindfulness that shrouds my profession sickened me. It seems hopeless to hear a few brave teachers blowing the whistle when addressed from this sociological distance. Even this great writer missed a need to look under education's rocks.

However, he didn't miss the connection between the lack of character formation in the schools and how Trump happened. He said:

> Expecting people to build a satisfying moral and spiritual life on their own by looking within themselves is asking too much. A culture that leaves people morally naked and alone leaves them without the skills to be decent to one another… After decades without much in the way of moral formation, America became a place where 74 million people looked at Donald Trump's morality and saw presidential timber…If you put people in a moral vacuum, they will seek to fill it with the closest thing at hand. Over the past several years, people have sought to fill the moral vacuum with politics and tribalism. American society has become hyper-politicized.

Recently, journalist Deborah Roberts appeared on *The View* to talk about her new book that discussed how teachers made a huge difference in the lives of many celebrities, including hers. She spoke about many teachers leaving the profession not because of money but because teachers want autonomy to do what teachers used to do—make a difference in students' lives. With no clue it exists and unable to force change, she identified the biggest casualty of WCCrime: the purging of teachers who won't compromise doing what they feel called to do and the muzzling of the rest.

Fox News pundit Watters said, "Trump won that election because of a laser-like focus on the forgotten man…A bond was formed back then that can never be broken."[3] I say, "I doubt anyone who had a dedicated teacher feels forgotten!"

Around 1980, the sanitizing of education to grease the way for WCCrime began, as had the tossing of bodies onto a pile of forgotten men. The stack became large enough to erode Republican officials' commitment to our Constitution and to support a person who admitted he wanted to end democracy. The army of forgotten men that our schools created is the autocrat's tool for ending democracy. The obvious solution for saving democracy, which none of these journalists recognized, is to end WCCrime.

Since the teaching of civics and critical thinking is incompatible with the system of organized crime that our schools have embraced, the scoundrels running our schools evicted it with the same intensity they cleanse great teachers from the system. Nothing replaced the framework of citizenship knowledge and skills used to keep democracy flourishing.

Most failed to notice its departure in our schools. It took years for democracy's skeleton to collapse. Academy Award-winning actor Richard Dreyfuss is an exception. He recognized this a decade ago and founded the Dreyfuss Initiative to bring civics back. His website described it as "a non-profit, non-partisan organization that aims to revive the teaching of civics in American public education to empower future generations with the critical-thinking skills they need to fulfill the vast potential of American citizenship."

He aptly depicted democracy's needs when he said:

We are the only nation in history bound by ideas only. We have no common ancestry or religion or commonly agreed to caste or class system. We're bound by those ideas born in the enlightenment and actualized in the Constitution, the declaration and the Bill of Rights, and they are the protection of individual civil liberties, and that people have the right to be protected by the law, the same law for all. And if each new generation of Americans is not taught those ideas and taught and taught and taught with rigor and pleasure, we are not bound. And we're not. We have about as much connection

43

to not just our neighbors but the people in the next state or the cops in Seattle, even if you've never been to Seattle, then I have to the man in the moon.[4]

He pointed out American exceptionality, saying: "We freed the intellect of the human race and rewarded mankind with freedoms and responsibilities once reserved only for kings and dukes, and how this meant that our schools were to create citizens worthy of what used to be only for royalty."

He declared that citizens must learn how their democracy and their responsibilities within it work, saying: "After fighting with England for the principle of ruling ourselves, the principle that WE Americans are the government, how did we attain such stupidity and arrogance to stop knowing who we are, and that WE are in charge? That is the essence of senselessness. It is the return to the way the world always was before our Revolution."

Like all outsiders and most insiders, Dreyfuss has yet to learn why civics is missing in schools. He sees it as an oversight he's dedicated to correcting. The truth is that those who embed democracy into classroom management rank as pariahs to WCCriminals. Where the fear of prison swirls, the need for unquestioning minds rules.

Teachers are not shirking their responsibility to teach civics and analytical thinking. To comply with their overlords, they gray out children's brains to create a haven for lawlessness. They go along with the amorality and immorality that WCCrime demands.

I was delighted to find another soul obsessed with democracy that I read Dreyfuss's 2022 book *One Thought Scares Me*. In it, he mentions that he can see the future but suffers from the "Cassandra Curse." In Greek mythology, Apollo, the god of the Sun, had a crush on Cassandra, a Trojan princess. He gifted her the ability to see the future. When she scorned him, he gave her the curse of never being believed.

I have a similar, but "not at all Greek god" curse. It has taken me forever to get this truth exposed because I have the Harvey Weinstein curse, a curse that predatory abusers inflict on their victims—no one will believe the victim. It works by adding years and making people give up.

We're a society that assumes we'd know if this lousy stuff were actual. Unbelievability is why the priests and the Harvey Weinstein types feel safe. It took the priest abuse victims about thirty years and the Weinstein victims about twenty-five. My twenty-nine-year-old mission makes this issue exploding before the 2024 election plausible. We need more than plausible to stop our democracy's death spiral, however.

About democracy failing, Dreyfuss said, "This is no accident. This is somebody's fault. People in power brought people, people in positions who can harm the public body through ignorance and treachery." He then went on, "You who are reading this. You may deny it; that's what you're good at. But it doesn't change the fact that you—as parents, as citizens, as politicians—did this stupid and horrible thing. And you continue to do it even as you read this book."

He admits his tone might annoy his readers but justifies it due to the gravity of silence surrounding this issue. I don't blame the public. It takes a book to understand what's going on in education, and reading about education is under the totem pole, not just low on it.

And even he got it wrong. He respects Arne Duncan, the former head of the Department of Education. Yet, Duncan failed to address teacher abuse in his district after a friend of mine reported it to him.

Nor did Duncan acknowledge a 2009 book filled with research documenting teacher abuse in the Chicago Public Schools, the district under his watch. I saw author Rosalyn Schnall on WGN TV speaking about her book, *When Teachers Talk: Principal Abuse of Teachers/The Untold Story*. Why didn't Duncan know about it? Plus, he was one of the leaders oblivious to the effects of women's liberation, an inexcusable oversight.

Because this many-layered, well-infiltrated form of corruption fools outsiders, it's hard to assign responsibility.

There's one exception. Those told about it and then do nothing deserve our ire. I have written to many who have brushed this off. I have offered to help them understand WCCrime so they can solve it. They owe it to us to learn what's happening since the general public assumes they do. And given its urgency, we need citizens on this ASAP. I offer the general public a pass, which I explain later in this book. But if you're reading this book now, consider your pass revoked.

In the 2023 article "Why-Trump-and-the-GOP-are -Burning-the-Entire-System-Down," Thom Hartmann said, "For democracy to work in human societies isn't some magic or organic thing; it depends on institutions and systems to function and remain free of corruption." Our schools have failed at that!

When I called the local library for a copy of Brooks's article about us getting mean, the librarian shrieked with delight, saying, "Twenty minutes ago, someone else asked for this very article." The popularity of a non-pop culture item was heaven to his ears. I, too, was glad others who lived near me cared about how we got this mean. It made local shopping seem emotionally safer.

The battle between ideas and materialism used to have teachers like me making sure that ideas like democracy won or at least held their own. We pushed these things: citizenship is a distant form of love; democracy is a moral agreement built on each person playing fair or going to jail; and law is nothing more than codified morality, with codified meaning "playing fair" put into laws with punishments when broken. Anyone who believes in morality believes in law. We taught decency. We developed people willing to participate in democracy.

We instilled ethical values, helped our students build an internal moral compass, and focused on their character formation and knowledge. We taught community, with schoolmates being their first opportunity to get along, rather than take on an us versus them attitude. Teachers with moral boundaries that wouldn't shift when the unscrupulous types began running our schools either no longer teach or no longer teach what their WCCriminal bosses do not want to hear.

In 1994, I discovered that my moral compass was as strong as the moral compasses of those running my school were weak. I lived by the Golden Rule; they lived by the rule of getting as much gold as you can.

The world had changed. I grew up having to wear a skirt to shop downtown. Now, getting naked and having sex on a video tape led to celebrity and billions of dollars. Our schools, the counterforce for these changes, were no longer a counterforce. Mom Kardashian easily scaled the abyss filled with WCCrime's dirty deeds and the severed spirits of dedicated teachers. The balance needed between what the Kardashians symbolize and what schools symbolize disappeared.

A Kardashian began dating a talented and presumed intellectual celebrity, which prompted an on-air conversation about whether Kardashians are smart. Some saw the couple as incompatible. Others said the Kardashians are smart too.

This was another time I wished they could hear me through the television. The difference between this bright clan and intellects is not intelligence but their choice of where to apply their intelligence. It is a value difference.

Intellectuals use innovative thinking to achieve ideals rather than to obtain things. They focus on accumulating good ideas, while the Kardashians focus on obtaining celebrity and material wealth. Democracy has me spending money to work at freeing our schools rather than on purchasing designer dresses. We're not organically harmonious.

Schools develop thinking about ideas. Most of what we encounter in daily life focuses on material things, other than religious organizations, which have also declined in influence due to the rise of social influencers.

The Kardashians are very smart. They model applying smarts to acquiring things and status. It is not that they have no place in society. They and social media have replaced what schools used to mold—balanced community members.

Materialism and the misinformation used to market it need an influencing counterforce. That used to be good schools and great teachers. Now, our country is like a scale of justice with one side dragging on the ground, creating sparks, and the other side so high that the air is too thin to breathe. We've become a society of opportunists, focused on what we can get rather than what we can do for others. We've lost the institution that contained our civilization's guardians. We're unbalanced.

The state of education I encountered was a system of accomplices with a "we-take-care-of-each-other" code that replaced the "we-take-care-of-the-children" code. It blanketed corruption ranging from embezzlements to kickbacks to all kinds of creative financial wrongs.

For instance, I worked at a district that had hired an architect to build a new library. He had no library experience. He failed to provide features, including a checkout station. Costly remodeling had to ensue. It could have been a kickback situation or someone hiring a friend. It wasn't a responsible use of taxpayer funds. Then there was a superintendent's wife, who they hired as a language arts consultant, whose knowledge and education were thin.

Although the list of financial wrongdoing is long, nothing is as detrimental as WCCrime's need for obedience over competence. It purges dedicated teachers. With the beloved image of motherhood and apple pie, WCCriminals block reform to maintain a twisted world. In a democracy, law is king. In a school, the administrator is king.

Teacher abuse destroys effective learning. Having to survive in a threatening environment, terrorized teachers become selfish teachers. Riddled with anxiety, they create a violent peace.

It's a brutal atmosphere where teachers know their smallness. They accept the psychological tracks that reduce them. With kindness drained from their hearts, loyalty to the villains remains. Having turned in their moral compasses, they lose the ability, even the right, to teach democracy. Can teachers accept unfair treatment like abused children and still convey critical thinking? I think not.

Kappa Delta Pi, an education Honor Society, has inductees sign a pledge that reads:

Education builds not alone for the present but for the future; not merely for self, but for society as well. Service incentive of the world's great teachers means that I will so live that others are empowered and enriched thereby. It means that as a teacher I will lose myself and so find myself in ceaseless effort to advance justice and peace for all people. All this I pledge as an ideal of Service.

Teachers break it, day after day, lost in the fury of the WCCriminals they serve.

Richard Reuther, a bullied Washington State teacher, used Facebook to teach what was going on with the 2020 election. It parallels what is going on in education. He said:

Trump is behaving just like a typical bully. You assault the biggest fish, the most respected person. Take that one down, and the rest will back off. When I was the target, my colleagues said, "If he can do that to YOU, what can he do to ME?" These were people, underpaid teachers, who had kids in college, who had mortgages on their primary residence... They NEEDED the money. They had no desire to be the next target. Many refused to walk in the halls with me on the way to lunch. They were terrified. Playing on the fears of those who don't want to lose is what they have.

Power is about having a platform. The quality of our democracy depends on who has the platform to watch over it. It shapes the nation. It hasn't been great teachers for multiple decades. Social influencers took it over once administrators took it out from under teachers. WCCriminals slant that platform sideways and let gravity take care of people like me. Teachers used to have a platform in the classroom. It was our sanctuary. It was democracy's sanctuary. It is time to return to our teachers' platform. Using wisdom and intellect, we must expand it so WCCrime, or anything like that, can't take it away again.

Our democracy influencers put their jobs on the back burner despite their love for their students. To explain why many kept quiet about the futility of the Vietnam War, Daniel Ellsberg said, "Most humans are loathed to be ostracized."

Whistleblowers are loathe to assist in the teardown of democracy. We chose to help children discover their gifts to become bountiful citizens, to pour our spirits into our profession to pay forward what good teachers gave us and to erase what bad teachers did to us, and to ensure that the scorn of those incapable of contributing to society does not take the lead. However, most teachers became puppets of darkness. Those in charge allow little that teachers honor.

Democracy is an agreement that we moderate our interests to operate together. The divisiveness that weighs heavy on our souls exists because too many citizens have not learned this. Magic doesn't make a democracy work. It's not organic, either. It depends on functional, corruption-free institutions. Education is neither.

My dedication to fixing education has always been for the sake of our democracy. This book explains why those in charge of schools have excluded teachers like me and thus weakened democracy. Keep reading. I promise our teetering on the brink of collapse democracy and the solution for restoring it will make perfect sense.

The altered two-page letter that the Board submitted on the next page, is starkly different from the actual two-page letter a parent sent to the Board and dropped off at my home. Notably, the sentence accusing the superintendent is conveniently missing from their version. To correct the record, I submitted the authentic version after they submitted the altered version. The authentic version is on the following page.

Take a look at these documents while considering the Illinois Criminal Code of 1961 - Article 17 Sec. 17-3. Forgery (720 ILCS 5/17-3) (a) A person commits forgery when, with intent to defraud, he knowingly: (1) makes or alters any document apparently capable of defrauding another in such manner that it purports to have been made by another or at another time, or with different provisions, or by authority of one who did not give such authority;

Friday, May 1, 1998

To All Members of the School Board

Dear Members,

Last Tuesday, April 28, 1998, the children of Mrs. Horwitz's class asked for a meeting with Mrs. Biancalana and the substitute teacher , Miss Palmatier. They were desperate to have Mrs. Horwitz back. The children wanted and needed their regular routine. A meeting was held and questions were asked. The children rolled their eyes when they realized that the truth was not being told. After the meeting, the substitut. asked if their questions had been answered and the children raised their hands and s id that Mrs. Biancalana was lying and they did not believe a word she had said. My chil. raised his hand and said that he had heard from one of his classmates that Mrs. Horw. · was suing the school for hiring all the new inexperienced teachers. Mrs. Biancal:na said that she wasn't suing the school. The children felt that as they were asking heir questions , Mrs. Biancalana was staring out the window "trying to put together he · next lie" before she answered their questions.

Today I asked my child how school was and he said he just wants his routine back and to be able to talk to Mrs. Horwitz. All year long the children have worked very hard to earn their special tickets which go to the end of the year Auction. He feels disappointed, let down and more importantly, he questions why it is acceptable for the Principal to lie to the children, but if he or any child is called down to her office. you had better tell the truth or be punished.

With only six weeks left of school, why are you as Board Members, supposedly in a position of power and representing the parents , not taking action by expediting Mrs. Horwitz's return?

Throughout this entire ordeal, please be aware that we are not fighting for the return of just any teacher, but for the return of an excellent, extraordinary. compassionate teacher who makes each child feel like they are number one. Mi s. Horwitz has a unique talent in recognizing and acknowledging each child's inal idual gift and self-worth. By not insisting on her immediate return, you are not just hurting Avoca's future but hurting our children.

BOARD EXHIBIT

As a parent with two younger children coming up through the system I beg of you to please stop hurting our children.

Sincerely,

Friday, May 1, 1998

To All Members of the School Board

Dear Members,

Last Tuesday, April 28, 1998, the children of Mrs. Horwitz's class asked for a meeting with Mrs. Biancalana and the substitute teacher , Miss Palmatier. They were desperate to have Mrs. Horwitz back. The children wanted and needed their regular routine. A meeting was held and questions were asked. The children rolled their eyes when they realized that the truth was not being told. After the meeting, the substitute asked if their questions had been answered and the children raised their hands and said that Mrs. Biancalana was lying and they did not believe a word she had said. My child raised his hand and said that he had heard from one of his classmates that Mrs. Horwitz was suing the school for hiring all the new inexperienced teachers. Mrs. Biancalana said that she wasn't suing the school. The children felt that as they were asking their questions , Mrs. Biancalana was staring out the window "trying to put together her next lie" before she answered their questions.

Today I asked my child how school was and he said he just wants his routine back and to be able to talk to Mrs. Horwitz. All year long the children have worked very hard to earn their special tickets which go to the end of the year Auction. He feels disappointed, let down and more importantly, he questions why it is acceptable for the Principal to lie to the children, but if he or any child is called down to her office, you had better tell the truth or be punished.

With only six weeks left of school, why are you as Board Members, supposedly in a position of power and representing the parents , not taking action by expediting Mrs. Horwitz's return?

Throughout this entire ordeal, please be aware that we are not fighting for the return of just any teacher, but for the return of an excellent, extraordinary, compassionate teacher who makes each child feel like they are number one. Mrs. Horwitz has a unique talent in recognizing and acknowledging each child's individual gift and self-worth. By not insisting on her immediate return, you are not just hurting Avoca's future but hurting our children.

Throughout the years, past experience has shown that what the parents want and what the children need is not important....It is what Dr.Sloan wants is what goes.

7066

As a parent with two younger children coming up through the system I beg of you to please stop hurting our children.

Sincerely,

54

5

YOU DON'T HAVE TO JUST TAKE IT FROM ME

"Knowledge is power. Information is liberating. Education is the premise of progress in every society, in every family."

Kofi Annan

"All the members of society have a direct interest in the manners of each of its individuals, because each one is a radiating point, the center of a circle which he fills with pleasure or annoyance, not only for those who voluntarily enter it but for those, who, in the promiscuous movements of society, are caught within its circumference."

Horace Mann

As I take you into the bowels of education, I'm trying to simplify what WCCriminals intentionally turned into a tangled, menacing jungle.

Imagine if administrators and school boards obstructed educators from following the laws that protect children from harm and guarantee a proper education. Imagine if they did this while making decisions geared toward their own self-serving interests, not the public's. There's no need to imagine. It's happening all over this nation, which is why our schools are spiraling further and further into darkness, unable to compete globally.

This raiding of our schools, which boards methodically conceal from the public, has generated such profound emotional chaos that our students use coping mechanisms with progressively more harmful outcomes, including shooting up their schools.

Our schools used to serve up spinach. Now, they offer a sweet table of addictive creations. An institution with the sacred mission of upholding democracy has pulled such a clever bait and switch on us that most remain reverent, incapable of grasping how fraudulent many schools have become.

I featured the two versions of a parent's letter, crucial evidence for my termination hearing record, on the previous page. The Board submitted the parent's letter after removing one sentence, unaware that I had the original letter, and I submitted the original letter with the missing sentence. The stark statement that my Board vanished with a black marker continues to evade accountability while speaking volumes about WCCrime. The erased sentence said:

> Throughout the years, past experience has shown that what the parents want and what the children need is not important—it is what Dr. [superintendent] wants is what goes.

Fealty to administrators, not children and parents, underpins education. A pervasive "I can do whatever I want" attitude is the foundation of the actions of administrators and boards nationwide. They seem to shun any association with democracy even though teaching it is its job.

But don't just take my word or Richard Dreyfuss, an acclaimed actor's word, when we say that education is the cornerstone of democracy. Our ancestors warned us. Thomas Jefferson said, "The most effectual means of preventing the perversion of power into tyranny are to illuminate...the minds of the people at large..."

Thus, dumbing down education is a straightforward route to tyranny. Even more on point, in the Republican Party Platform of 1888, Ulysses S. Grant wrote:

> In a Republic like ours, where the citizen is the sovereign, and the official the servant, where no power is exercised except by the will of the people, it is important that the sovereign—the people—should possess intelligence.

He had predicted in his 1875 "Speech to the Society of the Army of Tennessee" the following:

> If we are to have another contest in the near future of our national existence, I predict that the dividing line will not be Mason's and Dixon's, but between patriotism and intelligence on one side, and superstition, ambition, and ignorance on the other.

That contest is before us now because white-collar criminals, who have replaced competency with loyalty, have undereducated children for generations. Their failure to provide authentic education or to instill the patriotism that used to run through the veins of morally formed characters manifests as termites bringing a building down.

Think of our nation as a significant historic building with education as a substructure keeping it sturdy. Its foundation prepares citizens to support this "building" intellectually and morally. Since education produces future lawyers, leaders, and citizens and safeguards facts, keeping the building standing is crucial.

If our nation were an autocracy, schools would teach loyalty to the leader. Facts would be adjusted to those that pleased the leader. Since it's a democracy, it needs to develop each citizen's gifts and ability to think critically and play a role in governing, which includes voting, if not more. Facts need to be verified truth.

Schools once taught children how to know if the information was accurate and, more importantly, how to care if it was correct.

Brooks' article nailed where we are without a solid education foundation when he said in one sentence, "In a culture devoid of moral education, generations are growing up in a morally inarticulate, self-referential world."

If facts don't work for one's goals, many resort to what works for their greedy self. Alternative facts, a concept that could only live outside a democracy, now exist within. Once full of memories of the Golden Rules hammering our brains against making stuff up, our schools are now part of the world of alternative facts!

When education, our substructure, rots, our nation feels as it does today—slanted and broken planks under our feet. For many, it feels like we're falling between the floorboards. Our "building" is in turmoil with divided goals and differing "facts." Our schools existed as guardrails for democracy. Those running our schools have sold our precious guardrails for the raw steel and have pocketed the money.

Too many schools are run like HMOs, with decrees coming from the top rather than from teachers who know children's needs. Decisions are based on financial equations rather than on the welfare of the consumers, parents, and children. Stepford teachers, i.e., programmed robots, are the expected model. Worse, many schools are criminal enterprises, circumventing or, if needed, breaking laws while draining the life out of dedicated teachers. This wretched truth remains buried in a fog of disbelief with a trail of corruption linked to school shootings.

My goal is to educate you about the wrongdoings that few teachers dare discuss, including the theft of millions of dollars and the failure to provide authentic schools. I offer a framework for unraveling it and healing the nation with first-rate schools that will be within reach once the truth emerges. It's a truth that provides all of education's legitimate stakeholders a win while offering all those harming our children a loss.

I describe a war that attacks the soul of democracy, with no foxholes for teachers. It's the only way you'll know of this war. It matters not if you're conservative or liberal. A country that thrives for all must have real schools. You will learn how political parties and many of our institutions participated in the corruption, often unwittingly due to ignorance about WCCrime.

This corruption is as shocking as it's complex. It's about money, but so much more. You need to give me some time to explain it. It has stolen authentic education from us. It has created fertile grounds for school shootings. It has torn apart our democracy. Yet, it has evaded scrutiny because it's so much more complex than abusive priests or sexual harassment.

Furthermore, many think the government is intentionally dumbing down society for control. To that, I say the world of education is closer to a bunch of buffoons than a political strategy based on the cast of intellectually deficient characters running our schools. Perhaps many in government do not want a democracy and want to keep the people intellectually crippled. They may know about WCCrime and look the other way because it achieves their ends. The only way we'll know is if we blast the truth about our schools and the government continues to ignore WCCrime, signaling education does not matter to them. We can't say that isn't the case, but we know that what's going on in our schools has never seen the light of day. The media have completely missed this story.

Most reporters think it can't be that bad in the way most people think they can teach. Devaluing education brought us WCCrime and its tapestry of teacher subjugation. Education's history will help you see how democracy derailed.

Before women's liberation, other than nursing, teaching was the acceptable job for women. No woman in pursuit of a good marriage would dare use her brain and turn off men. Now that women are independent, few intelligent women will tolerate the brainlessness the education world demands. To WCCriminals, the exodus of bright teachers was perfect for WCCrime.

It was able to take hold since education is the stepchild of the social science disciplines. Few teachers earn an Ivy League degree. The only Ivy League connection is a program called Teach for America (TFA). It asks elite students to hold their noses and teach for two years so the people running the program can make lots of money. It created a temporary revolving-door teacher supply for underserved schools.

Do they help? This is a mixed bag. These children need continuity and roots, not teachers they'll never see again, who have had little teacher training. Plus, asking elite students to teach for only two years says that few would consider teaching as a profession, staining the profession more.

A degree from an elite college needs to be part of the world of education, not just a two-year stint that says: "People like us will only give two years to a career unworthy of intellectuals."

Also, schools associated with productive research are not among the teacher-training universities. Prestige universities have yet to realize that their marginalization of education has contributed to the downfall of our democracy.

Born before women's liberation, programmed to be background decoration, I'm making up for that by elevating education from the place where liberated women disappeared to THE discipline that will save our democracy.

This book strives to convince the powers that be that education needs to rise from the parenting section of our local bookstores to a valued discipline at Harvard or Yale. Its stepchild status is a key reason it has become corrupt. Yes, mafia-like corrupt.

While the Mafia with a capital "M" refers to blue-collar crime such as drug dealing, gambling, protection, and prostitution, amongst other vices, the education mafia with a lowercase "m" refers to white-collar crime.

These mafias have in common: a well-organized system of crime working as a team; durability over time, which resistance to reform epitomizes; use of fear to have their way; ability to commit a crime while an integral part of society; insulation from the law; parasitic existence off a host, which in both cases is the public; and a code of honor that maintains silence.

The main difference is that the Mafia accesses money via vice, while the education mafia accesses money via taxes. The Mafia uses physical brutality and murder to induce fear; the education

YOU DON'T HAVE TO JUST TAKE IT FROM ME

mafia uses psychological brutality and manipulation of the legal system to generate fear.

Although administrators drive teachers to suicide and rob them of their property rights, murdering and robbing are not part of their agenda, to the best of my knowledge. Another significant difference is that the education mafia enjoys the respect of the public and is insulated from scrutiny by bias that administrators have society's best interest in mind. In contrast, the Mafia is an object of disdain for most.

Society gravely erred when undervaluing a most sacred discipline. This intellectually disrespected profession has been fertile ground for exploitation. Resurrecting it must start with revering education. I hope to help you fall in love with it as I did.

TFA remains a candle in the wind education program associated with a university. Steven M. Singer's blog[5] devoted to the ills of TFA said:

> Watering down what it means to be a teacher is even less popular than actually being an educator. They recruit people in college who didn't major in education to become teachers for a few years before moving on to bigger and better things. The whole point of this scam is to serve the needs of the privatization movement.

> Investors want to change public education into a cash cow. They want to alter the rules so that corporations running districts as charter or voucher schools can cut services for children and use the extra cash for profits. If we allow privatizers to replace well-prepared and trained teachers with lightly trained temps, we can reduce the salaries we pay instructors. We delegitimize the profession. We redefine the job of 'teacher.' It's no longer a highly trained professional. Anyone can do it from off the street—thus, we can pay poverty wages. People who worked as temps in order to give themselves a veneer of credibility should not be treated the same as bona fide experts who dedicate their lives to kids in the classroom.

He then described how, subsidized by California billionaires, TFA alumni become paid staff for legislators, bringing the dark shadow of politics over education. He referred to Stephanie Simon's 2013 article, "TFA rises as a political powerhouse.» In it she describes how the significant money connections typically result in influencing education policy.

The important lesson here is: there's no way anyone connected to TFA has democracy's interest in mind because WCCrime is evident to anyone close to those running our schools. Since they aren't reporting it, they must participate or support it. They're pouring in money to make more money, not reforming schools. Only reciprocal wrongdoing could happen because thieves don't hand over their goodies.

Perhaps, once TFA discovered WCCrime, they threatened them with, "You share the stash, or we tell." More likely, compatible natures led to plotting together. I speculate with deep expertise on this topic and know that only the shady survive in education. Anyone who spends time working in a school infested with WCCrime knows something is very wrong. After decades, TFA has to know, so it proves that they're okay with it whether or not they're indulging in it. Fishy is the most accurate descriptor of TFA's participation in our schools. (There's more about TFA in the enhanced ebook version of this book.)

And the better universities have marginal education departments. Harvard University studied a teacher who was an expert in how children learn to write. Soon after that study, the principal placed that outstanding teacher in the "Rubber Room," the teacher prison you'll learn more about later. NY Union President Randi Weingarten, helped this irreplaceable teacher retire.

There's so much wrong here! Neither the union nor Harvard saved an expert teacher. They submitted to the district's harmful act, not what was good for our nation. At most universities, education is a Cinderella minus the fairy godmother discipline, with no connection to prestige or success. Lesser universities pretend otherwise.

I earned my Master's degree at National Louis University in Evanston, Illinois. It's considered good for education, in the way that McDonald's hamburgers are good for that class of hamburgers. In 2002, I wrote its president, who identified as LifelongDreamer. The email and the press release I sent him remain on my website,[6] unanswered, as silent complicity. This university follows the education world's "We take care of each other" code rather than we take care of the children code. In an email to him, I wrote: "There are more nightmares than dreams in this field...it is impossible to present yourself as a lifelong dreamer unless what you mean is that you refuse to wake up."

Having provided a sense of our universities' disregard for education, a climate in which education's intellect shrinks, I will take you back to 1963, when I graduated from high school.

Things were different before women's liberation. I was a before woman, a-little-before-Barbie woman. Given the limited choices, the brightest women chose teaching. Teaching, nursing, and secretarial duties were pretty much our world, no matter how smart or dumb we were. Luckily, I felt called to teach. Our careers were secondary. Our job was to marry well. There was no need for a prestigious school. Education was part of the inferior world of women.

I was a good student. I attended Oak Park River Forest High School, one of Chicagoland's top schools. Advanced placement classes were not a thing, but our school had an honors track where I dwelled. In my junior year, I took honors chemistry. I'm not sure how many girls were in the class, but I think close to none since I don't remember having a friend. The boys in that class were destined to be rocket scientists—real rocket scientists. The teacher challenged us with an equation-balancing contest.

This was a top school and the most challenging class. After a few days, I, not one of the rocket scientists, solved the equation. Instead of inspiring me to pursue a science career, I thought, "No one would want to date me if I did," besides, I liked children—the pre-women's liberation limited mind in action. I decided to be a teacher and make this a better world.

Creating an illusion that one can make an impact in education started at a young age, actually. In high school, I was a member of the Future Teachers of America, which, in hindsight, was an opportunity to recruit fools who thought teaching was about making a difference. The absence of clubs for fast food workers, manicurists, cleaning people, or waitresses meant that teaching was special. We thought God would not call us for something shallow or corrupt. Were we ever wrong!

I took all advanced classes. I had to share my college choice with Dean Swanson in my senior year. I told him that I was attending the University of Illinois. He appeared dismayed. I had the grades to attend a better school. He asked what I planned to study. I said, "Education." I will never forget his look as he muttered, "Oh, then it doesn't matter," and mumbled something under disappointed breath—"University of Illinois, that's good enough for teaching."

I wasn't surprised he looked down on a state school. I wondered why he would think a female would choose anything else. I knew I was Harvard material but programmed with non-women's liberation expectations, so selecting the nonintellectual world of education seemed perfect. It felt even better that he knew I was sacrificing my great brain and submitting—it made me an ideal woman. It took me until about 1965 to realize I could have had choices—when I read Betty Friedan's women's liberation blockbuster book, *The Feminine Mystique*.

He stamped my form. He meant well. I cannot accuse my dean of enabling male chauvinists, the predecessors of WCCriminals since the last thing they wanted was a person like me. If only he had saved them or saved me. Sorry, I'm digressing.

I'd still become a teacher if I had to do it all over again. I fell in love with democracy and somehow realized that teaching was a big deal for maintaining it, even if society hadn't figured that out yet. (It still has yet to!) I wanted to ride in a vehicle that built a healthy society. I had visions of what I could do as a teacher. Unfortunately, the vehicle and I ended up in a ditch.

I didn't write this book to brag about my scholarship or teaching ability. Apologies keep surfacing in my brain because of the socialization women my age had to endure. I've had to bat them down to do this work. Indoctrination runs deep. Men have always had a socially acceptable way to show the world they're smart. Women didn't since it didn't matter.

Since you need to know how anti-intellectual this field is, sharing the root cause of why teachers like me are incompatible with most of our current schools is bedrock information for reform. Plus, you need to trust my problem-solving skills, which are at the heart of my work, and why it's worth your time to read this. Most of all, you will better understand what needs to be done if you grasp that intelligence and teaching have become grossly incompatible. No matter how great I was at teaching, my brain made me a pariah to the antiquated, corrupted system in place.

In fact, intelligence is a curse in teaching. In my early twenties, a middle-aged male principal hired me, and during the interview crowed, "I'm unusual. I'm not afraid to hire smart teachers."

He had to have figured out that I was bright from my transcripts, as the interview was thin. His comment jarred me. His needing that mantra implied that most principals don't want intelligent teachers. I certainly had had enough rejection from men who don't want to date smart women.

"Why wouldn't they want smart teachers? Why was that unusual?" I wondered. Soon, I knew. Intelligent people are prone to figuring out and speaking out about incompetence and wrongdoing. It's a known fact that when teaching gifted children, a lack of fairness sets them off. They enter this world gift-wrapped in a need to make a difference, preloaded with an intolerance for injustice to make sure their gift wasn't wasted.

The "proud to hire smart teachers" principal was long before the days when a woman could complain about sexism. He'd put his arms around several of us as if we were the Rockettes—a chorus line about to kick in remarkable unison—and would say, "My teachers have the best legs." We did, and that's why we were hired! I'm sure he saw my eyes roll when he behaved obnoxiously and decided to replace me with an obedient girl.

My soon-to-come report to the Board about how he treated talented teachers with contempt, forcing them to resign so he could hire new ones each year, caused him to lose his job. I'm sure the "proud to hire smart teachers" principal stopped hiring smart teachers after me.

Years later, I understood why he wanted smart teachers. His abusive ways were more gratifying when foisted on attractive, bright women who'd have to put up with a short, homely man. This was 1970. By 1990, principals politically stacked boards, so no teacher had a chance to report their evil deeds.

What profession buries intelligence? The brightest people usually innovate and lead. I fell in love with a profession that was just plain wrong for an academic. Yet, I was born with an awesome gift to understand children's needs.

Success was elusive, having landed in a disrespected discipline with the few visionaries carefully gagged. With every modicum of intelligence cordoned off, WCCriminals went to town doing their lawless activities. Stranded amongst a bunch of followers with a bunch of criminals and no prestigious universities leading the way or bothering to investigate is not a starting place for something good to happen.

But it has, as you will see when you read more about my work in Chapter 13. I was in the right profession. Nothing moves me like teaching in a classroom did. I don't know how many unforgettable moments a human being gets. I've used up most of mine while teaching. Yet, I suspect that those of us who were called to teach got a bunch extra because miracles need to be remembered.

I remember the day I knew why I was born. An ordinary September day became etched in my mental diary. I was twenty-one years old. I had been teaching second grade for two weeks. I was indeed in love with my job. Each day felt too short. My soul was connected in a way it had never been before. I thought I had won the spiritual lottery.

Before I left for the day, I checked my mailbox. I have done many jobs, from retail sales to clerical work. This was not a job. I was living my ideals. Reality greeted my soul when I found my first teaching paycheck in my mail slot. Tears streamed as two worlds came together. I could make a living doing what I love! I nearly mutilated the paycheck, unable to stop tears of something more profound than joy. My soul became seated in this world of education, being paid for the work it came here to do.

I held onto a nearby railing, experiencing this blessed moment as a twenty-one-year-old, thinking no one had ever had this experience before. I write about it in my seventh decade of life, thinking no one will ever experience this again.

I knew I had the unique ability to help children find their perfect place as I had found mine. All my life, I had reached children few others could. My uncanny skill at getting children to cooperate found a purpose beyond the babysitting that filled my teenage years.

As a fifth-grade patrol girl, I dealt with a boy who exhausted all, including adults. I was able to reach him and tame him. Others would react with disbelief seeing him behave with me. A decade later, I read a newspaper article about this very boy being arrested for murder. I thought about that little boy who almost viciously drove all but me crazy. It validated the gift I had.

Often, a teacher would see me handle a student she had given up on the prior year. She would utter comments of disbelief. One said, "I had tried everything with Michael, but it was hopeless. I am shocked to see him showing you respect." She saw my skills as outside the norm. They were.

Then, there was anxious Ted in my fourth-grade class. My students' negative emotions were, for me, like skulls on bottles of poison. No learning happens when these warnings flash. I helped Ted devise a worksheet for when he worried.

Because I was also a reading specialist, I administered tests to determine my students' proper level at times. I checked Ted's since he was in a pull-out reading assistance program, and I wanted to make sure he needed extra help, given that the program was a source of anxiety for him.

The test showed he was at least at grade level and did not need that program. I recommended he stop. I zeroed in on anxiety, not reading, as his issue. His parents sent a letter expressing gratitude that someone finally figured him out. They were ecstatic. On the other hand, the special education director was almost as angry as during his years later videotaped deposition for my federal lawsuit when he turned red, an indication of lying. By the way, I still have the video if an investigative reporter looks into this criminal enterprise before the video ages out and turns all red.

I needed to be more knowledgeable about government funding. Still, I noted an eagerness to help a child eligible for ESL—English as a second language—while not wanting to help others, such as a child who was tardy eighty-five times. Decisions were odd and probably based on access to money, not what kids need. Otherwise, why were they mad that Ted stopped reading remediation?

Ted did well after that. I think about how a boy with deep worries felt being in remediation when he didn't need it. I'm glad I helped him even though doing so added incentive to get rid of me. I was there to help my students. I put them first.

Then there was Sally, who finished her work quickly and pulled out a favorite book. Students like that only alarm teachers like me since I was there to help my students grow rather than enjoy the easy ones like her. Her work was okay but could have been better, and I knew she was bright. I spoke to her about how I could help her use her free time to help her grow as a learner.

She told her grandmother that her teacher found a problem, and the family became upset as she had never had school issues. Her mom scheduled a conference with me, ready to pounce, at which I explained that Sally was too bright to be rushing through her work. I wanted to help deepen her learning. The mom quickly processed this as a positive step, mainly since Sally's math skills were not great.

In time, Sally improved in math and participated more in the extra credit opportunities I offered. The following year, the mom called me to tell me how great she was doing in math because of me.

I just described a positive example of how I teach beyond the lesson. You need to know where this led. This mom was so delighted that she met with the principal to express gratitude for my teaching and complained that no previous teacher had said anything about this. Immediately after that meeting with the praising parent, the principal wrote me up for diminishing my colleagues to this parent.

I had not said a word about prior years. The parent realized the previous teaching was deficient now that she met a skilled teacher. She met with the principal so she'd help her help these other teachers, not at all aware she would get me in trouble.

It crossed my mind to warn her and ask her not to raise this with the principal, but there was no way I could have asked that parent not to meet with the principal. Discussing the likelihood she would go on the attack was unprofessional. I accepted that I had to remain silent about the nature of the education beast, and I did for many years.

My doing my magic with children when the principal's favorite teachers couldn't compete was a recipe for trouble. Making sure my students each developed their gifts was the only path for me then, and I'm still on it. It's with adult students now.

Many years later, during my teaching dismissal hearing, one parent complained that her son's prior teachers were like stewardesses, whereas I challenged her exceptionally bright son. Other teachers thought the job was done while I helped him grow. I always integrated opportunities for my gifted students, such as leadership positions in our class newspaper. Another parent testified that our school had many good teachers, but Mrs. Horwitz was exceptional. She said I reached inside her child and found gifts like no other teacher had.

She was correct. As I reached, I saw inside my students. This allowed me to help them in ways no others had. When a movie about a horse whisperer came out, I realized I was a kid whisperer. I was using that gift to make this a better world.

My spirit had found its lounge chair. Although awe is associated with nature, while teaching, awe happened daily since education profoundly called me. Few are teaching with this same gift because those with the same profile could also reach inside our administrators and see criminality. That compelled us to report them.

My being exceptional with children is another thing you don't need to take from me. The parents' testimony is in my termination transcript. You can also take it from my ten-year-old student, who wrote an article for our classroom newspaper. The Board had abruptly banished me, leaving my students anxious. They had no idea I had a problem with my administration. I remained professional despite drowning in a most unprofessional job. I protected my students the way a mother protects her children. This fifth-grade student wrote:

> I am the most worried. The reason is that she has taught me the best, because she has gotten deep down to my thoughts to teach me the best (meaning that she taught everyone by their own personal needs, and not by her needs like other teachers do.) I think that she tries to get to everyone that way that is why I think that she is a very good teacher from all of the classes that I have been to. I know that Mrs. Horwitz has taught me the most…(This student's entire article is at the beginning of this book in "About the Author.")

I wasn't always able to teach. After having a child, teaching jobs became scarce. I worked as a teacher's aide for a year to be next in line for a teaching job. There were none the following year, so I gave up. I did various jobs until I became a marketing director for educational films. How that happened speaks both to my problem-solving capabilities and my deep-seated devotion to education.

I came across an ad for an educational film company seeking phone salespeople. I applied, figuring that at least there was an academic connection, and maybe it wouldn't be sleazy like my last sales position. They hired three of us.

Our boss explained that this company's educational division was failing because the plentiful funds for educational films available in the 1960s-1970s were drying up. While hundreds of film companies thrived for years, there were now less than a dozen, and this one's destiny would be bleak if they didn't figure out how to sell these films by phone. He explained that outside salespeople had always covered this market. As hard as they tried, their customers rejected phone sales.

I analyzed the situation and devised a strategy to avoid the usual phone seller's dreaded hangup. I changed our customers' minds. It worked so well that my boss made me Director of Marketing and Sales and increased my salary while firing one of the other two hired with me. I then hired about five others throughout my time there. (I had to fire the third original person soon after my promotion, an experience described in the Epilogue.)

A dozen of the other companies left standing noted my success, and a couple of years later, another local one made me an offer to save their failing educational film division, which became another of my accomplishments.

Succeeding in business failed to make me, a called-to-teach person, think, "Wow, I can make big money in business." Later on, it did tell me that I could turn our corrupt schools around just as I had saved a dying business. My problem-solving talent became part of my portfolio, which never saw the light of day. Still, it is what we need in education leaders. Our schools hire people who lack problem-solving skills, as those types are more easily controlled, and hire people who embrace and nurture problems to keep education as their private fiefdoms.

I earned many times more than a teacher—triple the salary plus bonuses. I traveled some, with an expense account, and met famous people.

When we sold the film series *Roots,* I had dinner with LaVar Burton. I met celebrated directors. I mainly hired teachers. One asked me if I still renewed my teaching certificate. I told her I hoped I could afford to teach one day, and she was stunned. But again, I was called to teach, and she wasn't.

Whenever I dropped my six-year-old daughter at school, tears formed. They were tears of sorrow that I didn't work where I belonged. At my daughter's second-grade conference, the teacher asked about my job, having heard about my glamorous life from my daughter. She said, "I'm so jealous," not noticing my sadness.

I can't call what I felt jealousy. It was closer to feeling hopeless that someone who didn't love teaching was teaching, and I couldn't. It felt twisted. Walking into any school and seeing all the school trappings made me sad. It does to this day. It's as if the lockers permanently hold part of me.

So, in 1992, when I could secure a real teaching job, it felt like I had won an Oscar. My principal's demand that our teachers' lounge had to be the "Happy Talk Cafe" or we'd be written up was a clue that there was unhappy talk needing a cover-up. Soon, I discovered the job was a dangerous travesty regarding what's suitable for children and our democracy.

The day I realized I needed to take the plunge that would end my career was when a parent complained about another teacher on my fourth-grade team. I told her to talk to the Board. She responded, "Parents are afraid." I knew teachers were afraid, but that day, it all made sense: gangsters were in control of my beloved profession. I set out to help parents and make a difference. I metamorphosed from an award-winning teacher to a whistleblower. Discovering that our schools were corrupt beyond anyone's imagination and talented teachers like me were outcasts to those running our schools, I knew I had to expose this. God doesn't give useless gifts.

I knew I was building a better world when I taught, helping each student find their gifts. I didn't see myself as a protector of democracy because there were few signs it needed protection. Not until I started my organization in 2002 did I realize it wasn't just my elitist school district that thought the law didn't apply to them. Teachers were reporting abuse and corruption from every state, every size district, and every socioeconomic level.

Then, when Trump and red flags of insanity and violence created a layer of anxiety in everyday living, I knew that I was called to teach for reasons beyond my students. Teachers like me protect democracy. It cemented me as an activist.

What made parents marvel at my ability to help their children has now made me a relentless reformer, ardently trying to reach citizens at a place far deeper than where political parties start and where divisiveness begins.

You don't have to take it from me, but who better could tell you what dedicated teachers do than an actual teacher? We lack civility or space to work out our differences without real schools. From my soul to yours, I ask you to delve further into the lost and wicked world of education. This book will lead to solutions for our nation that are only available with real schools, schools we will only have when we expose WCCrime.

6

COUNTERFEIT SCHOOLS

"Good people do not need laws to tell them to act responsibly, while bad people will find a way around the laws"

Plato

"The ultimate tragedy is not the oppression and cruelty by the bad people but the silence over that by the good people."

Martin Luther King

"Education is a better safeguard of liberty than a standing army."

Edward Everett

Before further discussing WCCrime, and at the expense of repeating what I've said, I want to clarify this. My concern about WCCrime is not just about money—it's hardly about money. The embezzlement of our tax dollars has hurt us far less than the collateral damage of pirates running our schools. Their lack of interest in education's intended purpose and their failure to keep children safe is what drives me.

The stolen money is of little importance compared to the effect generations of undereducated students have had on democracy, as well as living with school massacres. Too many of our schools are counterfeit.

For those who view schools as cash cows, WCCrime is easy money because it's corruption without consequences. However, WCCrime is more than stealing money. Its raison d'être, or reason for being, is to hijack public education and keep it covert. It's taking all of us down, not just teachers. Solving this is priceless.

Since you now know that WCCriminals pulled democracy's plug by duping, dumbing, and devouring the education world, you're probably wondering how prevalent WCCrime is. Although I cannot give you an exact count of WCCriminals, there are enough to have detonated our democracy. And since promoting and supporting incompetence is an aspect of WCCrime that evolved from education's missing intellectual leadership, WCCrime is widespread.

A more appropriate question is: Are there schools without it? That answer is yes. Former Connecticut Superintendent Dr. Armand Fusco wrote the 2005 exposé book *School Corruption: Betrayal of Children and the Public Trust* to save our education system. When I contacted him, he was shocked to hear about teacher abuse.

Why didn't he know about it? It's a tool for running crooked schools. It keeps teachers from reporting bad actors. This superintendent's agenda was the opposite. Although he knew of rampant corruption, he, like most, needed an education about what made fraud abundant enough to fill his book.

He later tried to attack WCCrime in another way. After he retired, he offered all Connecticut school boards a no-cost audit that could rise to a tax forensic investigation. Very few districts took him up on this generous offer. Not wanting to know if funny business was going on was the driving force behind turning down these audits.

Over the years, many educators contacted me. An administrator fessed up that he often lied to parents. He'd tell them their child didn't need a service that he knew they really needed. He read part of my book. He told me I was right about what was going on. I asked him why he and so many fell into line. He said, "It is like a drug. I was young. I walked around the school with so much power. It made me feel high."

Since he knew how treacherous it was, he left New York and got a job in California. Right before he was about to start, his new district sent him a copy of a letter saying he had resigned. They forged his signature, a popular WCCrime tactic. He realized they're a brotherhood of like-minded criminals.

His former district had extended their harassment to ruin his career. They make a phone call to a fellow mobster to do the job. They cannot allow any insider with information to remain standing and be a voice against them. They ruin their victim's credibility so they are no longer a threat.

His description that WCCrime and its kaleidoscope of fraud are like a drug sums up why it infiltrated our schools. However, it's a drug that ruins society, not the person on it. And in the same way, drugs are not a problem for everyone, there are high-functioning schools. However, great schools are a minority. Even before WCCrime took the reins, education's disrespected profile and inability to deal with intellectual ideas meant limited success.

Some successful teachers will resent what I am exposing. Their careers worked. Those fortunate few great teachers, oblivious to what most of their dedicated colleagues have endured, are not blessed with luck. They're cursed with blinders that will keep them from saving the profession they hold dear.

We need widespread investigations to determine the extent of teacher abuse and corruption. Instead, we have a widespread cover-up. WCCrime is in over 50% of our schools, but it sometimes feels like 90%. Only an honest survey will determine this, and that will be only after teachers feel safe to tell the truth.

And how ruthless are these administrators bent on having their way? I'd say not as bad as Charles Manson, but behaving better than he did is easy. And, it's hard to consider a school shooting better than Charles Manson if you consider the outcome rather than the intention. WCCriminals don't intend to afflict harm. They do whatever to grab every perk available to them.

Investigations do not occur when predators are in control. Predators abuse to have power! Research suffers the fate of being up against very organized crime; it's complex and scary. The following two examples are the only serious research I've encountered in my three-decades-long, diligent education study.

While teacher Rosalyn Schnall, the author mentioned earlier, was teaching at Chicago Public Schools, teacher abuse disturbed her so much that she conducted careful scientific research to document its prevalence. She found that 85% of the five hundred teacher research participants experienced career-harming abuse. In the description of her 2009 book, *When Teachers Talk: Principal Abuse of Teachers/The Untold Story*, she said, "Teacher abuse may very well be the most significant underlying cause contributing to the decline of public education in America today."

Before her, Education Professors Joseph and Jo Blase of the University of Georgia had conducted groundbreaking research on teacher abuse. They reported their findings in their 2002 book, *Breaking the Silence: Overcoming the Problem of Principal Mistreatment of Teachers*.

It validated the existence of teacher abuse and described its harsh nature. It wasn't intended to determine its prevalence. The professors hoped to spark further investigation. They would have if educrats weren't experts at keeping the silence the Blases tried to break.

A few years ago, I came across an article by an unknown education writer parroting what I've been saying for decades: teacher abuse is the key cause of education dysfunction. He celebrated the Blases' unknown exposé and deduced that no one knows about their work, showing that teacher abuse is the root problem. Meanwhile, I have a prolific website that screams its existence, not just mentioning the Blase book but selling it since 2002. He's right. A teacher is no one.

I blame the lack of respect that envelops the world of education. It is understandable not to respect this world as it exists. Had prestigious universities maintained intellectual dignity for this discipline and led the way with teacher-validated research, the Blases's significant research would not have fallen into a black hole. Follow-up research by a network of scholars would have encouraged more in-depth study and ignited real reform.

Instead, it is unknown since education is not a serious discipline or practice. It is undeserving of dignified status as women were at one point. I needed to carve a new path in this once empathetic but now pathetic world. Unlike most of my colleagues, who express concerns quietly with tortured acceptance, I could not allow education to lapse from disrespect to worthlessness. I made saving education my career and welcomed ostracism from a coterie of people who were outright stealing education from our democracy or abetting the theft with silence.

Education is both art and science. It needs talented experts to practice it. It is an ideal rather than an opportunity to make money. Idealism stemming from skilled teachers must lead the way. Administrators must be in place to organize teacher findings and needs. Its leaders must be career-driven, idealistic teachers, not opportunistic administrators who erase idealism.

Teachers learn to observe children's needs. Their observations and requests are crucial for success. Teachers are like mothers observing their children and determining their needs. Good mothers are continuous problem solvers. WCCriminals not only do not listen to teachers, they squish the life out of them so they'll stop sharing. Rather than lead with ideals, they lead a political empire that has little to do with the ideal for which it exists. They ignore these children's other mothers, thwarting their ability to problem-solve.

Were you aware that great teachers love your kids as if they were their own? We do. Are you aware that great teachers are nearly extinct? We are. We need to save education together.

A teacher's career is over if a teacher does what I did. Despite my efforts for almost three decades, education remains ineffective and toxic. One person, like me, needs to succeed for another to find courage. There's no point in teachers joining me in this darkness I have inhabited since 1995. I need citizens to help me find power so teachers can join me.

Think Harvey Weinstein. He did as he pleased for decades because he could ruin the career of anyone who reported him. Those in that system found it easier to endure him than lose a career like those in the education world who endure WCCrime. Only when one actress spoke out did a few others help build a voice.

When the next voice saw Goliath on his back, she spoke. Then, when Weinstein was on trial, many more spoke. Because Ronin Farrell investigated and reported the truth, it broke open. If not for one brave movie star, Harvey would still be having sex with his obliging harem instead of with—you know what goes on in jail.

Think priest abuse. Because *The Boston Globe* investigated it, it broke open. Watch the 2015 movie *Spotlight,* which is about how they almost gave up. It's hard being a David. That's how abusive situations work. Predators hide behind silence, born of fear until someone explodes the truth. This sinister strategy of silencing teachers guarantees you will not hear of WCCrime elsewhere. It's ruthless and hell-bent on keeping the status quo.

And keeping the status quo is more than just a WCCriminal goal. Ending democracy, what WCCrime does, works for those who prefer that socioeconomic status and class remain as is.

White supremacy is rooted in economics. If the elite and powerful were tired of dealing with others who had not achieved their status, they would want to close off their special place on this earth. They'd like to limit competition amongst their peers by annihilating the road to the top.

It is agreed that education is the underpinning of a democracy. It is the only way for those not born into a wealthy family to find success. It is an equalizer. It allows social elevation. There would be no better way to end the sharing of their resources than to end the institution that allowed so many people to start with nothing and become one of them—our public schools.

In a recent email, Robert Reich said:

> In 1994, when I was serving as Secretary of Labor in the Clinton administration, I gave a speech warning that America was becoming a two-tiered society and that rising wealth inequality would eventually tear the fabric of our society and bring democracy to its knees.

He was correct. Yet, he did not know that WCCrime was chipping away at the institution that was to promote wealth equality. He still doesn't know or he would have mentioned it in his writings.

Nevertheless, he cares. Some do not want wealth equality. The Supreme Court decision, *Citizens United,* combined with the "destroy public schools" agenda, is a joy to the hearts of those tired of carrying the needy, the unsophisticated, and the foreign. Those obsessed with money and power can create the life they believe they deserve or plan to obtain. To them, life is about material and social gains. School choice—gut public education—is their solution, not democracy.

Some books warn the public against the privatization of schools, particularly the charter movement. Diane Ravitch's 2013 book, *Reign of Error: The Hoax of the Privatization Movement and the Danger to America's Public Schools* ranks high among them. However, she only explained where we are, not who brought us to this democracy-destroying dance. WCCrime paved the road to privatization. To arrive at a solution, all must know the WCCrime history behind this power grab to grasp how schools got to the point described in Ravitch's book.

The dysfunction of our schools allows many to accept the charter movement as the only solution. Once educated about the free-for-all in our public schools, citizens will know they must turn this runaway train around, not give away its railcars.

The personal ambition of those in power has replaced community ideals. Education is the road to democracy. Dismantling education is the road to an aristocracy, where power is held in the hands of the privileged few. It is a one-way road if we do nothing.

We can't just stop the privatization movement. We must identify the players who opened the door for this destructive movement. We must go back to education before WCCrime, something we can only do if we acknowledge what brought us to today. We need to learn how evil took over education so we can restore democracy. I think doing nothing about the exodus of talented women due to women's liberation left a hollowness ripe for crime. The question is: did they do nothing about that issue so they could hijack our schools, or were they not bright enough to anticipate the vacuum women's liberation would surely cause?

We must shame many and punish some for their role in WCCrime. That will redirect rather than obliterate them. We must view WCCrime as a mistaken path that was easier for most. It is not proof that good leadership does not exist in education.

We need to understand that education has been the Wild West. So many inept and immoral types held the reins. Good people had to go along or go away. The solution isn't to end public schools, a pillar of democracy, but to clean them up. That will only be done once we know the facts. We can't throw out the baby with the dirty bath water.

A friend described her substitute teaching experience in an elite suburban high school. Her students thought Reconstruction happened in Europe and had no idea what it was. She was aghast. Earlier, I mentioned removing civics lessons and lessons to help students form proper character and become citizens in a democracy. Combining that with sparse history lessons, schools are launching missiles, not citizens.

I became an activist in 1995 to prove that these power-mongers abused the best and brightest teachers and turned them into puppets or forced them out of the profession. I co-founded the National Association for the Prevention of Teacher Abuse in 2002 to find like-minded educators.

I created a website with humorous graphics to balance the seriousness of the topic. I didn't have to deal with it being too soon, having done the writing several years after my termination, but I did think about readers being confused—it's not funny. Yet, the topic is so depressing that I decided that humor would help the reader stay with it. I decided to have it reflect who I am as a person. Humor has always helped me keep my spirit intact; since this work comes from my soul, it belongs.

And I still enjoy the rolling eyes on the page describing the altered documents that my district put into the legal record found at http://www.endteacherabuse.org/alteredl.html. Usually, it's called forgery. In their case, it's called nothing. They violate laws with abandonment. Those eyes, not the wheels of justice, have been rolling for the past twenty-two years.

Over 2200 people joined our group, sharing their horror stories. They expressed gratefulness that our group existed. I met a nation of dedicated teachers whose presence in my life almost made up for the torture I'd experienced. I posted their stories online. Their voices shouted that our country was in a race to the bottom due to sham schools buried in a facade of deception.

Then I discovered that nearly half of the bright, dedicated teachers who joined my group voted for Trump. Their wondering about the out-of-control state of our schools turned into disgust; they elected a disruptor. It became clear to me that the corrupted system was why our democracy was falling apart and why people fell for Trump.

In his book *Audacity of Hope*, former President Obama said, "Throughout our history, education has been at the heart of a bargain this nation makes with its citizens." Reneging on this promise caused many to lose faith in the government. They knew that both political parties allowed our schools to become tools for the powerful. They wanted change even if it meant the end of democracy; to them, it was a farce. They disbelieved that a legitimate government would allow these swamp-like schools.

For targeted teachers, teacher abuse was deprivation wrapped in biohazard plastic. It made our calling a sham. Parents, reacting to the sham forced upon us, made us their enemies. The education landscape crumbled.

A memorable conversation with a parent member was when one told me she found our site and had an epiphany. She uncovered why teachers behaved as they did. She had thought they were Satan since she had no idea what their administrators were doing to teachers.

Our group identified the real "Satans." They're scoundrels who order teachers to let down parents to spawn prejudice against teachers, their faithful cover. The more parents and teachers hate each other, the less chance any would figure out who the bad guys are. Our site ended her hate.

The story of Houston ISD, detailed in Part Three of the enhanced ebook, sheds light on what WCCrime is and why government accountability became one of my impelling goals. It contains the reporting of phony scores to gain power and then blaming it on an innocent victim while harassing all who tried to expose them. It included a courageous administrator, Robert Kimball,[7] who spoke out but whistled in the wind like the rest of us. A US president and two education secretaries rose to the government's top on lies.

WCCrime is hard for parents to figure out, so they deduce that teachers don't care, not that teachers are hostages. I did not talk about what was happening until I decided I needed to go public one day. A parent confronted me in the hall, asking what was happening after seeing me cowering at the meeting about her son. She knew something was wrong, and she demanded I tell her.

By now, you can tell I am not a cowerer. The fact that teaching did that to me shows how effective WCCrime abuse is. It penetrates deeply and secretly like infrared waves. There was nothing too low for administrators.

Soon after that I chose a career of exposing the truth about our schools to force change, and then in 2015, Trump made change more urgent. Although I could not support Trump, members who voted for him remained in agreement about our schools. We were able to still talk.

Not just angry teachers turned to Trump. Parents have, too. I had many discussions with an active parent member, who joined because the principal had tormented her son for supporting a bullied friend. She ran for office on a stop bullying platform and received an unexpected check for $10,000 for her son's schooling, saying in their mob-like way, keep your mouth shut, and we will take care of you.

She returned the check with a piece of her mind. Later, she told me how she had found Qanon and how Trump was going after the pedophiles. Can you blame her for falling for that with what she had experienced: children mistreated and administrators covering it up with money?

It was 2016. My failure to expose WCCrime since 1995 convinced her that she needed Trump. I could not persuade her or others like her that my path had promise. To them, a bombastic strongman, not a former teacher, must uproot the corruption.

I hoped if people wanted to understand what led us to Trump, whether for or against him, they'd read my book and a counter-movement could begin because I understood them. Many believe that Trump's followers are all white supremacists. Yet, many of the teachers who joined my group are black or have black partners, yet support Trump. Many described agonizing attempts to help disadvantaged children yet support Trump.

Yes, there is racism. It is expected with hollowed-out schools. But teachers join my group because they care about educating children. They know effective education is close to being outlawed and express deep concern about the school-to-prison pipeline. They're stressed out that they're prevented from saving these students by teaching them how to stay out of prison.

I know what buoys Trump beyond his irrational cult. Take a look at my online dialogue with a Trump-supporting member I had known for years. https://www.whitechalkcrime. com/fake-news/ These people have had it!

Since so many of our members chose Trump, some of whom I knew well and respected in every other way, I knew if the powers that be admitted to failure in education and began a clean-up, we could win them over. We could bridge the divide as well as decrease Trump's support.

With Trump, we are up against a cult of delusion and others who have accepted authoritarianism and lawbreaking. They believe our democracy is dishonest. I get how the concept of a corrupt deep state caught on. They think: how else did so many people allow our schools to become this phony?

There is a deep state of pretense and anti-democratic behavior in our schools. The hidden corruption that has hijacked our schools proves them correct. They believe that Trump is the only way to grab back power. They see what's going on in education as part of the deep state. I see it as a democracy that's lost its way and needs its citizens to rescue it.

Many are parents who feel threatened by our schools. Schools pull politics in to create distractions from their wrongdoing. They become overly "woke" or overly conservative—whatever works for them. Schools should be as neutral as possible on these issues so educating children takes center stage. Instead, they jump into fads so they don't have to do what they're supposed to do but can't do without allowing teachers to take the lead.

We have diverse views about issues. Schools used to be the place where people learned how to live together with their conflicting opinions. At their core, schools were where compromise grew. Now, they're where it dies.

Understandably, many feel as unsafe about the values being taught at our school as they feel unsafe about schools due to school shootings. Understandably, many parents want to protect their children from these schools. WCCriminals have made our schools unsafe by disempowering the force that is used to make them safe—powerful teachers.

The growth of homeschooling was a natural outcome—a red flag. Had the souls of great teachers remained in the driving seat, our schools would have been on an entirely different trajectory.

85

Since WCCriminals made sure they stuffed these loving souls into trash cans, schools have become a threat to moms and families.

Democracy thrives on compromise, a principle that WCCriminals blatantly disregard. The surge in homeschooling and the growing unity of moms and families against Democrats is widespread rejection of our schools, a direct consequence of the detrimental influence of WCCriminals.

I can scientifically prove that our schools are a key reason many vote for Trump. From the onset of my group to expose teacher abuse in 2002, we regularly received a few members each week. We thought that was terrific since many told us they were afraid to join and had visited incognito for years. Each year until around 2017, about a hundred-fifty people joined. Our membership exceeded 2100. In 2018, it slowed down so much that I had our webmaster check for technical problems. I wondered if some clever tech person from a school district had figured out a way to hijack our membership form. However, our tests worked. It wasn't that.

Then, in 2020, membership plummeted further. Realizing I had mountains of testimony, I chose not to investigate. It took me time to comprehend the reason, probably because it was so disheartening.

My 2019 book, which highlighted Trump as a perilous fraud, led to a drastic drop in membership. The number of members now stands at around 2200, with only a hundred new members since Trump's rise. My democratic approach to ending teacher abuse was not the popular choice among those disillusioned with the crime in our schools. Trump was.

Our schools are indeed toxic for children. Many parents and teachers who know this are willing to give up a democracy whose leaders do not know this. Moms and families feel unprotected. Their mistake is who they run to for protection. The problem is genuine. Trump became their solution.

Many would agree that Trump is a cut-off-your-nose-to-spit e-your-face solution. But right now, it's the only solution because those in power have missed WCCrime and why school shootings are happening. They offer no solution, no change in this arena. That is a key reason many parents justify Trump.

He represents doing something for families even though running into the hands of a valueless person to protect their values is irrational, particularly since he did nothing about WCCrime when he was president! When people feel the need to run, they become illogical. They are right to run but wrong to run to him. Changing the balance of power at our schools would eliminate their need to run from our schools and our democracy at the same time!

In all my books, I point out that the documented wrongdoing in our schools flows from both political parties. It is deeply situated and has been impossible to expose. I know because I've been trying to tell the story since 1995. Whereas some see this state of affairs as needing a strongman to fix it, I see it as a nation that lost its way and needs deeply spiritual people to fix it.

Where would these profoundly spiritual people reside in a society? You won't find them trying to make a lot of money. You won't find them seeking fame. You will find them signing up to work at low salaries with minor status because they innately value others equally or even more than themselves.

Education is their destiny because education exists for the sake of others. They will be called to teach. However, we must separate them from opportunists who see education as more accessible money than business. We must distinguish people with education in their hearts from those with education in their wallets.

It's challenging to get people to understand what our nation needs to do to save democracy. Choosing Trump seems easier to many. When I told my doctor about WCCrime, he responded with the corruption-is-everywhere slogan.

If words could scream, the next sentence would. Don't tell me there's corruption everywhere! That's true, but much of it exists since education's deep state of rot forms the foundation everywhere.

He told me how they eliminate great doctors who put medicine over politics. He described how they had fired a brilliant doctor who led a department that is now on its third replacement, as they still haven't found someone to meet his quality.

He made the mistake so many make—dwelling on the corruption they know rather than learning about the source, the root cause, of corruption: a society of underdeveloped people. I know corruption is everywhere, but our lost education system is a significant factor in why it's everywhere.

Education is the deep state. It's a profoundly spiritual ideal. Its purpose is to create a more perfect society. It's now profoundly corrupted. It has destroyed democracy and contributed to all the other deep states of rot. Education is the leader of spiritual paths. Thus, we must address it first and expect others to follow. They will.

Consider this to show his argument's fallacy: His hospital realized the replacement doctors were not up to the job and kept replacing them. They knew that competence matters, an awareness not anywhere near education.

I had tried to explain how detrimental it is that WCCrime has pushed out good teachers, and he countered that corruption pushes out good doctors. His example is not parallel. He didn't understand the issue. His example demonstrates the normal good vs. evil that goes on everywhere. Politics often wins. But rational forces bring back balance. The wrongdoers pay for their political mistakes. In my example, WCCrime dictates all. Politics and all its mistakes run the show, and eventually, in its utter dysfunction, it takes down everything.

A strongman cannot fix our messed up deep state. Learning about where and how education became a scam can and will fix it. To the extent we work on this together, those who thought Trump was the answer with those who, by not looking for an answer, enraged those who knew we needed an answer, will begin to repair this broken nation. Once we work together and recognize the toxic deep state that does genuinely exist—our hijacked education system—change has a chance.

My greatest hope is that it's not that people are so shallow, but that they have not had access to the information needed

to identify WCCrime and that our president, or other authority, reads this book as President Kennedy read Rachel Carson's
1962 book on pesticides, *Silent Spring*, and does what President
Kennedy did—lead. Nothing will show those who have given
up on democracy a better reason to vote for democracy. Not
ending WCCrime is such a monumental failure. Its reflection
on democracy is blinding.

WCCrime fools most because it is pretty clever. It has grown
deep roots in the fertile grounds of so many other-centered people.
Way too many public officials have no clue about it or dismiss it as
not the big deal it is. Knowing that a Supreme Court justice was
clueless about the need to scrutinize those running our schools
convinced me that this is due to naivety more than complicity.

Former Supreme Court Justice Stevens stated with stunning
prejudice, "The courts must operate from the basis that school
administrators are acting in good faith." You will see this quote
again in this book. It's important. It must be known that our top
court doesn't get WCCrime or holds prejudice against teachers
and doesn't want to get it. This means most don't get WCCrime,
and it's up to we, the people, to make them stop operating from
assumptions and start investigating.

Not investigating for corruption, knowing how common it
is, is like never cleaning your house. Over time, dirt would pile
up, and you would no longer have a viable house. The corruption
has piled up, and we no longer have real education.

I want to believe the Supreme Court Justice would have figured this out, but his reverence for schools blinded him. I could
be wrong. Officials might support this mob-like takeover of our
schools, and the courts might be pretending to be naive. Either
way, we must build a force to stop it. I do this work because I
believe in democracy. I hope the good people leading our democracy will wrap their arms around ending WCCrime once known
and understood. The thought of a dictator deciding the television
programs I can watch also keeps me at this.

We need to create a force for democracy as the solver of
our problems as passionate as the force for Trump. That was

my mission in 2002 when Trump was only a shyster who had built a condo building in Chicago. We didn't consider buying a condo there when we moved into the city in 2003 due to who built it. He was too far over on the bell curve for our comfort. I also knew then that we needed a force for democracy to get our schools back. I learned how dangerous our schools had become, but I did not expect the danger to morph into so much more than our schools.

It might not have if my 2008 book had gone viral and fewer citizens needed a grenade-like leader. I knew that a president, or presidential candidate, who admitted the truth about our schools would win over many people because of how admired they'd be, compared to the presidents and candidates who have missed or avoided a grave issue plaguing our nation, appearing not to care.

WCCrime is a big reason not to trust the government. Allowing it to take over and take away our cherished and deserved education feels like a deep state plot against us. In reality, ending WCCrime so we could reform education would be like restarting a computer or pressing a button that restores trust.

We've all agonized for hours dealing with a dysfunctional computer only to do a restart and think, why didn't we try that hours ago? Computer fiasco solutions are often simple if you know the restart button. I'm giving you a restart button to reform education.

Watching the courts trying to solve the problem of Trump, an authoritarian who operates above them, using his cult followers as ammunition, we see how challenged our courts have become. This would not have happened if our democracy influencers had still been influencing. We must restore their power by pulling the curtain on the malfeasants now running the education reality show. Good schools are a vaccine against a demagogue. The government that provides the vaccine will win back the hearts of many who lost faith in it.

Some believe we need a get-out-the-vote movement. Reconnecting to democracy—how we lost it and who is worthy to lead it—is our only path to counter the cult of authoritarianism.

A cult is about to swallow a nation that didn't realize WCCrime, with teacher abuse as its hidden hallmark, had seized its institution for maintaining its democracy.

We must bring back our democracy influencers—our dedicated, masterful teachers—by exposing WCCrime and elevating education to a regarded profession. By assuring these called-to-teach teachers that the tyrants holding our schools hostage are no longer in charge, they will reclaim their desire to teach.

That's me speaking about teacher abuse and WCCrime at the Washington, DC Mall in 2008.

Above are two of the handful of teachers at the 2008 Washington, DC March to expose teacher abuse. The *Washington Post* reporter in attendance reported nothing. She thought it was not newsworthy that only a few teachers showed up despite the preparation and costs for a mall presentation. She also ignored my speech, which you can find at http://www.endteacherabuse.org/epic.html

A picture says a thousand words and shows over fifty pounds gained while teaching.

2008 New York Terrorized Teachers—This is the only way teachers tell the truth about their schools.

Go to https://www.whitechalkcrime.com/#vid Here You will hear them say that their principal called students "retarded" and operated in other shameful ways.

NAPTA NAPTA NAPTA
National Association for Prevention of Teacher Abuse

STAGES of ABUSE

General Goal: Maintain an organization whereby the hierarchy has absolute power and neither the teachers nor the parents can interfere, thus hiding incompetence, maintaining lucrative positions, and control over the budget.

Methods/Goals-in order of intensity (Most teachers not aware it is intentional bullying until level 8.)

1. Avoid hiring older experienced teachers who are thinkers./Keep a staff of young revolving door teachers so roots and opinions won't establish.
2. Praise conformity./Staff of Stepford teachers who won't question anything.
3. Give perks to a small group of teachers that form first line of defense against other teachers./Create a barrier clique between administration and teachers by rewarding a few good soldiers who will serve as positive voice pieces for the administration.
4. Overload with work./Create inability to complain about issues - keep too busy.
5. Limit assistance with difficult children or purposely load certain teacher with difficult children./Create inability to complain about issues keep too busy to speak out.
6. Limit support with difficult parents and create barrier between teachers and parents./Attack self-esteem so won't feel empowered and won't trust their own thinking while eliminating parent allies from forming.
7. Place children of high profile parents with teachers who conform./Avoid having parents form allies with strong teachers.
8. Write up false reports./Flex muscles so teacher will know they are being controlled and will become confused.
9. Create files with false and negative reports; create separate file in case contract requires teacher is to be informed, and keep documents out of teacher's view./Build a case against teacher.

10. Threaten- directly or through rumors or innuendo by designated staff messengers./Create wall of fear to silence teacher.
11. Threaten others in presence./Set example; increase fear to point where teacher will report other.
12. Humiliate./Keep divergent thinker as dysfunctional as possible; weaken self esteem.

13. Torment./Affect psychological health so easier to control and teacher will quit.
14. Demonstrate clear demarcations between favored and unfavored staff;lower evaluations of teachers who befriend administration's target teachers./Encourage teachers to choose party line so undesirable teachers will quit.
15. Let union people know they must support administration./Avoid records that can be used against administration in case there is tenure hearing.
16. Ostracize - divide and conquer./Create system of quislings to force unwanted teacher out.
17. Suggest resigning to avoid termination./Hide bullying pattern from Board, save money on hearing, frighten teacher into last chance for any reference or future teaching jobs.
18. Banish with leave or ordered doctor visit, especially using testimony for fee psychiatrist./Use fear of psychological report to encourage resignation.
19. Terminate and settle with a gag order not to talk against district./Don't pay teacher so desperate teacher will give in.
20. Promise good reference; destroy reputation so they will never be in a position to bad mouth former district./Secretly inform other districts so teacher won't be hired elsewhere in area or even same city.
21. Politically control tenure hearing; submit altered documents; arrange for colleagues to give false testimony for status; call witnesses and directly and indirectly warn them; drive teacher to despair so she will give up./Good Ol Boy Network protects each other knowing the system depends on silencing - witness tampering and altered documents won't be noticed.
22. Politically control tenure decision. /stall/War of attrition: hope for natural death.
23. Threaten or entice union into selling out teacher./Guaranteed absolute power so no teacher will speak out.
24. Your guess is as good as mine.

7

THE ESSENCE OF TEACHER ABUSE

"Nothing is more despicable than respect based on fear."

Albert Camus

"A lie doesn't become truth, wrong doesn't become right, and evil doesn't become good, just because it's accepted by a majority."

Booker T. Washington

"What sculpture is to a block of marble, education is to a human soul."

Joseph Addison

I get that it's hard to believe this has been going on. You'd think you'd know of this, knowing many teachers. I will dive deeper to explain why teachers won't tell you. The intimidation into submission strategy is staggering. Insiders know they cannot discuss anything in this book if they want to keep their teaching career.

As mentioned, I grew up in Oak Park, Illinois, where many infamous gangsters raised families. One boy in my fourth-grade class was friends with Tony Accardo's son. One day at Show and Tell—our social media source in the olden days—he shared that he had a sleepover at Accardo's house. They were playing in the backyard, and he saw a flower he liked. As he was about to separate it from its bush, Tony Accardo, who had served as Al Capone's chauffeur and guard before he took over the mafia boss role, appeared in the yard and said, "Don't pick the flowers."

Accardo said it like any dad, but it scared my classmate, which was his point in sharing what was a frightening experience for him. To most teachers, administrators are Tony Accardo.

Only a few speak out. Society disregards those who blow the whistle since we are scarce. To grasp why you know nothing, I will help you understand teacher abuse. Drowning teachers in work is part of the abuse. It leaves teachers too exhausted and too buried in work to fight the system. I remember not sleeping at all one night to complete a task the principal assigned me. She knew it took way more hours than I had before its due date. She ignored my requests for more time, adding my lack of sleep to her list of things to make my life miserable.

I discussed teacher abuse on a radio show once. A caller asked why I wasn't more specific about what teacher abuse was. It was impossible to spell it out in the few minutes I had. He wondered why I hadn't seized upon a legal aspect of it, such as age discrimination, since, according to him, that has remedies. I could have explained that he was wrong if I had had enough time since I had pursued that route. Their conniving ways block teachers from the law.

It takes a book to explain an issue hidden so well. It's like learning about an alien from Mars. There's so much no one knows. Those in power in education operate above the law at their pleasure, and there's no way to stop them. Using teacher abuse, they eliminate their adversaries.

Education is like a 10,000-piece puzzle with a monotonous background and missing corner pieces. One completes a complex puzzle by starting with the corner pieces that have a distinguishable shape. The cornerstones of this "puzzle" deal are hidden in

WCCrime issues and hinder one's ability to even start. Some try to figure out how the schools deteriorated, but few have figured out why.

I'll take up jailed, movie-mogul Harvey Weinstein again to explain the abuse. It took years before anyone spoke out about what he was doing. Many obliged him just as many teachers service administrators' requests that harm children. Going along to get along is the point. As far as I know, and I have spoken with thousands of teachers, WCCrime does not include demands for sex. Yet, teachers would do almost anything other than harm children.

The Weinstein saga unraveled because an actress took years to find the courage. I found the courage in 1995. I found many others who found the courage. The difference is we're teachers. We live in a no-money world. No investigative reporter sees us as worth their time. Plus, what happened to us is not as black and white as sex. I can help you understand what happened to us by sharing a workplace situation before teaching.

As mentioned, I belonged in the world of education, where the goal is to help others, unlike business, where the goal is material gains. After I had a child in 1970, there were no teaching jobs. I had to enter the business world. Several years into my new career, an executive of the corporation for which I worked raped me—rape as defined by the New York legal code!

I left the business world soon after, more confident I was not designed for it. I didn't report the rapist because I knew I would lose my job. Aware that rape was about power and accepting that my journey in life was not about acquiring power, I moved on. I figured I would get back into the moral world of education. I was sure that they would never permit power trips at the expense of children or in betrayal of the public trust. I blamed myself for being in the money world rather than the "idea" world. Everyone expects power trips, money worship, inhumanity, selfishness, back-stabbing, and deceit in business. I wrapped the rape in, "I didn't belong there," so I could move on like a business world tourist.

Soon after, I remarried and no longer needed an income. I needed to follow my calling, though. In 1992, I earned a master's degree in reading. I could return to the world where other-centered people like me belong. Unsure of what degree to pursue to secure a teaching job, I asked an admission counselor. She responded, "It doesn't matter which you choose. You won't be in the classroom long. You are too dynamic."

At the time, I assumed that she meant I would rise to a higher position. Applying hindsight, she may have been trying to spare me. Either way, it's depressing that dynamic people are incompatible with teaching! And beyond heartbreaking, it's our nation's biggest problem. It's not just about not fitting in when I was so effective with children. Other teachers don't get a chance to grow when mediocrity is a goal.

Some teachers enter teaching like artists whose paintings sell, and others become great over time. If there's no place for the gifted, called-to-teach teachers, there's no sharing of the gifts so others can become more.

Disillusionment was not a strong enough word to describe what I experienced at my teaching job. A litany of power trips, money worship, constant lying, brutal competition, inhumanity, selfishness, backstabbing, and deceit flooded my life. I, like so many others, and to the detriment of our children, had misjudged the world of education, buying into the façade that fools so many. In comparison, business was child's play. What I unearthed in education was hard-core, infiltrated, sinister darkness with persecution at its core.

The psychological rape I experienced in education was more painful than the physical rape. It cast me out of my assumed world for not being compatible with my school district's nefarious ways. It meant there was no place for a person like me. I had accepted that working in business was a mistake. I couldn't fit in where ideals were not the driving force. So when my presumed "home" turned out to be more brutal than the place where I knew I did not belong, it was a disconnect—a soul rape.

My spirit entered a world of inhumanity and ended up adrift. Education turned out to be psychologically brutal. I am a person who values ideas over objects. I had moved on after a short period of depression after a physical violation. The abuse I experienced as a teacher pierced my soul. It meant children were at risk, and my gifts had no value in teaching. Even though it hadn't happened after the physical rape, I found that I needed that sense of closure about which I had often heard spoken by rape victims. "We need to get our lives back."

Before the internet, isolation made this impossible. I now had a group of like-minded teachers. Getting our lives back meant attaching meaning to our suffering. Forcing change upon this corrupt institution was a powerful avenue for healing. We followed our emotional compasses to turn these horrendous experiences into something good. Yet, our voices remained muzzled.

We licked our wounds with little hope for support or understanding. "This couldn't have happened to us," reverberated through our minds. We adopted other people's perceptions of our situations, as no one else had been through this hell. We lost touch with our souls. In time, we blamed ourselves, the ultimate goal for the predator, so that they had no consequence to bear.

Teacher abuse has many faces. I included a chart at the beginning of this chapter and my before-and-after teaching picture to help you understand it. It wears down teachers like an overflowing river taking over the land. It destroys confidence. I had an incident right after my district terminated me that illustrates how much.

Depression had settled in, and a heavy fog settled over my dream career. I learned that one of the best ways to dispel this fog was to bring light to someone else's life. So, I decided to volunteer at the nursing home where my grandmother had spent her last days. On the first day, I spent time with a woman, getting to know her and reading newspaper articles to her. They scheduled me to return the next week; a voice message from the nursing home left me anxious.

My heart sank as I listened to the voice message. I was sure I had done something wrong. I shouldn't have read the news or gotten to know that lady. I felt like I had failed at this job. The thought of being rejected at a nursing home, a place where most can't bear to volunteer due to its bleakness, was a new low for me.

I returned the call and prepared for another termination. The volunteer coordinator wanted me to accompany that lady to her podiatry appointment downtown in a taxi and was hoping I would do that for her. Teacher abuse takes your self-esteem to places you've never been and never want to revisit.

This book could have been filled with more outrageous incidents I had to endure. However, had I done that alone, you wouldn't believe them. You need to understand the why behind abusing teachers to grasp that these insane and heinous incidents happened to me as well as to other teachers. I've told you how they made me feel. I've shown you how they made me fat. Now, I'll let you know about one hideous avenue of abuse that the principal wove throughout my last two years and into my legal saga.

Most parents were wonderful. When there was one that wasn't, siccing her on a targeted teacher worked like a charm. It gave a principal a partner in crime. My principal got lucky. The one she used on me was to parents as a hundred-year snowfall is to a weather event.

This parent had so upset the principal at her former district that the former principal called my principal to warn her about this parent. She had not exaggerated a bit. While her daughter was in third grade, this parent insisted on observing all four fourth-grade classes, including mine, to determine who deserved her daughter. The mother decided on Mr. P. Guess who got her? Me, the teacher she did not want.

Before my year with her began, teachers had complained about how this mother trapped them in the parking lot, sticking her head in the window of their car and keeping them there for over an hour. It was common knowledge that this parent was bonkers.

It's been a lot of years with many buried incidents. But many are still vivid, such as when I was administering a test. The mother enters the classroom with a cheat sheet for her daughter to make the test easier. After she left, I walked over to the child's desk to see what she had given her. From afar, it looked like that. I needed to confirm. Plus, I wanted to ask her to put it away without embarrassing her. Across the room, accusations are not good teaching!

The next day, the principal wrote me up for hovering over that student's desk to see what her mother had given her. The mother must have complained to the principal after the child complained to the mother. I'm sure she was embarrassed about the cheat sheet. I doubt the child thought what I was doing was wrong when that's a teacher's job. What if a mom did a drug drop-off—or a gun drop-off?

Besides, ignoring cheating contradicts what teachers are supposed to do. The child was not manipulative, as far as I could see. She could not have known what an easy target I was. She had a right to complain to her mother. What's more, she was brilliant. Very smart. She didn't need it. The mother needed the cheat sheet.

Can you imagine a teacher being accused of hovering? The principal was so desperate to find fault with me that she left no issue rational. She didn't care that the mother was trying to help her cheat on a test. She didn't care that a teacher always hovers to attend to individual students. She needed to get me.

Close to the time when my days were over, I remember her accusing me of not doing something—I can't remember what now—and I replied, "I would have had to hover to do that. Are you now permitting me to hover?"

She stomped away so she could write me up for something else. It wasn't my sarcasm in her write-up, but it was my sarcasm. I'm sure. After a couple of years of her harassment, it was the only tool I had left.

In addition, this unfortunate child often roamed the halls after school because her mom hadn't picked her up. She was tardy eighty-five times. But the principal accused me of making her anxious. I decided that even though everyone had warned me never to write up a kid no matter what, since the special services team was where teachers lose even more, I wrote her up. I thought that these obvious issues would engender support for me from other colleagues, who, up to that point, had been decent.

Writing up is what schools call creating a referral for help from others, from social workers to psychological testing. It's intended to help a child beyond what a teacher can do. Since helping children is not a welcome part of the WCCrime agenda, the special services team is a unique combination of mean girls who meet the Gestapo.

The team decided that I was making her anxious—not her over-the-top mom, not the cheat sheet, not the tardies or the after-school abandonment, and not the principal for putting her in the class her mother didn't want.

Teachers have no choice but to avoid write-ups. Think about having a firing squad in place when you write up a student with issues. Who wants to go there? Indeed, not the teachers that have had school shooters in their classes, a topic I get to later. Those in control determine what's wrong with the child in a way that benefits them with a team of mediocre and warped minds more suited to politics than to helping children find their purpose in life.

And the horror of this parent is another issue you don't have to take from me. She was an integral part of my federal lawsuit, now a legal record. She kept disobeying rules and made taking her deposition impossible. My attorney appealed to the judge for assistance. The judge ordered her to appear in his court to take the deposition under his watch. This rarely happens. This intolerable parent was a gift that kept giving to my principal. And it paid dividends. The attorney fees needed to deal with this unbearable situation added to the abuse.

During my termination hearing, the fact that I had given this child an X in "School Regulations" for having been tardy for twenty-seven out of sixty days became an issue. The principal changed the X to satisfactory before the parents received it and accused me of not telling the parents in advance about this X to justify why she changed it. One can look in the record at Exhibit 190, the parent's letter arguing about that X, to know that I had told her. How could the parent argue about something that wasn't on the report card and that I had never told her? Dealing with twisted lies was my life.

Then, if a parent liked me, she did her best to create tension. Keeping teachers and parents at odds by using hatred to build a wall between them is a WCCrime fundamental. Teachers and parents in alliance threaten WCCrime like nothing else, which is, in essence, the goal of this book—forming an alliance against it.

One incident of my principal stirring the pot sticks with me despite thirty years between me and that memory. It was so warped. I had a boy in my class, Steve, who required an exceptional amount of upkeep, including detailed weekly reports for his parents.

That was a challenging year for me. My father-in-law died, my brother-in-law died, a car hit me from behind on the expressway, and I was sick with something I can't remember. (Amazing how good my memory is about my teaching experience. My brain must have known I needed this information to accomplish my life's purpose, so it saved it while letting go of so much else.)

At one point that year, the principal called me to her office to admonish me. She told me that a parent had attended a luncheon with Steve's mom, who told her I had complained that my job was too hard. The tattling parent was appalled that I was complaining and wanted me to know that if I wanted an easy job, I should apply to Elk Grove Village—a district far beneath our elitist district. I remember the exact district. It's close to where my principal is now that she's left behind a trail of WCCrime.

I hadn't complained at all, not to the mom or anyone. It was a challenging year, but I loved teaching. I had a recurring dream of being back in the classroom for years, so when a job is a dream come true, you don't complain. (I still have that dream, believe it or not.)

I could not understand why a parent would misrepresent who I was as a person. She acted as though she really liked me. I was distraught, but I was not about to confront that parent. It would have been unprofessional. I was glad when her son was no longer my student. I felt confused.

Two years later, she wrote a letter requesting that her daughter be in my class. When I saw that letter, I was speechless. Why would she request me? I thought she must be unstable or, worse, sadistic. It made no sense. The year with her daughter went well, and I kept thinking about the movie *Three Faces of Eve*. The mother was a delight. I liked her. We got along fine. Her nasty comment swirled in my brain, though. I batted it down to remain professional. I felt more confused.

Somewhat later, when my parents knew what they were doing to me and took action to keep me employed, this mom discovered that she had been a source of my demise. She was outraged. She remembered the get-together where a parent had spoken with her about me and what she had said. It was: „Mrs. Horwitz is the hardest working teacher she has ever known." She then wrote a letter to the Board to squelch any opportunity for that false statement to be used against me.

The parent, who had alleged I was complaining, was now on the Board. She pretended not to remember. She either knew that the principal had made that up or knew she had made that up.

A superintendent stacks his board with those who speak the same language, the language of lies, so his questionable business will be smooth unlike those of us who teach. Except for those on the administration track and most boards, people who value public service dominate the teaching profession. Choosing this low-paying profession validates this. This truth, combined with a typical teacher's nature and the inability of the world to believe us, devastates us. It was much worse than physical rape.

To make matters worse, when I appealed to the Board for protection from what the administrators were doing to me, I used the term "psychological rape." Rather than investigate and protect me from it, they held my use of the word "rape" against me.

Turning our calling against us is a rape of our ideals. Our schools hand us personal deprivation wrapped in the ideals that made us teachers. They leave us with an almost Sophie's choice. "Do what we say even though your students will suffer, or don't do it, and you will no longer be teaching."

They take us down before we have an inkling about how corrupt education is. They bury us in an orchestrated ambush.

WCCriminals push our souls into a dark hole. They turn our lives, once filled with the joy of teaching, into a struggle to escape unfathomable darkness.

The second time I cried as a teacher, I was with my class taking part in an astronomy demonstration. I was lying on the gym floor, observing the stars. Their ramped-up abuse and the darkness in the room made me think about the bad acts the principal did to my students to punish me. It tormented me to remain in the classroom and be the cause of their pain.

The "classroom with the quietest line after lunch got a treat" contest bothered me. One after another, my students said, "Mrs. T's class was fooling around, and we were perfect, but they won. It's not fair." My class wanted to see a particular movie for a party day. The principal denied us a movie that many other classes had enjoyed. The message was clear. Revenge knows no boundaries.

I understand why this is all so unbelievable. The principal doing mean thing after mean thing knew every child's name. She had the parents eating out of her hands. She seemed so caring. When the parents visited the school, her great dog and pony show soldered already rooted, faithful beliefs.

This is not an honored institution. The military adheres to a duty to disobey unlawful orders. Teacher abuse erases any duty to disobey that one would expect is in place. That's why you don't know.

I was where you are. I went back to school to get back into this heaven-on-earth profession. Motherhood and apple pie oozed from every school I entered until education revealed itself. It's a monster that devours the souls of those dedicated to it. Only the shallow or those who contort themselves into shallowness survive. I gradually understood this.

That's why I set out to expose this years ago. I told myself it took thirty years to expose priests, so expect decades, not years. It takes a nuclear-powered, emotional steamroller to understand that people they had trusted could be this dreadful. It's been tough to expose this pigpen of corruption, but it's far easier than being part of it.

Court Documents from Horwitz v. Avoca School District #37

Now, let's see. The Board of Education used 8,476 pages to bury Karen Horwitz. Tactics replaced substance. Do you really think the taxpayers needed to spend all that money on all those pages if they really had a case?

Compiled from data in the local paper, the *Wilmette Life*: For ten school years starting from June of 1997 and ending in June of 2007, the period in which we engaged in legal conflict, a district with 676 students reported expenditures of close to $750,000 on legal fees. (This applied to my tenure hearing; it does not reflect legal fees paid for my federal case for which the Board had an insurance policy and possibly increased insurance rates due to claims involving my federal case.)

Between the 1997–2000 fiscal years, during the height of their compilation of bogus charges against me, [District] spent $168,000 with their regular law firm, Robbins, Schwartz, Nicholas, and $55,000 with Scariano, Himes, and Petrarca, a law firm they hired just to litigate my case. A district of this size typically spends approximately $20,000 per year. The legal fees paid to Scariano et al., hired just to litigate my case, totaled $291,000 and do not include expert witness fees or the cost of the extensive bogus psychological report and other court costs.

They reported an $8,000+ payment to Dr. Hazard, the Education "expert witness," to say he knew nothing of teacher abuse. The Board squandered public funds of over $400,000, cleansing me from their system despite my parents' protests while squandering funds on undue legal fees in general. Unaware, each parent contributed at least $1000 to keep WCCrime thriving.

8

WHY WCCRIME IS SO HARD TO GRASP

"The greater the difficulty, the more the glory in surmounting it."

Epicurus, Greek philosopher

"Maybe you are searching among the branches, for what only appears in the roots."

Rumi

"A brave man is a man who dares to look the Devil in the face and tell him he is a Devil."

James A. Garfield

The obstacles to teaching about WCCrime make my journey a mission almost impossible. The unpopularity of reading about education ranks high on that list. Then, the distance between reality and what parents think is vast. What makes a good school is complex. So what makes a bad school is too.

People don't know, and trying to tell them when the power is so skewed is nearly futile. WCCrime, an unthinkable tyranny, has a buoyant life, as did priest abuse, which took thirty years to expose. Piercing the veil of secrecy when power has its grip is Herculean. I am revealing WCCrime via memories rather than just a downpour of facts to keep you in the passenger seat! I hope you're still there!

This is hard to convey. It's so hidden. A significant reason for this is their ability to pay to destroy the reputation of any teacher who threatens their existence. If settlement offers don't work, they pay attorneys to bury their enemy. I used "enemy" rather than enemies as they take down one at a time to use other enemy teachers against the chosen target.

I politely told them where to place their generous settlement offer. I don't remember the exact amount, but it equaled almost six years of my salary. My attorney said he could double it, to which I replied, "This priceless information is not for sale."

The previous page is a picture of the ridiculous, extensive record they bought to silence me, which didn't work either.

My calling to teach caused me to take on this mission to teach you about WCCrime. But I'm not sure it was only my being called to teach since I'm a parent and grandparent, too. What distinguishes me from most parents is that I know the inner workings of schools. The 2023 article, "Politicians and pundits say parents are furious with schools. Polls say otherwise,"[8] said, "…In general, people also tend to give institutions that they interact with directly, including schools, the benefit of the doubt" reminded me how far I am from you.

This isn't a hot dog dilemma. People like hot dogs, But they tell us we'd change our minds if we saw how they're made. Most prefer to hold our ears and eat them. And that's not so bad because we don't eat them often, and the bad stuff is likely more disgusting than harmful.

This situation is different. There's now a book telling you it's not like the hot dog I just ate. The harm is monumental, including school shootings, the end of democracy, and a lousy future for our progeny, who will blame us for this once they find out. They will find out because I'm told I should use TikTok.

TikTok it will be if it's still an option and if that's what saves us from an autocrat.

I get why parents failed to develop an appropriate amount of disgust for what our schools are doing. WCCriminals have replaced their skill at educating effective citizens with evolved public relations skills. WCCrime demands a magnificent coverup since no one wants to go to jail. They are excellent at acting like they care. They have those who know otherwise reduced to sound bites of approval. They have you despising teachers.

Suppose you overheard a teacher in a confessional telling a priest how guilty she felt about deceiving her parents. You'd be sure she was lying to the priest.

WCCrime has a unique brilliance that attracts con artists and those seeking power and money. They know what parents want, so they pretend to offer it. They unleash trust on the level of grandma taking care of your child. From knowing every child's name to having constant smiles every time you see them, they dwell on the "you-have-nothing-to-worry-about" status. If something made you wonder if your administrators were for real, you'd toss that thought away, not considering for a second that they're duping you.

In fact, their specialty is public relations. Parents liked my principal. I liked her, too, until she started lying and overloading me with issues. Outgoing, personable, and excellent at pretense described her. WCCriminals are two-faced and careful how they abuse those who might report them.

WCCrime has flourished under the radar. They're experts at hiding the negatives it causes. Teflon-like, everything slides far enough away for them to dodge. They can count on their staff pretending not to notice since they know that those who do notice end up targets. I know what you think because I was a parent and had the same naive thinking. Here are some typical parent thoughts:

1. The bad guys go for the big bucks, so they aren't in education. Truth: These aren't the Ivy League guys with a

ticket to top jobs. These people would manage a Denny's if they chose the business/money route. It's more money than elsewhere. Second, there are big bucks to embezzle.

2. A school is much closer to heaven than a business. Truth: My rape story erased that thought.

3. The failure of school reform is not intentional. Truth: When they embezzle and purge dedicated teachers to cover up corruption, their goal is to ruin reform so they can keep things as is.

4. Schools fail because they need more business minds. Truth: Schools don't fail at corruption. They're very successful.

5. Schools are strapped with awful teachers because it's impossible to fire them. Truth: The impossible-to-fire-a-teacher lie has you and the courts rooting for WCCriminals. I'm proof they can fire us. They prefer to pocket the money it costs to conduct a tenure dismissal hearing. They give your tax dollars up to terminate political enemies, not to keep your children safe.

They thrive on the sympathy earned for being stuck with bad teachers while they keep perverts with our children to prove they can't fire teachers. There's no better story than tenured teacher Darlene Goodman's. http:// endteacherabuse.org/Goodman.html They banished her for accusing her principal of assault—accused by

others, http://endteacherabuse.org/Carastud.html too —but claimed they were stuck with the science teacher who showed pornography to his students. Here's a local television station's online report:

KOBTV.com Eyewitness News New Mexico—Parents file suit over teacher accused of showing inappropriate picture Last Update: 04/30/2002...Los Lunas police are investigating a teacher accused of showing an inappropriate picture to students. Parents say the teacher at Raymond Gabeldon Intermediate School was showing his students pictures of his sixth grade class that were on his computer. They say that's when a picture popped up showing the teacher with his pants down holding his genitals. When parents complained to the school, they say the teacher was placed on leave. But they later learned he was teaching at Manzano Vista Middle School in Los Lunas. Parents have filed a lawsuit against the Los Lunas School Board. The school district could not comment on the case.

Not only did her district not protect the children, but they lied to the parents. Her story also shows that the press missed the essence of this story—Goodman was no longer teaching, but the pervert earned a place in the classroom and in these WCCriminals' hearts.

6. No one talks about teacher abuse or crime in our schools. Truth: Considering how ruthless teacher abuse is and how hard it is to expose, they're wise to remain silent!

7. Horwitz is describing a conspiracy, and I know better than to believe a conspiracy. Truth: conspiracies have taken a hit of late. So many are so dumb that it's embarrassing to entertain them. They say you're not paranoid if someone's after you. It's not a ridiculous conspiracy theory if there's an actual, illegal takeover of an institution.

The other points are short. This one needs to be long. It's a big one. An authentic conspiracy is unlawful, and many people work together to keep it secret. So many need to work together to expose it. Plus, a ton of proof that our schools are a hot mess validates this.

Are we the country that cried "conspiracy theory" so much that an actual conspiracy profits? A big yes! We can't afford to be so prejudiced against conspiracies that we overlook a real one that's creating unthinkable damage. Unlawful acts by a group of self-serving administrators are illegal. Hiring others with similar dodgy values to turn teachers and other educators into their worker bees to violate laws is unlawful. It's a conspiracy; it maintains secrecy to avoid consequences.

Our nation has become fearful. If we admit to a real conspiracy, all conspiracies will become real. That's as wise as never going to the doctor so you won't have cancer. All it takes is an investigation to know if it's real.

There is solid university research about teacher abuse and a couple of altered documents in my record that have yet to be scrutinized. These people get away with everything. I have dozens of teachers ready to testify about WCCrime and its connection to school shootings. Besides, the utter failure of our schools proves they are not into educating kids. And our democracy—their responsibility to keep together—is falling apart.

Believing that education reform has failed because no one has figured out education reform is ignorant. It failed because the people who want to take advantage of this gold mine pretend they cannot figure it out. They make sure people like me have no power. I had to overload this book with receipts to prove the WCCrime conspiracy! Conspiracy theories flourish because real conspiracies happen!

Erik Pevernagie said: "Let us not get scooped up by gaslighting manipulators stealing our emotions and taking possession of our inner child to carry out their dark agenda. Let the light of our intuition guide us subtly and wisely along the path of trust and suspicion."

For our children's sake, do not abandon suspicion. This is an authentic conspiracy. It's as foolish to not investigate conspiracies as it is to trust unverified conspiracies on the internet.

As mentioned, many abused teachers bought into Trump and his deep state lure because what we saw in education feels like a deep state. Since it is a conspiracy, those who lived it believe in conspiracies. Our government needs to wake up and realize how easy it was for Trump to entice people living in an actual conspiracy to follow him. Becoming a Pied Piper was there for the taking.

It's as stupid to believe all conspiracies as it is to not investigate a conspiracy. Ignoring this group of whistleblowers is as foolish as believing "Pizza Gate." And unlike most conspiracy accusers, we have the receipts—lots!

8. People who choose education are good guys. This is another long one since it's so wrong. In my first book, I mentioned Superintendent Paul Vallas' wrongdoing dozens of times. There was so much, and they were so shameful. (They are also in the enhanced ebook, Part Three, with the extensive documentation about WCCrime.)

You can imagine my joy when he was a finalist for Chicago's mayor in 2023. If he had won and I hadn't already moved back to the suburbs, I would have moved back to the suburbs. It is unbearable to see him handed power while a person like me has none.

Who holds power is at the core of our mess these days. Shame on us for almost electing Paul Vallas as Chicago's mayor after his scandalous history.

And it wasn't just him. There's also Dr. Rudy Crew. In my 2008 book, I referred to two scandalous rapes that occurred under his watch, one in New York and one in Florida. I included lots of other misconduct that did not stop his rise to power. A 1997 New York incident produced a scathing 28-page investigative report: "OPPORTUNITIES LOST: How Personnel At August Martin High School Mishandled A Breach Of Security And The Rape Of A Student In Classroom 324."[9]

There were mentions of other articles about his immoral acts that I put in the Appendix. This creature is still standing strong. People hire him to speak. I saw a 2018 article: "Crew Named Co-Chair of Major Justice Initiative." Google him; you'll see. There are many more dodgy characters in my 2008 book, who I bet are still flourishing. I don't know what's worse: that education supports wicked people, or it doesn't support great teachers. Thinking they're good guys is a problem that takes a book to solve.

Administrators are good liars, though. I take that back. They aren't good liars. I never learned body language, but I have become an expert in veins telling all. As I watched Trump's lawyer spout an absurd defense, I noted veins near his eyes pop slightly.

I recalled the day my principal called me to her office. She told me that a teacher had reported me for yelling at a parent while on the phone in the teachers' lounge. I knew I wasn't yelling because I could hardly breathe. The only teacher in the lounge became concerned and offered to help me to the office. That teacher wasn't a perfect human, but it would have been evil for her to twist things like that.

The accusation that I knew to be false startled me, but reddish wormlike things appeared all over my principal's chest and neck as she accused me. They ambushed my thoughts. Her fair skin and her expose-all sundress offered a mesmerizing view.

Later, at my hearing, the teacher, alleged to have reported me, testified that she didn't hear me yell at a parent and that she saw me gasping for breath. The principal's body had told me she was lying, but WCCrime veiled any chance that it mattered.

The principal wrote me up as insubordinate for leaving her office that day. I did do that once chest pains brought me back to earth from the spellbinding effect of those strange worms.

The pains reminded me that I had asked my doctor if I could put off the angiogram he had ordered in April until the end of the school year in June. My workload was so strenuous. The principal had at least a three-point plan to drive me to quit. Taking time off for the procedure combined with the principal's subterfuge would indeed end my career.

My doctor's "Beware of the Pain" letter said to stop what you're doing if you get chest pains and call me. He used dancing as an example. He could not have imagined a principal operating like the wicked queen in "Snow White" as what I needed to end, nor could I have a few years earlier.

At my termination hearing, I submitted a medical document showing I had a 97% blocked artery in my heart at that time, which explained the gasping and the need to exit her office. The hearing officer refused it as irrelevant, banishing the document that proved the principal's outrageous, upsetting lie and my need to leave her office. Not allowing it in the record also allowed him to opine that I had faked a mysterious health issue. He likely had worms under his suit, finding my document irrelevant. Veins don't lie. WCCriminals do!

WCCriminals are diabolical in so many ways. Embezzling money is a biggie, but it's a lot more than the usual financial crimes. For instance, one teacher spoke about a district in Wisconsin. Students kept complaining they were hungry. She went to the head of the kitchen to start an investigation. The next day, she found a huge bag of vegetables on her desk with a note saying, "Enjoy."

The mafia way is put little in writing. People get the message. The message was, "Look what you get for keeping your mouth shut," Now you know why the kids are hungry. They risked scrutiny big time over a bag of vegetables. How many people would even want vegetables? Then again, there's built-in fear, and making soup was probably her best bet. And I can even go from soup to nuts to describe kinds of WCCrime.

A member of our group worked in the Atlanta Public Schools before the test cheating scandal that exploded in 2009. We're hearing much about that case due to the Trump, Georgia, Rico racketeering indictment. I've known of it for years. He had experienced harassment from the principal, who was part of that indictment. He tried to report her abusive ways long before the cheating scandal.

Racketeering describes WCCrime. It's a well-organized crime. The teacher said the Atlanta cheating issue was only the tip of the iceberg. He said, "Jackson operated like a private school funded by the taxpayers." He appealed to organizations in DC. They pushed him out of teaching. He sued, then concluded, "It's rigged." His lack of being able to do anything about WCCrime made him leave teaching.[10]

All the teachers indicted for cheating in that Rico case were not nuts to follow orders. They would have been nuts if they didn't follow orders. Bennet Packman, a physical education teacher in Florida, found that out the hard way. He refused to take a suspicious driver's education class that he realized would make him an illegal driving teacher. Administrators made his life miserable, including limited bathroom visits.

He uncovered that the course was a sham while being targeted for abuse. They then terminated the teachers who took the course. No teacher won.

If unscrupulous administrators get caught, they sacrifice you in a New York minute. But you are a nut if you don't follow orders. Nut butter is a better description of a teacher who doesn't go along with illegal acts. The "when in Rome" way of thinking is the only way a teacher can survive.

It's hard to know how many great teachers figured this out, kept it to themselves, and left the profession. I only know of one such teacher since those who choose this exit keep a low profile. At my school, there was a teacher who made a silent exit. At some point during her second year, I heard through the grapevine that this was her last year. I asked where she was going, and the person said she was starting a new career. They seemed to suspect that she was turned off.

Unlike every turned-off teacher I knew, she knew to walk away. Almost every other teacher would huddle in the hall and discuss the abusive ways of our administrators. They were like battered wives determined to make the marriage work and needed to vent. But that one teacher never vented. I have often thought about her. My thoughts faltered, "I wish I was more like her—of course, I couldn't have done that since I haven't been able to end my devotion to this profession decades after I stopped teaching."

For me, it wasn't a lack of street smarts. I knew these people were terrible, and the profession embraced them, so I needed to escape. Yet, teaching was not a job to me. It was a commitment to public service and making this democracy strong. Silence is complicity, whether due to teachers who endure and complain in secret or teachers who ditch the profession. But silence is understandable since the truth hasn't mattered. WCCrime is an industrial vacuum cleaner that sucks truth up before it has legs.

WCCrime can be macabre, too. In an article,[11] "Investigation into Georgia teen found dead in gym mat is closed without charges," the sheriff said, "In closing, I am quite sure that there will still be a contingent that will believe there was foul play."

He said that based on the facts of the case rather than knowing about WCCrime. This article also omitted a pertinent fact reported in earlier articles. The security video that might have shown what went on in that gym was blurry and had a suspiciously missing part. I tried to find the article that detailed the blurry and missing tapes. I make sure every word of this book is documented. I was unable to find it, even after contacting the source.

I found a different article that said, "…According to King, the family attorney, the school's gym had at least four surveillance cameras. So far, only a few still images from one angle have been made public. They show Johnson walking in the bottom right-hand corner of the frame, but they don't reveal how exactly Johnson got inside the mat. Lt. Jones said the remaining footage does not shed any light on how Johnson got there either. School officials have said they must get consent from other minors in other parts of the video before they can release it."[12] The article also expressed funny business with video documentation.

I found my description of that unattainable article in a 2014 email to a psychologist studying wrongdoing in schools. I had included a link (now dead) to the article mentioning the blurry videotape. I wrote her the following:

> Recently, there has been a story in the news about a high school boy who was found dead rolled up in a gym mat, 'Benjamin Crump talks about Kendrick Johnson case in Albany—Macon Political Buzz|Examiner.com.' His parents didn't believe the autopsy and hired a lawyer and arranged

for an exhumation. It turned out that the boy not only had marks showing he had been possibly beaten, but all of his organs had been replaced with newspaper.

When I heard that, my first thoughts were, 'I don't think they are killing kids for organs. They probably just needed to hide evidence, yet who knows what this will come to if left in the darkness—my motivation for doing this work!'...this new attorney asked for the videos in the gym. As I predicted, they came back all blurry when that murdered boy walked to the mats. And another part of the video was missing. And someone said, 'Of course, the school wouldn't tamper with them.' You see, this is what we are up against. There's an undying belief that good people run our schools.

You can hear my frustration in that ten-year-old email. In 2022, they closed the 2013 case with a determination of no foul play. They wrote off missing and possibly altered videos that suggest shadiness. They were confident that the people running our schools were doing the best they could.

It could have been a fight and an accidental death. No one will ever know. They mentioned two other boys. Someone may have killed him by accident, and he might suffer guilt his entire life. Truth is liberating and is best set free. But where there's WCCrime, there's a coverup.

It is impossible to lead a fair investigation when it starts and ends with, "No way would a school do anything unethical or criminal." This prejudiced statement proves that democracy's promise of justice cannot be found within these schools. This sheriff investigated with prejudice, as did our US Supreme Court justices. This must change, or losing our democracy is inevitable.

Examples of WCCriminals not being good guys are endless, but this book cannot be. So, I'll include one more, which beat me down by the spring of 1999. My doctor recommended I take a couple of weeks off before I subject myself to more inescapable abuse.

I prepared careful lesson plans for those two weeks. Knowing the criminal minds I was up against, I made an extra copy, put it in a large envelope, sealed it, and signed my name over the seal. I went to the post office to mail them to myself. That verified the date. I figured they'd accuse me of no lesson plans. They did just that.

At my termination hearing, we presented this never-opened envelope as proof that what was in there was left on my desk. The district stipulated this as accurate.

What an achievement, I thought! I got her. Power tried to register within me like a faraway radio station struggling to broadcast. Although it was not my life's game, I realized I had to find power for this job. I was up against people who worshipped and lived for it. I had to seize it to level the playing field they had shoved on top of me and all the teachers. I thought about how all their gaslighting allowed them to own education. Their psychological manipulation made others doubt their own perceptions, memories, or sanity. It was their tactic to gain power and control. Now, the absolute truth blared in the face of this queen of gaslighting.

If I had met power, it soon slithered away like an unwanted introduction.

Under oath, my attorney asked my principal about these plans. This woman, who cracked oversized wads of chewing gum as she led our meetings, deserved judgment rather than authority. Yet, this skilled fabricator with an irrational share of power, which also allowed her lack of etiquette, testified that nothing was on them. She said, "The lesson plans were blank."

There was writing and instructions on each page—there still is on these pages this board buried with my career. On a scientific level, there was writing. Still, as my union lawyer told me, which revealed the union's worthlessness, "There is only truth in math and science.» This was neither. Truth did not matter.

Her testimony met no skepticism in this WCCrime court. She knew she could create the record she wanted by lying under oath. Gaslighting, twisting truths, and creating alternative narratives to control the victim's understanding of reality had no boundaries. She was right. She's still haunting school districts to this day.

I noted one prestigious district hired her a few years ago, but this unprincipled principal was gone in a year. Some districts still have authentic goals, but far fewer than needed to maintain a democracy. I know that is true since she has been inflicting her immorality on districts for all the twenty-nine years I have been trying to expose WCCrime. The last I checked, she was doing her evil in an unimpressive district that is more unimpressive because of her.

Everyone in that room knew she was lying. No one in power cared. Lies that in a democracy would accelerate a bonfire of consequences rest comfortably on my computer. Those courthouse boxes could experience a fire if anyone who participated in the dirty deeds about my case were still with a sound mind. I should have said not demented with age. Their minds were only sound then if you count operating with lawless acts as sound.

No one worries about getting caught after participating in WCCrime, the perfect crime. So they don't bother destroying the evidence. However, if enough of you decide to do something about this now that you know, someone from my old district might do something to destroy this telltale record if their WCCrime mind still works.

Psychologist Linda Hatch said, "Gaslighting, brainwashing, cults, hostage situations, and totalitarian propaganda have a common basis. They use similar techniques to confuse, intimidate, and disempower people. These methods are used by abusers of all kinds to control other people and promote the abusers' interests." Hatch described that hearing well.

Bad people are running our schools. She lied under oath, and a state was okay with that. I wrote everyone you can imagine in Illinois, including the governor who later went to prison and the one who had been in jail. The fact that many of the perpetrators are still in trusted positions helps you understand how so many people gave up on democracy and decided that doing what the

Germans did in the 1930s—trust an autocrat—seemed like a good idea.

Phew, we finally got to 9, the last typical misconception.

9. Watchdogs are watching over our schools so we'd know if wrongdoing was going on. Truth: I found out that there were no watchdogs for our schools in 1995. I called the Illinois State Board of Education (ISBE) about wrongdoing I had observed in my district. It was the caucus' job to create a slate of board members. I saw the Board strong-arm the caucus so they couldn't change the board members when the caucus was the safeguard for assembling a democratic board. To eliminate the safeguard, the Board spread misinformation about the caucus leader, the information I verified and found false, as was the information used against me.

The ISBE told me there are no watchdogs. I must have asked the gentleman three times. I was stunned. He said that the only method for dealing with wrongdoing was voting. Since people don't pay attention to school board elections, there's no method to stop them. They ensured their political allies who were participating in the wrongdoing or looking the other way ran for their board. The superintendent handpicked board members based on loyalty to him, established with under-the-table privileges.

It shocked me that nobody was assigned to watch over our schools. I'm sure you are, too. It seemed impossible that they could have so much taxpayer money yet have no one checking on unethical behavior or lawbreaking. In the enhanced ebook, Part Three, you can read about a WCCriminal theft of over 12 million dollars at Roslyn School District in New York as one example proving this.

All an administrator needs is a rubber stamping board to disassemble the guardrails, and his wish is his command. We base our trust in schools on misconceptions and assumptions.

And much of our mistrust stems from unions, when they are like Patty Hearst, victims of Stockholm's syndrome, as are so many teachers. It's not that Patty Hearst, like the unions, didn't side with the bad guys. I do not condone what the unions did to help my district trash me. They tried to manipulate me to do what the district wanted. They were deplorable. Everyone up against WCCrime falls into line. A shroud of fear holds their brains and hearts hostage. In my mind, their criminality is secondary, however.

The path from my brain to your brain is a perplexing maze. We've discussed the believability issue. What I am telling you takes that to new heights. It's easier to finally accept that priests did what they did to boys than to get that WCCrime flourished right under your noses, and you didn't have a clue. What I am saying here is a step beyond. People who have known me for years and trust me act like I'm discussing the theory of relativity when I try to explain WCCrime.

I often do not discuss what I do with social friends, aware that explaining it takes a village of words. The bridge between my work and almost every human being who hasn't been a dedicated teacher seems more extended than when a scientist endures explaining a new theory. The unbelievability factor haunts my work.

Shocking acts performed by out-of-control, influential people hide under cover like an unborn baby in a uterus. When what they do is too unbelievable, it's not believed until it's blown open. If not for the media, Harvey Weinstein would still be sexually abusing actresses. If not for the press, depraved priests would still be sexually abusing boys. We need our if-not-for!

It would help if you sailed through an unbelievability maze to save democracy. The corruption bewilders most. Most say, "We'd know if this were going on. We know administrators steal money, but how does that affect democracy? It's impossible to believe they are making stuff up about good teachers since they so need them. Teachers must be the problem."

Ten years of substitute teaching didn't clue me into WCCrime. It took working at a full-time job over two years to get what was going on. It's not at all what you think. I've discussed misconceptions. I will now discuss barriers that need crossing:

1. People tend to defend their lives rather than examine them. Introspection makes them feel less than others. When my children were young, I found parents praising their child's teacher even when the teacher was lacking. It's hard to think you sent your children to the schools I describe. Rejecting the truths in this book is more comforting.

2. There are some excellent schools. But 95% thought the school where I taught was exemplary. They were breaking laws and putting children in harm's way. The coverup is superb. Most believe their schools are excellent.

3. If your school is an exception, it's still your problem. Children from good schools must live in a world with children from schools who aren't doing their jobs. It's not good enough that your school is fine. In a democracy, we need all schools to do their job.

4. Bad administrators end up in good districts. Things change. A good school can suddenly become a bad one. WCCrime does not infiltrate every school, but any school can slide into it. It can be temporary, but the chunks it takes from students' lives are permanent.

5. Motherhood, apple pie, and schools exist anchored in virtue. It might be easier for me to convince you that your parents did a lousy job raising you than many of our schools are shams and scams. All are one step from hiring a WCCriminal. It happens accidentally at good schools; it is intentional at bad schools. It's close to finding out that a beloved uncle molested your child. It's hard to accept.

6. Then there's the embarrassment of you not realizing this. Can you imagine how hard it was for parents of boys abused by priests to even consider that might have happened? It

was thirty years hard. That's how long it took to elevate an accusation to an issue worthy of belief and action. Sinners' harmful acts hide behind veils of victims' shame. Many believe that devotion to Trump, despite his criminality, stems from a similar human frailty. It's hard to be wrong.

7. This embarrassment multiplies when you consider those precious children gunned down while you are oblivious. So it's better to think Karen Horwitz can't be right, as no one wants an ounce of that guilt.

8. You have friends or relatives who teach and never told you anything about this, so it can't be true. I've explained how teacher abuse terrorizes teachers into silence. They won't discuss this. Then, there are some genuine schools. The principal who hired me wanted a successful school. Had she not left, I would have had a great career. I would have been one of those who never said a word about school corruption. Granted, the superintendent had issues. However, the original principal provided a healthy barrier. I could have had a blissful career at that school.

9. Teachers are afraid. Teacher abuse is ruthless. Once our staff listed issues to discuss at our next union meeting. On the list was "a more democratic atmosphere," something I didn't add. Yet, no one spoke about how undemocratic things were, not even at that meeting. It was as if it wasn't on that list. No one claimed it, and the president pretended it wasn't there. Only with close friends will teachers dare speak of their administrators' abusive ways.

10. Victims of abuse don't talk about abuse. That's the secret sauce that makes abuse so effective. It's what makes it abuse rather than harm. Embedded in abuse is the bully-is-king concept. Terror increases determination not to be next. They help the bullies to not become targets. Shame and silence are best friends. Some are drowning

in an abusive environment but know there's a high price to speak about it

You didn't hear about the priests or Weinstein before investigations blew those issues open. And until investigations begin, we won't know how pervasive it is. We do know our children's scores lag behind children's scores from other countries, our democracy is imploding, and school shootings are on the rise. We know investigations are missing in action.

11. Teaching is a complex practice viewed as simple; people think anyone could teach. This is the most challenging barrier. They don't think anyone could paint like an artist or well enough to sell a painting. They don't think anyone could be a scientist. They believe teaching doesn't need a book, *Teaching for Dummies*, since dummies already teach.

They're only right when describing weak teachers. Every profession has people who could be better. Some change with experience. Talented teaching requires both creativity and skills. Some take longer to acquire skills. Inexperienced teachers might be less effective. But some are masterful.

12. The prevalence of female teachers with male bosses coupled with pre-women's liberation thinking existing before the 1980s set an oppressive environment for a women-dominated career. The historical top-down structure is a slippery slope for WCCrime. Non-liberated women's unquestioning acceptance of authority erased resistance to its takeover. When equality began, teacher abuse escalated as liberated women started questioning what men were doing. When what they were doing became WCCrime, teacher abuse was WCCriminal's stay out of jail card.

Even where WCCrime did not take hold, education remained a patriarchal stronghold. Often, law-abiding administrators operate in a top-down, dictatorial style, incompatible with great teachers who need a creative setting to do their magic. A great teacher is a great problem solver. Repressive authority inhibits creativity and innovation. Although WCCrime is worse, authoritarians suffocate greatness out of teachers, compromising schools, too. Low pay, low status, and assuming anyone can teach are ingredients for suppression.

13. Learning is what most people overlook when they diminish the act of teaching. Anyone can be a teacher, but it takes talent, skills, and training for students to learn. Those of us who studied brain-based learning know how learning takes place.

Some teachers delve deeper to make sure learning happens. Because this "profession" requires pleasing the authoritarians in charge in so many schools, fewer and fewer teachers bother to develop as professionals. They realize that the teachers who do are the first targeted. Professional drive and initiative serve as red flags to WCCriminals.

From studying brain-based research, I learned that no one learns anything not connected to prior knowledge. A person who isn't a doctor can only absorb a little when reading medical literature. A good teacher ensures that new knowledge is scaffolded to something the learner already knows. Understanding this explains why teaching to standardized tests without the ability to scaffold is futile and damaging. It also explains why it's been so hard to expose WCCrime.

Only some insiders experience it, while others are treated with kid gloves and covered with false information that serves as plastic in the rain. Then, many insiders are so naive; the torrents of abuse confuse them. Some blame themselves. Most have gentle natures. They leave teaching bewildered. Few have the street smarts to identify WCCrime.

14. This is the first time you have heard about this. Books discuss financial wrongdoing, the mistreatment of teachers, and the blame placed on unions and teachers. Few connect the dots between these issues. I'm one of the few putting abuse together with WCCrime. New ideas take time. They have to become believable. Reporters can't report what they can't believe.

My story includes a reporter in the year 2000 who told me she couldn't believe I did nothing wrong but then called my state board of education when I pointed out to her that THEY had done something wrong. They violated the statute mandating a decision in thirty days. You'll hear about this reporter all over this book.

Her call was powerful. It forced their hand. I got my decision too late to use for my federal case—they manipulated that loss—but I got my hands on a case filled with fraudulent, altered documents that could prove WCCrime once someone with power cares. Yet, the reporter did nothing more. She was too sure I was the problem.

That incident taught me how alone I was. When the truth is disconnected from society, the solutions are, too. That reporter could not do her job in a world lacking essential facts. She couldn't even reach a point of suspicion against our state education leaders and do her job. Mountains of lies kept her dysfunctional. Thus, she, like all reporters, has failed at this—and you don't know about it.

15. Figuring this out has been too complex for our leaders, who aren't education experts. WCCriminals have been able to keep them from whistleblowers like me. If a progressive Supreme Court justice could be fooled, anyone could be fooled.

16. People think all corruption is parallel. When I tell people about WCCrime, most roll their eyes and give

a tell-me-something-new response. They insist that there's corruption everywhere. That's true, but everywhere isn't democracy's foundation.

Corruption in medicine affects health. Corruption in business affects finances. Corruption in education affects our entire society. It deteriorates its underpinning. Education will earn the protection it deserves only if it becomes a respected discipline.

Ulysses S. Grant did not say we'd become a nation of morons if medicine or business became corrupted. He knew the momentousness of education. Few others get this.

17. Then there's the fumble grasp—this can wait. Some comprehend that it's an issue but not the 9-alarm fire that it is. People think that real schools will only help democracy over time. To them, it's a back burner, not an immediate solution.

All of these barriers have contributed to the loss of faith in democracy. Many are about to vote for a person who will end it. We need a proactive democracy instead of one that looks the other way at something as serious as WCCrime. We must prove that it isn't a deep state depriving us of proper education. Instead, it's a profoundly dysfunctional state allowing this due to ignorance.

Democracies make mistakes that let people down. However, unlike autocrats, who don't care about the people, a democratic leader corrects these mistakes. We must restore faith in democracy so more will vote for it. The government and the media must fix this education disaster to regain their lost trust.

President Biden promised to save the soul of this nation. As schools mold character, they protect our souls. Allowing WCCrime has left our souls abandoned. Yes, educating a new generation as solid citizens will take time. But if we fail to show those who've given up on democracy a reason not to give up, we may lose our democracy. And even if we dodge the Trump bullet, we will continue to have the ugly division that darkens everyone's existence. We will remain divided souls with these schools as they are.

I would like to provide you with a sure-fire method for detecting WCCrime, but it's like dealing with cockroaches. They are impossible to find, and they run for cover when you turn the lights on. They aren't going to fess up. They are too afraid of consequences. Let your administrators know you're onto them and watch for sabotage. But they're skilled at it, and you aren't. That's why we must take care of this problem as a nation. This has to be a movement with solid educators as leaders. These educators must come from outside the education establishment. A great starting place is NAPTA members.

You could use a copy of this book to ignite discussion when amongst teachers or administrators and judge their reactions. You'll be surprised how many sigh with relief that someone's doing something about this. WCCrime benefits only a few but affects everyone. You're more likely to find educators who want it to end than those who don't. The bottom line is once it's known, it will free sycophants and weaken the predators. There are so many dedicated educators that once they're safe, WCCrime won't be safe.

Why believe yours truly? Someone had to figure this out, as with every new idea. People do hard things. Steve Jobs invented the Mac and iPhone, born in his mind. Zuckerberg/Facebook. Bezos/Amazon. They meshed needs and ideas to form a new phenomenon. I figured out the relationship between bad things happening in our schools and solutions.

My calling to teach transformed into a calling to figure this out. Or my ability to help children, my seeing deep inside them, morphed into seeing deep inside education. I'm a skilled problem solver. No child failed in my class. So, I applied my problem-solving gift to our failing schools. I knew if this "student—our schools" failed, so would our democracy. Don't let that I'm female or a teacher get in your way of accepting that I've figured this out.

I know what's wrong with our schools and what needs to change. Thousands of others who've experienced WCCrime firsthand agree. We are powerless, voiceless educators. The sooner others accept this truth and share their power, the sooner our nation will be on a healthy path.

No institution can withstand years of corruption and still fulfill its intended purpose. This book will enable you to become a watchdog. It will bring back the influencers who used to expand children's minds, turning our children into citizens rather than hollow souls. The coverup is outstanding. It takes an insider with colossal passion to figure this out. You did nothing wrong. Our leaders did nothing wrong. But that was before. Doing nothing now is wrong.

9

DEMOCRACY - A CLOSER LOOK

"At his best, man is the noblest of all animals; separated from law and justice he is the worst."

Aristotle

"Yesterday is not ours to recover, but tomorrow is ours to win or lose."

Lyndon B. Johnson

"A problem well-defined is a problem half solved."

John Dewey

People fall in love with a sport. Others fall in love with a profession. I fell in love with democracy. In 1995, most were taking democracy for granted. Not me. I discovered that my school district was operating above the law. I inquired about government watchdogs and learned there wasn't even a toy poodle that fits in a purse watching over us. Nothing is in place other than the teacher as a lapdog model.

Why was I worried? Democracy is a promise that each person counts. Each person agrees to follow laws in place to maintain civility and morality. It creates a path for the American dream. It's what I signed up to teach. Yet, each of us began counting less and less as both political parties and the media let us down. The path became overgrown with poisonous plants.

Both parties blame the other for destroying democracy. I don't. There's one institution that led this downhill journey: our schools. They failed to teach what democracy means and the skills needed to keep it. They ended democracy within it. The few insiders that would dare tell you about their dismantling of democracy stand no chance of being heard.

I'm not saying the people running our schools are intentionally taking down our democracy. It's happening because they are not running authentic schools and haven't been for decades. Intentionality is a topic for another book. And to the extent it exists, there will be a counterforce once the public knows the truth about our school. Once resurrected, outstanding schools will take care of that, too, since education is not only where people learn to read and write. It's where people learn their role in democracy.

Democracy doesn't intersect with our schools. It is at their core. Education exists to promote and preserve the continuity of a government. An autocracy uses education to teach submission to the ruler's absolute power. A democracy uses education to introduce the role of the individual. Each person has some power. Our education system needs to prepare citizens. Thus, misinformation, the vehicle of the autocrat, has replaced the teaching of critical thinking or one's life raft in a democracy. It's no wonder that so many people are easily conned. Inferior education has left individuals suspended in a sea of disinformation without a floating device.

Democracy means everyone counts. By not educating children about it, or the skill required to live within it, critical thinking, they cannot grow up to make sure it's in place. They cannot distinguish between facts and conspiracies, leaving them vulnerable to a wannabe dictator.

They know not to fly in a plane piloted by a movie star or great singer who never flew an airplane. Still, they need to understand government more to avoid a reality TV star president. Democracy and its primary tool, critical thinking, requires teaching to endure. The end of democratic schools has produced generations of shallow-thinking non-citizens. Democracy now flirts with its demise due to WCCrime, the fraud upon America that drove me to take on this mission. We need innovative people to force the unraveling of this. I haven't given up trying to find them.

There are significant issues made more problematic by our shell-like schools. At the top of that list is racial inequality. A functioning democracy solves problems such as inequality. It educates away prejudice in many. It respects all. Our nation's challenge with racial equality has become more consequential with the absence of authentic schools. However, there is no issue of racial inequality when it comes to teachers. WCCriminals discriminate against exceptional black and white teachers equally. The enhanced ebook, Lesson Seven, discusses outstanding African American teachers being trashed and other racial inequality issues.

This topic is a huge reason why WCCrime is so destructive. However, I am confident that exposing WCCrime and bringing back real schools will offer a bonanza of progress toward equality—maybe more than most issues given its journey from slavery that many are trying to hide rather than respect. When called-to-teach teachers run this show, all children will receive what they need.

When I put together my list of visions in Chapter 15, I only mentioned diversity a little. I focused on the top structure that we need to reach all children. Dedicated teachers care for each individual when the system allows them to as doctors do. I focused on a structure that will solve democracy's issues—authentic schools.

Every child needs good schools. Some have ways to compensate for bad schools. Those who don't suffer more. However, based on our sinking nation, even compensation stopped working, landing us all in a sinking ship. We must end WCCrime and change the structure. Diversity needs will then fall into place.

One issue that has haunted me for years is the gangs in Chicago. I know that the best path for eliminating them would be to provide engaging schools for those gifted black boys who see our schools as the joke they are. These gangs are like Trump followers—people who reject what our democracy is doing and turn to violence.

I know many teachers who could help these young boys connect to education, the secret to success, but this system is as lost as those boys. I recall a California high school teacher who was forlorn over not being allowed to teach her students how to avoid jail. She believed that her district wanted to provide inmates rather than achieving students.

A synopsis of former Secretary of Labor Robert Reich's 2021 book on democracy, *The System: Who Rigged It, How We Fix It*, said, "Reich's objective is not to foster cynicism, but rather to demystify the system so that American voters might instill fundamental change and demand that democracy works for the majority once again."

I think that more than just demystifying and demanding is required. Exposing and then fumigating WCCrime is the solution for change to happen. We must name the specific, unlawful practice we need to end to level the playing field. Culprits hold up this field, turning it into a giant water slide, forcing anyone without power into a rut at the bottom. The rut is a grave rather than a springboard to success.

Reich got warmer in "Civic Education, Foundational to Democracy,"[13] his article reiterating the need for civic education:

America's founders knew that the new republic's survival necessitated a public wise enough to keep power within bounds. It required citizens capable of resolving the tension between private interests and the common good—people imbued with civic virtue...Ignorance and despotism seem made for each other, Jefferson warned. But if the new nation could 'enlighten the people generally...tyranny and the oppressions of mind and body will vanish, like evil spirits at the dawn of day.'

He mentions that Horace Mann, the father of public education, also connected public education to democracy. He includes Mann's thinking: "'A republican form of government, without intelligence in the people,' he wrote, 'must be, on a vast scale, what a mad-house, without superintendent or keepers, would be on a small one.'"

Our country is a madhouse. It never had to get this way had we heeded Mann's warning. I attended Horace Mann School through the eighth grade. Mann's spirit must have captured mine. Although people my age have long retired, I am gripped with teaching this nation about how WCCrime has bulldozed our democracy. Reich says:

> If the common good is to be restored, education must be reconnected to these public moral roots. We must stop thinking about it solely as a private investment that may lead to a good-paying job and revive the founders' understanding of it as a public good that helps train young people in responsible citizenship.

WCCrime has turned education into a private investment on steroids. WCCriminals keep it confidential, given that there's jail time if known. Reich, like most, needs to learn about WCCrime as the reason for eliminating civic studies or what all words sharing its root, *civilis*, which relates to citizens, describe. That includes civility, which, if absent, feels like madness. Reich adds:

> Such an education must encourage civic virtue. It should explain and illustrate the profound difference between doing whatever it takes to win and acting for the common good. The difference between getting as much as possible for oneself and giving back to society. Between assuming everyone is in it for themselves and understanding that we're all in it together.

Between seeking personal celebrity, wealth, or power and helping build a better society for all...It should enable them to work with others to separate facts and logic from values and beliefs, and help them find facts and apply logic together even if their values and beliefs differ.

He's right. However, an education requires role models. A staff of souls saturated with WCCrime from partaking in it or going along with it out of fear fails us. Bringing back civics education with covert WCCrime would be as productive as having Donald Trump teach morality. A hypocrite can try to teach, but profound learning only occurs when the teacher's soul is aligned with the lesson.

As long as WCCrime thrives, teachers submerged in it must padlock their souls to remain in teaching. They may be able to teach a subject, but their strangled souls thwart their ability to teach proper human interaction. And we must also question how well they teach subjects like math and literacy when teachers have closed-off souls. Test scores suggest: not well.

Spiritually crippled teachers diminish the American dream as well. @ProudNavyVeteran tweeted: "The biggest threat facing America today is stupidity. A significant portion of our citizenry has been indoctrinated rather than educated."

Our schools, drowning in WCCrime, leave students "radicalization-ready" by not developing their minds and hearts. Those who grow up to be rational, problem-solving citizens do so despite, not because of, our schools.

Schools once were the keepers of the facts. Having tossed that responsibility in the same garbage bags—not the see-through kind—with the discarded teachers of substance, they helped to label what the establishment offers as fake news to a vast segment of our population. The lack of depth that criminally minded types possess permits the takeover of brains and the erasure of moral sense.

As you further understand that education is no longer braided with democracy, as patriotic leaders warned it needed to be, you'll know how we've become such a hot mess. We now have a nation in chaos with education swept under the rug rather than serving as its pillar. We must bring that pillar back. People you trust have unplugged democracy—the plan that makes your life count. Keep reading and roam the authentic education landscape so you'll understand.

Dreyfuss, like Reich, longs for democracy to be taught in our schools. In his book *One Thought Scares Me...*, Dreyfuss points out the various ways of teaching democracy. He speaks about teachers telling stories so children fall in love with America. Most primary teachers include art projects with these stories and still do. As teachers less guided by specific curriculum goals fill the classrooms, these lessons have less intentionality. Instead of weaving an ongoing love for democracy, these lessons remain disconnected from art projects and stories.

Then, without teaching basic to more complex civics lessons over the years and without teachers who practice classroom management calculated to infiltrate democratic participation, students do not develop a love for democracy as before. It's a concept that fails to penetrate the brain when not embedded by design into teaching as analytical thinking teachers always did.

I agree with Richard Dreyfuss that we need to bring back civics education. We first need to expose WCCrime and the why behind its removal. In his book, he said, "The absence of Civics is behind all the rage that accompanies our uncontrollable partisanship, which doesn't allow for the legitimacy of any views contrary to one's own. That in itself opposes this idea of America." I agree with that.

He says, "No wonder even our best thinkers can't get a handle on what's wrong with America." That's where I disagree. Our best thinkers do not know what's going on in our schools. They need to learn about WCCrime. Or they know it too superficially to care. That's the missing piece that leads them astray and why they need to read this book!

He said, "We have reduced our respect for their teachers, viewing them as sly, defensive cheaters instead of the few remaining heroes of our culture." He's correct, but he doesn't know why—WCCriminals need them voiceless.

He said, "If I were pitching a film to a studio with a story about all of this, I would make the villains the ones who are seeing big profit in privatizing the school system and taking down the public school system altogether."

His discussion of privatizing schools was brilliant. Besides diluting our public schools, shifting to privatizing facilitates WCCrime. Public schools have more laws they need to break to do their evil deeds. Privatizing removes many. In Part Three of the enhanced ebook, you'll read about Kandise Lucas, a private school teacher who reported her school's neglect of a severely ill child to a state child protection agency. Her employer sued her for defaming his business.

The only right I had, and still have, is to report wrongdoing even though nobody in power cared or did anything about it. Public schools must abide by the First Amendment. They cannot sue me. She didn't have that right.

Dreyfuss is right about private schools in more ways than he listed. Besides, education is a service. We all profit by having a solid democracy. Once you turn it into a business, only the owners profit. All my ideas for great schools would not work once making money ran through it.

Top-notch students who can go to any college and do any job won't work for a lower salary to enrich the owner. Many bright students choose government jobs knowing they will make less than in private business but do so because service fits their humanity profile. Helping an owner make money in a company intended to be focused on upholding our democracy but isn't would not attract quality educators. Schools need to attract people of the caliber of lawyers who want to serve the Department of Justice rather than go into private practice.

Privatizing schools is an expansion of WCCrime. Money cannot be the goal of running a school. All decisions have to evolve from protecting our democracy. Let people who focus on money run businesses. Keep them out of the protecting democracy world unless the spiraling to its death democracy we now have is the goal. On his website,[14] Dreyfuss says:

> Civic values such as civility, clarity of thought, and the importance of dissent are not inherited at birth. We must teach the ideas; the younger, the better. In light of the changing demands on the education system due to an increasing focus on Science, Math, and other academics, civics has seen its allocation of time greatly diminished, resulting in younger generations having little connection to our founding documents and political system.

He's right about civics missing but wrong about why. Administrative arrogance, essential to WCCrime, has no place in a democracy yet has replaced civility. An article from the hill.com[15] described Dreyfuss' view of what abandoning civics does:

> Despite having a political system that highlights individual freedom and responsibility, we fail to provide individuals with the skills they need to successfully fulfill the role of citizenship. Civic values have been absent in certain events of our country's recent history. We have experienced conflicting political parties unable to compromise, violent protests showcasing a government unable to foster peace, and new generations falling behind their peers in education rankings.

> Extremism has plagued our government and caused shutdowns, fostered resentment between political parties, and generally caused inefficiencies. The lack of civility in debate in our political bodies is destructive and must be addressed. On top of that, the average American citizen needs a better understanding of civics and the nuances of our political structure. We must teach civics so that our future leaders have the skills they need to run our country effectively and future generations have the skills they need to be informed, active citizens.

In his book, he mentions a 2018 Rhode Island lawsuit filed on behalf of students who sued the state for not providing sufficient education to participate in a democracy. He said that in 2020, the judge threw out the case. Rather than rule that a school district had a duty to provide a proper civics education, the judge found, "We may ignore these things at our and their peril."

The judge took it as seriously as the court took my 2007 Petition for Writ of Certiorari on the US Supreme Court docket that asked if teachers have a right to use teacher abuse as a defense, which I did not, and whether school boards have a right to abuse teachers, causing harm to students. It ignored these things at our and their and democracy's peril! Education moves through our lives like a foreigner in a country that says foreigners are not welcome here. Is it ignorance or intention?

While Dreyfuss was dedicated to bringing civics back, having founded an organization for that purpose in 2006, I was on that too. I exposed the reason it went missing. My fellow democracy lover tried hard to get your attention with equal disappointment.

Is education the only thing that brought our democracy down? No. But it's the biggest and is part of why the following weakened democracy. Social media, TV celebrity worship, conniving political parties, technology, inequality, and many more played a bigger role, having occurred without the benefit of critical thinking to deal with each.

Artificial intelligence is soon to cause havoc without authentic schools. Education was to balance those things that WCCriminals, too busy counting their money, ignored. Our teacher influencers were to make sure nothing compromised proper learning.

The hijacking of our schools made balancing extinct. Our schools offer little protection against the ills of social media. In Chapter 12, I describe an uneducated parent who was able to help her son unlearn how to identify reliable information. That parent thought anything on the internet was factual. Due to WCCrime, she foiled my research lesson and my career, as many others like her did to teachers nationwide.

All my principal needed to do was inflate a couple of complaints to justify my disposal. A parent's opinion was a grenade against the learning of facts. It meant nothing to my WCCrime-infiltrated district. WCCrime's strangling of democracy included sticking a knife in media literacy so that the learning of facts no longer remains at the core of education. WCCrime turned most people into craven souls, unable to contemplate how undemocratic schools will destroy our democracy.

Experts describe YouTube as a beast contributing to the January 6 insurrection more than any other social media factor. Do you think the shallow-minded teachers that the thugs running our schools prefer will bother to tame this beast? Maintaining and designing an ongoing curriculum that reflects society's needs requires intellect and critical thinking. Pariahs like me, whom no lawless authoritarians want in their midst, are the ones equipped to do the job. WCCriminals abandon society's needs as they trash us.

While teaching fifth grade, I worked alongside teachers who promoted popular television programs. I concentrated on widening my students' horizons and critical thinking skills and helping them become productive citizens. I cringed at my colleagues' shallow focus on popular TV. My ten-year-old daughter was too often glued to the television. Why would they provide more?

My fourth-grade teacher had introduced me to ancient history. I wanted to be like her. With schools fixed on the frivolous, children grow up unable to cope with complicated issues such as ensuring we provide the education required for an informed electorate.

They hunt down teachers like me because critical thinkers are the enemy of the lawless. Yet we are the missing link to a healthy society, particularly a society up against social media. If I were still teaching, I'd be helping my students learn to decipher facts from fiction in social media, while my pop culture colleagues would be helping promote the chaos emanating from social media. They're unaware that teachers used to help children grow into citizens. And no WCCriminal cares!

If top universities participated in education in 1996, they, like I, would have worried about safeguarding accurate research and facts. They would have developed a curriculum to tame the beast and ensured schools implemented it. There would have been a counterforce, making WCCrime foreboding to administrators. National Louis University, our local go-to education university, dwelled on making my superintendent happy. And Harvard looked the other way.

As I pointed out, the top universities need strong education departments. The Ivy League universities put their toes in and run. The intellectual schools had little to nothing to do with us. I could have made only a dent in taming the beast had they not gotten rid of me.

People like me no longer choose to teach, and they ban the few who do from leading in education. It remains a perfect storm to take our society down. It's a discipline unmoored from elite universities, with women's liberation having removed most people of substance and administrators raiding the treasure chest, afraid to hire smart teachers.

This is why our democracy fell apart. We rely on universities to lead us. In education, they took a pass. Research continues in our universities but gets lost in a world where so few great minds survive. It lacks institutions that take the lead or administrators that care. The infrastructure to repair this does not exist except in the minds of people like me, who rank amongst the least powerful in society.

Incompetent teaching existed even before WCCrime took over. In 1966, my first teaching assignment—second grade—my entire class could not read. I mean, the whole class. They had a first-year teacher for first grade, and it seemed she didn't know how to teach reading. My second-grade students had the veteran teacher for first grade the following year. They were at grade level when they entered my class, which verified my assumption.

Had this been the elite school where my career ended, the parents would have complained. This was a working-class district that accepted things. It was up to me to solve the problem. I had a great reading instructor in college and was as prepared as any first-year teacher could be. That, coupled with solid problem-solving skills, I asked for first-grade books.

Had I not known to do this, I wonder if they would have been reading by the end of the year. I had them reading by mid-year. This shows how important good teachers are, plus how critical supportive principals are. WCCrime changed that.

By 1993, there was a chasm between me and my principal. She had no interest in what worked for me or my students. Based on my success with gifted students, she put me on the gifted committee. She said she wanted me to share the techniques I used to make learning happen for those students in my classroom. Her disguised motive was to end the gifted pull-out program, contrary to what parents wanted.

At one point, a parent of one of my talented students took me aside and said, "Teaching gifted students in the classroom works for you because you can lead a three-ring circus. You stay late and work hard. Teachers rarely have your intellect. They don't devote so much time to their job. They have babies at home. They aren't you."

What she said made sense, but I was too green to realize not to trust my principal. My principal acknowledged what I did in the classroom and knew I could teach other teachers. I expected to do that. I helped her end the pull-out program. She never had me teach anyone what worked for me. Instead, she trumped up charges to get rid of me the following year.

Among my best ideas was a vocabulary program I devised to address gifted needs in the classroom. A couple of years later, an administrator shared results from a standardized achievement test measuring a teacher's teaching ability. Yes, there is a test that does that, but for some corrupt reason, they don't use it for that purpose.

This standardized test[16] determines a teacher's progress by factoring a student's achievement based on that student's IQ. In other words, if Jonny has a low IQ but performs average or above, the teacher is successful. The teacher needs to be improved if

Jonny has a high IQ and scores average. Scores with intelligence factored in measure teaching, not low achievement that may have nothing to do with that teacher.

It was odd that the district concocting false charges against me to silence my ability to prove they were harming children used these more effective tests. It couldn't have been to ensure good teaching. They didn't care about that. Whatever, they handed me an academic pistol that proves my teaching prowess—something that meant nothing to them.

One can look at the scores in each subject area and see how many students perform below or above their ability. The data shows whether instruction ranges from poor to excellent. One adds all the percentage points in the "below" potential categories to determine the instruction level. Some "below" points are due to subjects not yet taught. One can judge teaching quality by evaluating several teachers' relative scores on this test.

There are results from my teaching, along with results from one of my principal's favorites. The honored teacher produced scores more than 200% worse than my scores. She had 370 points in the below potential category. I had 121 points in that category. The reading vocabulary shows me 30 points more in the above potential category. This was due to the program that the principal said she'd share but never did.

Bad teaching that advances administrative agendas to the detriment of democracy happens in other ways. The superintendent, who promised to make my life miserable if I said a word about the age discrimination happening at our school, decided to teach math using a year-ahead book. We had to teach fourth-graders fifth-grade math. He warned teachers to say nothing negative; we could count on him making good on his warnings.

Textbook publishers have intelligent mathematicians developing age-appropriate lessons. They structure math books for developmental learning. Using a grade level ahead is a recipe for disaster. It is like teaching reading before first grade. It hurts many children and helps a few.

I trusted the text developers. I learned that proper grade-level teaching is crucial when studying child development. It seemed wrong to me, but it looked impressive. And that's what the superintendent cared about. Based on how he treated me, it was clear that educating children wasn't his priority. He needed to impress or to cover up how much he wasn't into that. An animated Rolex watch discussion he had led with wanting eyes was my first and last clue to who he was. Doing math wrong was to be expected of such a hollow man.

These are but a few examples. This arena that great intellects and great reporters ignore has answers for democracy. This illegal education takeover is where we lost it. So, learning about what's going on in education is where we'll find it. WCCrime is not just criminals stealing education funds, although it is that, too. WCCriminals run schools to fill their needs rather than to fulfill the purpose of education. And one of their needs is getting rid of teachers dedicated to children, not to them. Another is a harmful curriculum that looks impressive.

Education exists in a fog. Until Covid, most parents thought they could teach their children. They thought it was an "anyone can do it, I prefer not to" skill, like cleaning your house. Having learned that teaching is more challenging, know this too: the key to the free-for-all corruption is the freedom to abuse teachers into silence. Richard Dreyfuss' unique appeal to the public that he included in his book speaks volumes. He said:

> You have no excuse not to insist on a better, more focused education for our kids or grandkids…They will know you didn't do it because the judgment of history will tell them. Those books aren't written yet, but rest assured they will be. [Your progeny] will be ashamed that you're related to them, even if you're dead. There is no amount of money, no act on your part, and no political opinion you hold that will excuse you. Nothing is being asked of you that you couldn't do in any given afternoon or a few afternoons. It's not hard, and it's not even expensive. Unless you are willing to support a complete

revision of the public school system so that it includes everything from Civics to the Arts, unless you pay teachers what
they are worth and resist any effort to structure education for
profit, then consider that you are a disgrace to your country.
That's not a maybe; that's how you will be remembered. And
forever despised.

He didn't stop there:

Let it be said right now that those responsible for undermining the American republic by failing to educate its citizens in
civic responsibility are guilty first and foremost. They should
be assured that one day they will be perceived as criminals,
and the institutions they corrupted will be rebuilt, brick by
brick—if time hasn't run out. Will it surprise the systems of
education, the press, politics, the courts that I am referring
to them...,

He said this way before talk of democracy in jeopardy became
mainstream. In my 2008 book that Oprah had in her hands but
not in her heart, I included a passage I wrote about the conniving
psychiatrist who helped the Board dispose of me. You can see that
I, unlike Dreyfuss, saw education as separate from democracy at
that time. I said:

Granted, he was an adult who made a choice, but a society can slide so far down into darkness that most members
lose themselves. I believe this happened in education. I
believe that we have created a tyranny within a democracy
and allowed that tyranny to fully cut all conduits of truth
so that the sane members of the democracy cannot rescue
themselves. To do so, they must make an admission of failure
unbearably shameful.

My 2008 thoughts now apply to our democracy as a whole,
but with a much worse destiny because of Trump. He has created a

tyranny within our democracy. If we elect him again, that tyranny will cut all conduits of truth so that even the sane members of the democracy cannot rescue themselves. Shame will keep Trump idolizers from admitting he was a mistake. Doing nothing about our schools will sculpt the way for a Trump takeover. Then, it will be much more than making amends in education to get our democracy back. We will need a revolution.

It's not just the disturbing Trump lovers that propelled me to finish this book before the 2024 election. My faithful volunteer webmaster became depressed over Trump. One by one, my friends were turning into Trump zombies—unable to talk about him while unable to not speak about him. Life just wasn't the same. It became clear that Trump had replaced some part of everyday life and that something was the sense of tranquillity that democracy provided.

Life became like flying acrobats who no longer had our safety net in place. Everyone's life was affected. I knew why. I had to work harder to solve what for years remained a calling but was now a calling on steroids. That giant trampoline-like structure that allowed our country to go about life with confidence used to be our schools, and we were all operating with fear that had replaced the comfort a good education had once provided.

Trump didn't make us all so unsettled. His attraction to evil found a home in a society orphaned from good schools. He personifies the loss. We became a society wherein a mere handful could remain in good spirits as fear and anger have taken so many out. Doing the right thing requires faith in others, which fewer and fewer people possess. Depression is anger turned inward. Anger has taken over.

Our choices have become democracy anger or democracy depression. We could count those operating above that on our fingers and toes. For every Liz Cheney who clings to what we learned in school, there are a hundred people depressed and another hundred ready to threaten a public official, and a few of them are prepared to kill them. If more people realized why life has become like this, that knowledge would return us to calmer waters.

Veiled criminality within our schools is taking down our democracy. Either it's unknown by those in power, or those in power haven't figured out that they are better off fessing up than losing our democracy. I never gave up on a student, so I won't give up on you reading and sharing this book.

To those, especially WCCriminals who see Trump as an answer: without our Constitution that Trump plans to end, a promise he's made, all that you've done for money and power, you will be doing for the king to line his pockets, not yours. And you'll get to fill his pockets only if you are lucky enough not to fall out of windows. I know. Most schools have two floors. Maybe you'll survive, but you'll be mutilated, and this supreme ruler doesn't like to look at ugly people.

10

FINALLY, THE WHY BEHIND SCHOOL SHOOTINGS - WCCRIME'S MISERABLE CURSE

"Education is the vaccine of violence."

Edward James Olmos

"A child must know that he is a miracle, that since the beginning of the world there hasn't been, and until the end of the world there will not be, another child like him."

Pablo Casals

"Every day, in a 100 small ways, our children ask, 'Do you hear me? Do you see me? Do I matter?' Their behavior often reflects our response."

L.R. Knost

All the children murdered since 2008 could be with us today had my first book been a best seller. As WCCrime has spiraled out of control, so have school shootings. A WCCrime-tainted education is not a vaccine to protect against anything! That's why you need to stay with me on this journey.

Your children and grandchildren attend schools with kids who are like canaries in coal mines. Since I'm not sure that people even know what that means anymore, I'll explain. Do you know that they used to send canaries into coal mines to check for poisonous gas? Maybe you don't. Besides being an old slogan, birds sacrificing their lives to protect miners is not "in" these days. Now that it's clear for some and redundant for others, its point blares. Living things dying in schools signifies something toxic going on.

The school shooters—who usually end up dead—are the canaries telling us something. Since no one has figured WCCrime out, dozens of children are killed, and I can't give up my mission. I can never, ever forget the Sandy Hook massacre. I know why school shootings happen. Those two thoughts make ending my mission unthinkable.

When the dark forces in education muzzled and banished the kid whisperers, they opened the doors to school shootings, a virulent form of bullying. School shooters are a natural outcome of these secreted toxic schools. We keep sending children into these "mines," clueless about the psychological poison that ensures nothing will change.

Lack of worth builds school shooters. Teachers who turn over their worth, what one must do to remain in teaching, cannot teach troubled children that they're worth more than the worst thing they've ever done. They cannot help alter their paths.

Our schools have given life to the ideal soil for growing school shooters. Due to WCCrime, they have morphed from safe houses to powder kegs. Once parents connect the dots from WCCrime to the mortal danger for their children our schools clandestinely hold, we can change this. Each time they purge a dedicated teacher, they exile a teacher who could and would have stopped a school shooter. Teachers like those who've joined my group are almost all that troubled students have in this world.

Power mongers immersed in WCCrime must bully teachers into silence. When an administrator does this at their school, and I mean "their" since they are kings, not leaders, they erode the support on which troubled children rely.

Great teachers are stepping stones for the unsettled waters of disturbed students. These students would drown otherwise. They are overloaded with toxic issues and deprived of a decent childhood. They drag others down with them. They are difficult.

Called-to-teach teachers are not in it to go along to get along. They are called to create citizens regardless of their students' issues. The unique, called-to-teach teachers are enemies to administrators whose lawless ways need cover. Since teachers who won't abandon children are dangerous whistleblowers, administrators purge them from their schools. They further ignite the rage in troubled children's souls when they take these teachers from them, leaving them on their own, abandoning these already dark, forsaken souls.

Furthermore, educrats sink these stepping stone teachers so parents will not expect excellent teaching. Since WCCriminals can't deal with teachers who put children first, they make parents think that unremarkable or even lousy teaching is the best it gets. Don't let those *Children First* pins fool you. My principal pinned them all over her as she started the day with a phony ethics reminder over the intercom. Remember the sawdust that school custodians used to throw on vomit? They needed barrels of it after her lectures.

Corrupt administrators destroy dedicated teachers to eliminate the threat of criminal indictment. As a result, children with needs that teachers who survive by playing politics cannot handle are abandoned. Troubled children's unmet needs become virulent, out-of-control grievances.

We used to count on dedicated teachers to love the smelly, antagonistic child whose life was a disaster. We were the only love they had. Now, we must rely on unique children able to love a messed up friend, rarer than a winning lottery ticket. Aaron Stark, who admitted he was about to shoot up his old school, could confirm this. He changed his mind, with guns in hand, due to the love of a friend.

FINALLY, THE WHY BEHIND SCHOOL SHOOTINGS - WCCRIME'S MISERABLE CURSE

Google Aaron Stork's TED Talk, "I was almost a school shooter," where he describes how close he came to shooting up his school. What Stark doesn't know is that called-to-teach teachers used to save children like him. Dedicated teaching used to be politically correct. He and you have yet to figure out that most administrators only pretend to want great teachers.

And think about the fact that almost every school shooter took their anger out at their past school. That was where their rage brewed for years in a caldron of justification to commit evil. We cannot have schools that fail to love each child enough to make them feel worthy unless we're okay with school shootings.

The story of Jack in Chapter 3 speaks volumes about why teachers step back from troubled students. Read it again if you don't remember how the special education team, where a teacher gets help for a troubled child at a WCCrime school, is like facing an evil firing squad. And it's more than likely inept, also!

Virginia teacher Abigail Zwerner's experience validates that![17] This Virginia teacher was unique. An article said, "The Virginia teacher who authorities say was shot by a 6-year-old student is known as a hard-working educator who's devoted to her students and enthusiastic about the profession that runs in her family, according to fellow teachers and city officials."[18]

She alerted her superiors that a student needed help, but they ignored her, and she ended up being shot by that student. Another article said, "In a $40 million lawsuit, Zwerner asserts that the school division's negligence allowed the shooting to happen and alleges specifically that the assistant principal ignored several warnings the boy had a gun that day."[19]

If you think many teachers would put forth the effort to help a student like this when administrators want them not to, and they incur the wrath of a disturbed child with no backup, you're dreaming. Her administrator ended up indicted. But most will think administrators like her are rare because that's what most assume about our schools. I'm here to tell you they're common. What's rare is accountability.

Educrat malfeasance that leads to "time bomb" students is hard on teachers in other ways. Ed Cobin, a former Teacher of the Year[20], underwent abuse for reporting guns brought to school. After two years of harassment, including a vicious criminal charge that HE told the student to bring the guns to school, he got his job back.

Think of the chilling effect teacher abuse has—an ability to extort silence and foment another Columbine. Despite the pain this caused, Cobin is in a better place today than the Columbine teachers, who avoided teacher abuse and have to live with the memory of what they could have prevented. (*School Daze*, his recently published book, includes a must-read chapter: "Preventing a Columbine.") An actual Columbine parent wrote a response to an article referring to Cobin:

As a Columbine parent, I want to tell all of you that you should be thanking this man every day. It is true that the disclosure of the gun sales is very important, but that is not the main reason you should be grateful. You should thank him because he is the kind of teacher that students will talk to. He is a contact. He is trusted. He relates to them. He cares. Teachers like this are the first line of defense against school violence. This is, in truth, the most important factor in preventing school violence.

There was, and I know this to be true, not one teacher at Columbine High School who was a possible source of such information. That is one of the main causes of the Columbine tragedy. There are thousands of families in Littleton who would have given anything to have a teacher like [him] in the school in 1998. He could have prevented Columbine. It is my hope that you appreciate and thank this man for his accomplishment. It is very possible that some of your children are alive today because of his actions.

FINALLY, THE WHY BEHIND SCHOOL SHOOTINGS - WCCRIME'S MISERABLE CURSE

> As someone involved in the Columbine tragedy, I can assure you that you owe this man, and teachers like him, a great deal more than you know. You have a hero in your midst. You should let him know that you appreciate his efforts. You should let him know, and all other teachers and administrators like him, that they are appreciated, that they are heroes.
> Randy Brown, Littleton, CO

Nevertheless, teachers like Cobin are pariahs to WCCriminals. The connection between WCCrime and school violence is stunning. A Columbine parent identified it vividly, yet we cannot get a media person to take on WCCrime, even in this context. There's a thread here that can unravel school violence like none other. But whoever disentangles it risks being labeled a boat rocker—a label avoidance that has our culture crumbling! Instead, we have shameless Trump sinking this nation!

Someone asked me if any good will come out of knowing what a toxic mess WCCrime is. My answer is whoever holds power will use it based on their values. Now, we have scoundrels exposing children to school shooters, hugging our schools—their treasure chests—not the children. We need good people in power to read this book and insist on replacing those self-serving types with those who care about others.

Those of us trying to report this will remain voiceless as long as the public trusts the leaders in power. The tragedy of our voicelessness extends to organizations such as Sandy Hook Promise or March for Our Lives, who have yet to figure out their core mission—eradicating WCCrime.

We need a powerful force like *The Boston Globe* that revealed priest abuse or a talented, courageous investigative reporter like Ronan Farrow, who exposed Harvey Weinstein. Disclosing this will be more challenging than those shameful episodes in America because teachers are so powerless. Teachers, who could have jumped on the Me Too Movement train to end their voicelessness, remain in a psychological fetal position, incapable of fixing their problem—and our nation's problem.

Learning this requires accepting how duped you've been. You need to feel some embarrassment and erase what you assumed schools are. Forget motherhood and apple pie. Schools are closer to abandonment and poison.

The 2024 manslaughter convictions of James and Jennifer Crumbley, parents of a school shooter, offer more insight. No one knew that Crumbley boy. The parents didn't know him. The teachers didn't know him. The school didn't know him. News reports blamed the parents and guns. I heard little mention of the school's lack. It wasn't only the parents who missed red flags. His teachers missed them, too. Or did they? They likely kept their mouths shut because that's what you do if you want to keep your job.

It's inconceivable to me that a child that lost could have been in my classroom, and I wouldn't have known. He could have been in my science class that I taught for less than an hour a few days a week, and I would have known to get him help. His parents could be oblivious and irresponsible. But a called-to-teach teacher could not miss the angst and rage that drove that boy to do what he did. A called-to-teach teacher would have spoken to those parents. A called-to-teach teacher would have given that boy hope, maybe not enough to solve all his problems, but enough to help him not take others' lives.

I think about my student Ted, whom I mentioned in Chapter 5. He was anxious because he was in a remedial reading class he didn't need, and it bothered him. I picked up on his anxiety and helped to get him removed from the class. Rage is far less subtle. I would have noticed it. I would have spoken up.

I think of Jimmy. A bright young boy with attention issues. He had Miss M for language, who was called to criticize, not called to teach. Often, when he acted up in her class, rather than handle him in a way that helped him grow, she'd call out across the class, "Jimmy, did you forget to take your meds today?" She evaded his privacy and humiliated him in front of the class. His mother was at her wit's end. The year after they trashed me, she sent him to a private school miles away. She knew that playing Russian roulette with teachers might break this boy.

To help him, I used to tell him that some teachers would be able to help him better than others and that if he kept the teachers who could help in the front of his mind, he'd be better able to deal with the teachers who couldn't. He knew he had issues. He knew he was hard. But no one deserves to be publicly shamed.

I never saw him as a potential school shooter, but a life of constant degrading has its way with young boys. What I did was take my students' mental health issues seriously, something the Crumbley's and apparently all their son's teachers didn't do. Teachers on eggshells can't do that. Their focus is on pleasing their bosses, not on their students.

And our courts have let us down. In The Supreme Court of the United States, 546 US 49 (2005), Schaeffer v. Weast, Superintendent, Montgomery County Public Schools, et al., No. 04-698, Honorable Supreme Court Justice Stevens stated, "I believe that we should presume that public school officials are properly performing their difficult responsibilities under this important statute." I warned you that I would repeat this troubling ruling.

Courts found that the Crumbley's failed at parenting, but they likely won't find that his school failed at its job because the court assumes that those running our schools are doing so for the benefit of our children. It's time our courts grew up.

In her 2014 book *Serious Repercussions,* Pennsylvania teacher Sallie Montanye documents unimaginable abuse for helping a suicidal student. Her book description tells why they need to grow up. It said:

The administrators stated the death of a child was of no public significance. The child's teacher disagreed. This is the story of the fight waged by one brave educator who believed a child's life did hold importance and was willing to sacrifice everything to protect a teacher's right to help a student in dire need.

Here's her story:
http://www.endteacherabuse.org/Montanye.html

Or listen to a podcast of five teacher whistleblowers:

At 34:14 you will hear why teachers don't come forward and the Parkland shooting mentioned.

Teacher Ed Cobin speaks about how to avoid incidents like Parkland. Instead of commentators asking, "Why does this keep happening in our schools?" they need to read my book and follow my work.

My 2008 book contained lessons about how unsafe our WCCrime schools are. The following are some segments from that book pertaining to school shootings that were part of those lessons. As you read them, remember they were written in 2008. Think about the children who would still be alive had that book gone viral. I still cry every time I see the Sandy Hook children's faces on TV.

Imbalanced Power A 2008 article, "Bullies' hidden danger: End the spiral of cruelty through intervention of bystanders,"[21] declared that we need a well-thought-out system against bullying, insisting that we cannot rely on bystanders. It said, "It may seem a stretch to link schoolyard bullying to atrocities such as ethnic cleansing and genocide."

FINALLY, THE WHY BEHIND SCHOOL SHOOTINGS - WCCRIME'S MISERABLE CURSE

Barbara Coloroso agreed. In her 2007 book *Extraordinary Evil: A Short Walk to Genocide*, she pointed out that imbalanced power drives bullies. Like everyone else outside education's impenetrable walls, she did not know about WCCrime. However, had she known, she would have recognized its hazardous, imbalanced power. She offered a convincing analysis that the structures of bullying and genocide are frighteningly similar.

What alarmed Ms. Coloroso most is that her research of anti-bullying programs throughout the world showed they "had as their foundation conflict-resolution solutions" when the problem is that bullying is not about anger or conflict; it is about contempt. Her outcry for bullying awareness programs included the following:

> They will not just be making the schoolyard and cyberspace safer for the significant number of kids that are traumatized by bullying, and who sometimes murderously snap—most infamously, but certainly not only at Columbine High School— or commit suicide out of desperation. They will be equipping a citizenry to recognize the toxic leadership that is bullying and refuse to be silent, collusive followers…This is especially critical for those who go into professions that are trusted with the violent power of the state. Failure to train such a citizenry sooner or later results, to our national shame…

She described a vicious cycle present in way too many of our schools. Teachers are held in contempt. WCCriminals will never train them to become experts; they need them powerless. Teachers are more than not equipped to recognize toxic leadership. WCCriminals make them as subservient as they can. Their powerlessness forbids any recognition, any mention, and any hope they will protect children. They become collusive followers. They, like all other WCCrime accomplices—with the unions topping that list—have no choice. They cannot help children accomplish what they cannot achieve. Since children learn from their esteemed models, children have little chance of dealing with bullying. Coloroso wrote her prescient warning in 2007.

The Columbine Syndrome, a genuine investigation of Columbine, will show that those teachers were psychologically manipulated into silence, and school life became volatile with psychologically troubled children not being serviced properly. Fuller pointed out in his 2004 book *Somebodies and Nobodies, Overcoming the Abuse of Rank:*

> An outcast starved for recognition who attacks others or himself is giving expression to the unendurable indignity of feeling inconsequential. A confidant of one of the boys who killed a dozen of their schoolmates at Columbine said of his friend,' He was afraid he would never be known.' (p. 49)

Deducing that teacher/administration tension existed at Columbine, I searched for documentation that proved that teacher abuse set the stage for violence. In the 2003 book *Guilty Until Proven Innocent: Teachers and Accusations of Abuse*, Mathew D. Olson and Gregory Lawler discussed Columbine social studies teacher Al Wilder, who was embroiled in a First Amendment federal lawsuit, whose ruling came down a year before the massacre. It left behind a contentious atmosphere—an atmosphere I knew well after I filed a federal lawsuit against my district.

They stated about how the two killers saw themselves as outsiders:

> While the boys' torment is only one aspect of the killers' psychology, the Wilder case gives a startling insight into an aspect of school life prevalent in schools across the nation. In America's push for higher Educational standards, society has inadvertently created the need for what Wilder considers fascist regimes within the Educational system. The result of this benign fascism is an increased competition among students." (p.140)

Competition fosters a student case system that creates a friction between students and between the faculty and administration…The Colorado Legislature held an inquiry into the Columbine Massacre and uncovered some of the WHYs that the boys' warning signs went undetected. The inquiry found that friction between the administration and faculty, along with friction between faculty members, had broken down the lines of communication in the school."

They reported failed communication; they said:

The [principal] "had numerous opportunities to facilitate a discussion between the teacher and the offended parents. The principal also had numerous opportunities to correct Wilder's use of controversial films, and he had a chance to offer Wilder a written reprimand and training for his non-compliance with district guidelines…[the principal's] treatment of the teacher led to the destruction of Wilder's career. (p.140)

Bullying creates a culture unwilling to converse due to a fear of more bullying, hot-wired fear. The authors said: "The sociological variables that drove two young men to massacre fellow students were bullying and a lack of communication." (p.141)

Communication is the language of love; the choice of silence or violence is the language of evil. Abuse leads to recycled pain that keeps recycling. Abuse manifests psychological nuclear war. As Fuller said in *Somebodies and Nobodies*: "The step from desperation to desperado is short." (p.131) In order to cope with abuse, people often make abusive choices born of desperation. Oprah wisely said: "The root of most evil is people's self-hatred."

Abusing teachers produces negative energy that sets in motion teachers abusing other teachers, teachers abusing children, and children abusing children. A NAPTA teacher called me concerned that their special education aides continually bully the Downs Syndrome students, calling them fat and making fun of them to make them cry.

When adults bully, one must look for a cycle of negative energy. EducRAT$ were likely mistreating these aides. When adults behave like children, abuse is typically the impetus. Then high school student Evan Ramsey is currently in jail in Florence, Arizona, having shot his principal. He replied that no one cared about him when asked what motivated him. Alienated students + unsafe communication = The Columbine Syndrome.

School Violence From Ed Cobin's story[22] about harassment for reporting that a student brought guns to school to the Columbine setting, where teachers were afraid to speak up, it is clear that mixing guns with WCCrime is a time bomb. Study any school shooting and find a connection to WCCrime: a disgruntled student left in an emotionally explosive state and/or a staff of emotionally paralyzed teachers.

Emotionally Unsafe Harvard Psychologist Daniel Goleman, in his book *Social Intelligence,* says, "Concern is the impulse that lies at the root of the helping professions, (p.97) …When people in the helping professions get little or no sense of having a secure base in those they work with or for, they become more susceptible to 'compassion fatigue.'" (p.257)

EducRAT$ have forced teachers to disengage empathy. This leaves children without the support and connections that Goleman identifies as needed to form healthy brain circuitry. Goleman explains that properly teaching wayward youths fortifies "their circuitry for self-control, thinking before acting, and the very ability to obey the law," whereas failing to do so strengthens their "hostility, impulsivity, and violence." (p.289) He wrote: "A great many of the people in prison are arguably there because of neural deficits in the social brain, like impaired empathy and impulse control." (p.289)

Goleman's emphasis on parents and teachers building supportive connections to produce socially appropriate citizens exposes the danger of EducRAT$'s puppet teacher model. He points out, «…To eliminate human values from social intelligence impoverishes the concept,…Then such intelligence devolves into the pragmatics of influence and control. In these anonymous and isolated times, we need to be ever vigilant against the spread of just that impersonal stance." (p.101)

Since EducRAT$ need influence and control to break laws, we have that very impoverishment, which generates out-of-control students and teachers as well as "group narcissism." To avoid abuse, teachers cater to leaders who demand to "hear only messages that confirm their own sense of greatness," thereby agreeing to acts harmful to students.

Goleman describes WCCrime: "Everyone tacitly colludes to maintain their shared illusions...Work devolves to a charade." (p.121). "...those who imperil the group's grandiosity are typically demoted, upbraided, or fired...[it] becomes a moral universe of its own, a world where its goals, goodness, and means are not questioned but taken as holy writ. It's a world where doing what-ever we need to to get whatever we want seems perfectly fine. The ongoing self-celebration fogs over how divorced from reality we've become. The rules don't apply to us, just to the others." (p.122) Creating "an emotional stew" that is lethal. (p.278)

This "stew" he described leaves students to fend for them-selves; teachers dare not anger their leaders. He says that Elliot Aronson, a social psychologist who examined the Columbine tragedy, described high school as a "living hell" for children taunted for not being in the in-crowd. (p.307) And that social ostracism impairs learning and "disengaged students tend to have higher rates of violence and disruptive behavior in class, show poor attendance, and drop out at higher rates." (p.306)

A 2007 article entitled, *I'm Worried About America*,[23] reminds us how unsafe children are without meaningful relationships. This article illustrates how safety starts with interpersonal relationships solidified by quality teachers who inculcate good decision-making in children. It said:

> Why is it that kids are shooting up schools? They don't seem
> to attack video arcades, bookstores or houses of worship. Per-
> haps they don't feel as "connected" to school as we might
> like to believe...urban schools need to be an oasis in a sea of

poverty, deprivation, violence and depression. Schools have an obligation to be the best part of a young person's day; a place so wondrous, beautiful and engaging that a child feels wanted, respected and part of something bigger than themselves…Such an environment would be inviting, personal and filled with…most importantly, adults who know each child and can maintain a meaningful relationship with them.

Instead, we have the business crowd—the New York EducRAT$—"buying" students with cell phones, following the advice of a Harvard economist rather than Goleman, a Harvard social scientist, when the latter said: "consider those who staff these institutions,…[which] are vulnerable to the accountant's delusion that social goals can be assessed by fiscal measures alone. That mentality ignores the emotional connections that drive our very ability to be—and work—at our best." (p.315)

Had these leaders read Goleman, they might have realized that children's brains needed addressing. This means quality teachers need to guide students' emotional growth by making special connections to their students. Goleman said:

> Mounting research shows that students who feel connected to school—to teachers, to other students, to the school itself—do better academically. They also fare better in resisting the perils of modern adolescence: emotionally connected students have lower rates of violence, bullying, and vandalism; anxiety and depression, drug use, and suicide; truancy and dropping out…Good teachers are like good parents. By offering a secure base, a teacher creates an environment that lets the students' brains function at their best. (p.282) …whenever teachers create an empathic and responsive environment, students not only improve in their grades and test scores—they become eager learners. (p.284)

In the helping professions, compassionate leaders are a necessity. Goleman masterfully explains how social interactions affect our brain wiring and body chemistry. Yet, educrats are guilty of ignoring Goleman's warnings. They also fail to learn from history. They take not learning from history one step further than conceivable. They punish teachers for using it—for even mentioning it! The following segment from my 2008 book shows how far they take that.

A desire to protect children is the core of a teacher. Indiana school counselor Marlene Knispel *sued her district, protesting that her free speech was stifled. The Journal Gazette* article said: "…School officials threatened to discipline her if she continued trying to garner support for efforts aimed at addressing school violence…their actions caused her to fear for her job and damaged her reputation."

The article continued: "[The Student Services Director] criticized Knispel's letter on several grounds, saying he viewed her actions as insubordinate and that discussion of Leo and Cedarville schools in the context of the shootings at Columbine High School in April 1999 was in poor taste…Since the October 5, 2001, reprimand, Knispel has not spoken out about school violence for fear of losing her job…"

The fact that they reprimanded her for mentioning Columbine offers insight into the demented viewpoint our EducRAT$ take about their charge. Perhaps a Columbine teacher expressed similar concerns before the massacre but, like Knispel, was silenced. More likely, the Columbine teachers knew their possible fate and kept their mouths shut.

Even more chilling is a Pennsylvania teacher's story, including constant harassment to keep her from speaking about a potential Columbine situation at her school, an inability to speak publicly until life circumstances freed her, union collusion, a good teacher leaving the profession, and missing police reports.

Her story shows that the cover-up of violence is endemic. This teacher had a written death threat. Nothing was done to protect her, but something was done to silence her. If you check out her story, you'll see that after she retired, she sent me an email with language to add to the story, including her name, showing how sincere she was about forcing change.

This is how EducRAT$ "Think"—if you call it thinking: Cautious thinking is for fools, as are laws. Public relations cover-ups are far more financially expedient. Horrible things rarely happen; if they do, since you hold all the power, use damage control, and you are money ahead.

Those were mere segments of my 2008 book's lessons. You surely noticed that the subject of guns is nowhere in this book despite the prominence of the topic of school shootings. You won't find a mention of guns in my prior books either. My work as an activist is not about guns or the Second Amendment. This book is about what our schools are doing wrong that has sent democracy into a death spiral and established school massacres as a way too familiar horror.

Even if we managed to limit assault rifles, where there's enough rage, a school shooter will find one. I'll leave dealing with guns to others, not because I don't care or have no opinion, but because doing what I do is hard enough as it is. And I know the solution. My focus is to eliminate the force that grows school shooters—WCCrime. I am confident that since school shootings are connected at the hip with WCCrime, they will vanish once we outlaw WCCrime.

You know, school shootings keep increasing. You know, kids usually shoot up the school they attend or once attended. Yet, you never ever could have figured out why they're happening without knowing about WCCrime and how administrators are holding teachers hostage—disconnecting them from their calling to help children, forcing them to work in a muzzle, or casting them out of the profession.

Given your prejudiced view of our schools, you never would have figured this out. You just wouldn't think they'd be this fraudulent. You might have thought they're inept, but few would consider they're dealing with out-and-out criminals. You needed to know me to connect the dots to school shootings.

Now that you know the why behind school shootings and that all we need to do is banish selfish, immoral administrators, do what I do. Start blowing a whistle. Eventually, our combined sound will turn this into a kitchen table issue, end this shameful cover-up, and make schools safe again.

Look at it this way. The inhumanity and unfairness I experienced in the school where I taught, which still passes as an ideal school, made me an activist. Think about what living within this cold-bloodedness does to a young child's development. There are consequences for a society that allows evil an honored home. One of them is school shootings.

Need I say more? I haven't stopped trying to teach why we have school shootings. I can't stop trying, knowing this is an unneeded tragedy. Help make this book go viral so no more precious children will be gunned down!

11

WHY A BOOK?

"Learning is not compulsory... Neither is survival."

W. Edwards Demin

"Education is simply the soul of a society as it passes from one generation to another."

Gilbert K. Chesterton

"To learn who rules over you, simply find out who you are not allowed to criticize."

Voltaire

You hear a lot about teachers' unions, but you'll discover very little truth about them other than here. Unions, like WCCriminals, have little concern for truth. When my union attorney told me there is only truth in math and science in his attempt to stop me from revealing the truth about my teaching experience, I responded, "Yes, there is an ability to make the truth, not the truth, using the law. But there are people like me who will keep making the truth resurface. You can depend on that."

He said don't bother trying to fight this. He had represented many other teachers who felt as I did. They wanted to expose this. But the system is way too powerful, and employed teachers are too intimidated to stand in support. And parents move on with their children. The union's advice was, "Give up. That's the way it is."

Before his capitulation advice, the union's surrender to WCCrime had been crystal clear to me. A brave teacher who did research on abused teachers tried to buy an ad to sell her book on the union's website. They refused her money. The union, like everyone else, chooses survival—that's why I call them secondary WCCriminals.

Administrations have unlimited funds to cover this up. They create enormous, cluttered records to bury teachers in legal fees. Furthermore, teachers must pay to educate lawyers in education law since our cases exist in the disrespected, non-profitable education arena where few can afford to hire them.

Also, there are no laws to protect teachers, as there are to protect most workers. Decades ago, legislatures nationwide designated teachers as "professionals," grouped with doctors and lawyers. They realized the long work hours required to be a good teacher would lead to costly overtime.

So, they made it so teachers cannot ask for overtime pay and aren't eligible for protection by the Department of Labor. These "professionals" must rely on their salaries to obtain legal help.

Before the internet, we had scattered, wounded teachers without a voice and frightened teachers focused on keeping their jobs. NAPTA created a new truth. We posted teachers' stories so others could hear their despair. Many abused teachers are like hamsters on wheels trying to seek justice and build a voice. They put their lives on hold and expend energy and money in an endeavor that has been and remains hopeless.

There are hundreds of thousands of teachers employed with holes in their hearts. They know that they sold their souls to keep their jobs and that they are cheating children by remaining silent. They have given too much money to unions that have sold them out. They have given far too much of their souls for a job that bullied them into submission.

Keep in mind when actresses endure physical rape and say nothing to stay employed, they suffer. When teachers tolerate the rape of their souls, the suffering extends to their students. The abuse keeps them silent about harmful acts. The dual nature of teacher abuse makes it much worse!

Administrators brand teachers' souls, making them theirs rather than spiritual forces called to teach as was intended. They purged those who resisted this branding. Those who speak out exist only outside our culture's norm.

Now that you understand how swift and devastating teacher abuse is, it is easier to understand why you know nothing about it. This is why I decided it needed a book.

Before 2000, I started a book named *Mama, Don't Let Your Babies Grow Up to Be Teachers*. It was designed to warn others about this pseudo-profession. That was before I realized it was much more than male chauvinists having their way—something closer to a mafia with male chauvinists having their way. The book needed to be more than warning people not to become teachers. So, I put that aside despite loving the title.

I developed a curriculum to help the public understand the takeover of our education system. Researching other worlds of corruption helped me determine what to do.

I read Kurt Andersen's informative 2020 book, *Evil Geniuses*, about how the business sector created a more unequal society. "The one book everyone must read as we figure out how to rebuild our country," said Walter Isaacson, referring to *Evil Geniuses*. His review inspired me to read it, and I hoped to find education somewhere in it.

My book is a companion to this best seller, in which Andersen mentions, in one sentence, that the evil guys did something similar in education. Boy, was he right! At the same time, he, like everyone else, had no clue what they did. Plus, I do not recall him mentioning Project 2025, the icing on the evil cake! I could be wrong since, had he mentioned it, my mind wasn't ready to grasp it yet. Those of us not born with selfish minds take longer to absorb the diabolical plans the wicked concoct!

The Business Round Table, a villain in his book and mine, when called upon to reform education, failed to scout out quality teachers and create a competence power base that would thwart what they deemed the unions' alleged political power base.

These business gurus did the exact opposite. They aligned themselves with WCCriminals and exalted teacher abuse. It would be great if my book stood next to his at a prestigious publishing house, shouting about the issues as his book still does. But I am a teacher. And as long as teachers are low on the totem pole, the voices that could change the world are mere whispers.

Making a difference in education was always my plan. Besides programming me to be a marginalized woman, my parents filled me with extreme values. There was the rule I had to be fair to summer employers—a rule I mention again because it says so much.

Then, my father hand-wrote a letter to President Reagan, admonishing him for lowering taxes. That cursive, lined stationery sits in my mind, reminding me of my father's ardent act. He predicted it would destroy our democracy. He didn't care that he was in a high bracket. He cared about democracy. He had to have loved it to want to pay more taxes.

I didn't fall far from that tree. As mentioned, I grew up in Oak Park, Illinois, home to many infamous gangsters. That's why, when I discovered many of our schools were closer to mafias than places to educate, it took less time to feel submerged in evil. A child programmed and seemingly born to do good is incompatible with mafia-like wickedness. I knew to fear and avoid them, but I never expected that they'd be part of my destiny in education.

Thus, I needed to make that known when I found these gangster-like creatures on my doorstep. And when I say doorstep, during time off per doctor's recommendations, I had to deal with a custodian ringing my doorbell daily, intimidating me with written messages.

I asked their messenger to please put the letter through our mail slot. The autocrats admonished me for speaking over the intercom and not opening the door. They obviously instructed him to put the notes in my hands, but he was embarrassed. I was to remain locked in my home only to open the door for their daily messenger to upset me.

I then ordered a doormat that said, "Go Away." The smart-ass, not welcome mat, provided some balance—a bit of power? My superintendent lost it over the mat, but then again, he never had it. I must admit, I enjoyed watching his wrongdoing backfire.

He had bragged about how C students like him were better leaders. Twenty years earlier, a principal had bragged about not being afraid of intelligent teachers. The announcement of his C grades felt like I revisited an obsession with intelligence unique to educrats.

It broadcasted a severe problem in education. C's might be better when leading something simple. An education leader who needed help understanding the curriculum was not a good thing. Remember, he thought teaching math a year ahead was okay. Besides, he was likely a D student. He was not a truthful person.

Back to the gangsters on my childhood doorstep, so I can finish telling you why this book. My high school expository writing teacher, Miss Barclay, taught us about the miracle of a book. She explained that a book could make a difference, using Rachel Carson's *Silent Spring* book as an example.

Carson's mission was to control dangerous pesticides. She succeeded. I had to write a book to "control" dangerous administrators contaminating the world of education. Ernest Hemingway had attended my high school. I had often climbed the worn marble steps, hoping to absorb his writing skills.

So, in 2008, I wrote a book exposing the corruption in education. I designed it for a serious investigation, not a mass-market read. I was hoping what happened with Rachel Carson's book would happen to mine. President Kennedy had read about it in a magazine. Pesticides no longer enjoyed a free rein.

A few influential people knew of my book. One thanked me for it, but no one instigated an investigation. (In Chapter 13, I share the famous person who thanked me and sent it to Oprah.) I then realized I needed a mass-market book. The big guys, my original audience for the book, wouldn't help us.

It doesn't get much bigger than Oprah, so I had to rethink a new book. It had to be shorter. The first one was okay as a dense textbook since its intended audience was an investigative reporter. But now, it needed to fit into busy schedules.

I started a new pile of notes, awaiting the momentum to finish a book. I had to remove most of the teacher's stories to shorten it. I kept the lessons as is. The documentation proving my points had old dates. I wanted readers to see that this was happening years ago, and there had been a book detailing it. They would know that they could have stopped it. Even so, I added links to current corruption to prove it was still happening. No one needed them. The nation was so much worse.

As expected, things devolved. We ended up with a dangerous con man as president. What better proof that something is amiss in our schools than the desire to elect Donald J. Trump? Our schools engineered too many ignorant, gullible people.

Turns out that stupidity is more contagious than COVID-19, or more people would have figured out that Trump's a con man. He said he was rich but grabbed poor people's money. He can't pay his debt, but he's so rich. Indeed, stupidity is more contagious than COVID-19.

At the end of 2019, I published a more reader-friendly book entitled, *Why We Elected a Dangerous Con Man: White Chalk Crime, the fraud in our schools that is destroying our democracy.* I planned to attract readers who are open to understanding how our country went insane. I hoped that the desire to understand our country's mess would allow me to lead readers to the boring topic at the heart of this wreck—our fraudulent schools.

If it had potential, Covid destroyed it. The battle of marketing a shocking concept without a publisher while living like a hermit made me revisit my goal. The mass market book had to happen in the future. Taking on pesticides is child's play compared to taking on the education mafia. And Camelot is no more.

This is my third book. This time, I focus on the connection to democracy. What you are reading now is a bridge to my past books, which contained the receipts to end WCCrime. You will find the eighteen lessons from my 2019 book in the enhanced ebook version. The ebook also contains QuickNotes, a way to avoid reading a book you must read for a college course. (Later, I offer a free PDF of the ebook for those who join our movement to expose WCCrime.)

This book, which is also Part One of the enhanced ebook, is a memoir of my teaching days written to help you understand what is shocking and complex in a more reader-friendly way. This book's Epilogue contains part of the memoir I wrote about my termination journey. The enhanced ebook contains the entire memoir, *Court-Assisted End of a Teacher's Life*.

Trump, the man who wants to be king, announced he'll end democracy. All the king's horses and all the king's men cannot put democracy back together again. But we, the people, can put it together. It was made to crack and sway and change by the people and for the people. Democracy isn't a Humpty Dumpty issue. It allows us to break it as long as we don't desert it.

Handing it to Trump would be desertion. Holding onto it and reinvigorating it with a new generation of students who will learn what almost happened is a terrific lesson. This will only happen if we fumigate WCCrime so real educators, our pillars, once again fill the halls of democracy's foundation.

What has happened to our teachers has happened despite our legislature, courts, and presidents. Ulysses S. Grant had it right. There will be no democracy without education. Education with WCCrime is without education.

I was called to teach. I grew up amongst gangsters who drain society for what they can get for themselves. That made me want to be part of the landscape that raises society for all. I wanted it that way before Trump sat on life's seesaw and left most of us suspended in the air as if on a stalled gigantic Ferris wheel. And now my mission is teaching you.

The last thing I thought I'd grow up to be was a warrior. Yet I cannot stop fighting to expose what's happening in education—what few teachers dare to speak. It feels like it's pretty much me, a former teacher, and the school buildings crying out in hopes of saving our beloved education.

Over two thousand teachers joined my group so we'd be heard. They're talking to me, but not you. Their voices are woven within this book, giving you confidence this is not one person's delusion. Who are we? We were called to teach in the most profound way, so we reacted to what we saw being done to children in the most profound way, despite the cost.

Since there are no spiritual mistakes, those born to teach cannot keep quiet about wrongdoing. We are here to fight those who would turn schools into bastions of self-interest. We are nature's balancing potion.

Since it takes a warrior to get you to realize that education has morphed into darkness, I've been at it since 1995. As a teacher, my insider status allowed me to see what those running the show made sure would never leave the building.

This book contains all that you were never to hear. You were to go about your life blessed that your children were in schools that obliterate the dedicated teachers in a similar way that devout Catholic parents were to offer up their children to abusive priests.

Education, the dynamo we could have used to soar as a culture, is now buried in society's unkempt closet. It's the ultimate equalizer. WCCrime guarantees unfairness.

Great teachers do more than put out the rage in troubled children's cauldron-like minds, even though that alone makes them sacred. They know how to make learning, what children resist, fun.

When my principal assigned me to teach fifth-grade hard-core science—using science as a teacher elimination tool, hoping I'd quit—I took a graduate science course to confirm that my teaching techniques were appropriate for science. I didn't know. I hadn't taken a science course for thirty years at that time.

Soon my principal condemned my science teaching due to a parent's complaint that I had students read biographies of scientists, a National Science Foundation recommendation. My principal's desperate need to make my teaching life miserable fanned any flame to bury my career.

Vito M. Dipinto,10/29/97 7:46 PM,the world of education is filed with small
Mime-Version: 1.0
Date: Wed, 29 Oct 1997 19:46:50 -0600
To: horwitzk@newtrier.k12.il.us (Karen Horwitz)
From: vdip@evan1.nl.edu (Vito M. Dipinto)
Subject: the world of education is filed with small minds

karen
one narrowed minded myopic parent can't seen the benefit of the truly
innovative and authentic hands-on opportunity you provided and the
principal gets on your case? this is a district that needs better
administration; but your assignment is right up there with the most
innvoative stuff being advocated by All the science ed commcuntiy (national
science standards, Project 2061 and NSTA stuff); the only suggestion that i
would give you is that I would require the students to perform an
investigation that demonstrates some of the person's discoveries, ideas :

My Science Professor's Encouraging Memo

I asked my professor, Dr. Vito Di Pinto, Chair of the Science Department at National Louis University, for support. He sent a memo entitled "The world of education is filled with small minds," praising me for that lesson. I included it in a later presentation to the Board, asking them to save me from her wrath. My professor not only validated that I was on the right track, but he also questioned my principal's knowledge of the current

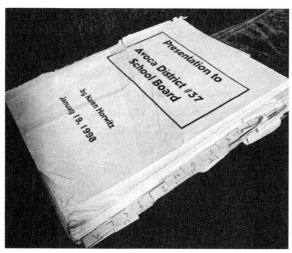

The Detailed Presentation that My School Board Ignored

science practices. He didn't matter, it didn't matter, what was right for my students didn't matter, WCCrime mattered. His memo helped me, though, as I had to teach the same curriculum as the experienced, majored-in-science teacher. I needed help to get it right.

That year, a parent started an after-school science club. I need to remember the exact enrollment. I do remember the only girls who joined came from my two classes; no girls were from his two classes. The size of the club was close to twenty-five students, and about twenty were mine. I may be off a bit, but I know he had only a single-digit number of enrollees, and I am sure it was six or fewer.

The actual science teacher whined about how hard it was to get students to learn science. He graded on the curve since they did so poorly. This was different for my students. I taught the scientific approach in a way that my students loved. They gobbled it up. He knew science, but I knew how to teach.

Excellent teaching is like good art. Only some people can do it, and those who can need to be revered, not trashed. We buy great art, not that which is hard to look at, but our WCCrime schools place no value on excellent teaching.

When they eliminated those of us who knew how to engage children, they also eliminated our ability to teach others what works—a double whammy. When you read about frustrated teachers struggling to teach challenging subjects, like this colleague who complained about his impossible-to-reach students, know that some teachers could have helped them reach students if the bullies running our schools cared.

I was born with an awe for education; even the soulless principal who did her best to destroy it failed. In 1995, I sat in her office listening to her give a reference for a teacher she had employed. I heard her strategically drop in his ear piercing—it was when a man's ear piercing signaled sexuality—to prejudice the prospective employer. She hung up the phone, cupped her bony hands, and extended them. With a horror movie narrator's voice piercing the room, she said, "Nobody knows the power I hold in my hands."

She was right. She was also giddy with joy being able to ruin the career of a teacher who had worked under her. Inflicting pain meant winning to her. That she enjoyed her victim's misery was clear. Thoughts, like rusty lancets, pierced my mind. "Fortunate that she had only taught a few years before landing an administrative position. Better to harm adults than children. Why did they hire a cruel person like her? What has happened to the world of education?"

A colleague on the principal search committee had told me that the committee chose someone else. They didn't like her. I wondered why the Board hired her rather than the committee's chosen person. "Did they realize how inhumane she was? Is that why the committee chose her? Do they know and not care? That's not possible." Later, I learned that hiring tyrants in education is prevalent. It helps them brand the profession to fill their needs.

I remember feeling like I had won the lottery when this fabulous district hired me. It began to feel like my vulnerability in the business world, but worse. I was so sure this was the humane world. "How could I be so wrong?"

I wondered how my teaching life under her would be. My dream-come-true job transformed into deep worries. "Was she going to be another savage boss?" This limited, non-human being was about retribution and did not care about others. She had too much power. That day added the need to expose an education world that could hire someone like her to my plate!

Peace activist Betty Williams said, "Governments do not have the answers—indeed, quite the reversal. A lot of times, they not only do not have the answers, but they themselves are the problem. If we are committed to helping our world's children, then we must begin to create solutions from the bottom up."

I'm still in awe of what it would be if teachers like me had even a smidgen of the power that she abused daily. I wrote this book hoping you will help set free the power of real education via called-to-teach teachers. We must release this potentiality so democracy has a chance. A book to reach the masses and ignite their passion to save our democracy is a bottom-up approach for when a top-down approach doesn't work. With WCCrime at the top, need I say more?

WHY A BOOK?

There are so many reasons for you to read this book, such as:

- Save our democracy. Understand how our country became such a mess.

- Help put an end to school shootings. They are, beyond any doubt, connected to WCCrime.

- Enable successful education reform and resurrect the American Dream.

- Help build equality by providing real schools for all.

- Feel good about yourself by giving time to something that will fuel your soul.

- Help end the political divisiveness that our corrupt schools help produce.

- Help teachers avoid a crushing career. Show teachers you appreciate them.

- Empower teachers so they can protect your children.

- Show your children that education is worth your time and, thus, theirs.

- Earn street "cred" with your children for caring about the place many of them dislike. With so many spirited teachers driven out of teaching, it's not a joy to be a student these days.

- Protect your grandchildren and great-grandchildren.

- Help them thrive in great schools.

- Help end decades of corruption that made education so much less than it could have been.

- Help recover billions of dollars for the common good rather than for WCCriminals' pockets.

This book helps broaden your views about the devolution of democracy. Contrary to popular opinion, white supremacy is not the sole reason that Trump has converted so many. It is also anger with the establishment having let us down, particularly in education.

It's so unbelievable that the media has missed it. I've spoken with many reporters, and I can tell you they cannot believe it. We need to make them smarter. Our society is filled with under-developed brains that will remain as such until we examine what has happened in our schools.

If you watched the HBO movie *Bad Education*, you probably thought the Roslyn, New York superintendent who stole over ten million dollars was an aberration. Hugh Jackman was perfect for the part. This charming man had an entire community thinking he cared about them. Yet, I saw the actual Roslyn superintendent's picture. He reminded me of the creepy principal who lined up his female teachers with great legs, Rockette's style, and made us kick. He was no Hugh Jackman!

Believe it or not, a Roslyn educator joined our group soon after I wrote the first draft of my 2008 book. He validated my prediction that WCCriminals abuse their teachers. He shared that the superintendent harassed him big time after he reported fraud in his department. He was confused. It was bewildering.

Why didn't the superintendent honor him for discovering it? The unexpected fury of wrath shocked him into searching the internet to figure out why. He found out at our site. He had happened upon the financial books that were part of a money laundering scheme. They needed to abuse him into silence.

Thousands of others who don't look like Hugh Jackman are snatching education from you. This deserves to be repeated: rescue the hero teachers from horrific abuse for their sake and for ours. They are the missing pillars of democracy. They deserve their Me Too Movement, which is impossible without knowing the truth.

Every worker deserves freedom from abuse. However, you'd be hard-pressed to find a more deserving group of humans than those who chose to become teachers and harder-pressed to live with a strong man controlling your life. If enough of you help this truth go viral, we will get our *Boston Globe* or Ronan Farrow. There is no better gift you can give a teacher.

I could not include the hundreds of teacher stories in this book as I did in my original book. Go to http://www.endteacherabuse.org/background.html#twenty and read enough stories to become part of the solution.

And consider this. I discovered that in 2023, I sold one copy of my 2008 book—a fifteen-year-old book. It surprised me. Why would anyone read it now? The answer is that I'm the only one who put together the pieces for accomplishing reform. That book explained it all. This book explains why you need to read that book. Now you can do so by reading an abridged version, which is now Part Three of the enhanced ebook. (Keep in mind, later, I offer a free PDF of the ebook for those who join our movement to expose WCCrime.)

My list of leaders contacted within both political parties who did nothing proves that WCCrime is a bipartisan blunder. Their lack of concern about the evil our group of teachers tried to relay speaks volumes. The ACLU, the courts, and the media would not give us mental space. It does not matter if anyone goes to jail as long as they run from education, as cockroaches run from the light. This book will let the light begin.

Here's hoping that my need to write books is over and I can retire and paint in a thriving democracy.

12

MEDIA ILLITERACY

"The goal of education is the advancement of knowledge and the dissemination of truth."

John F. Kennedy

"If any man seeks greatness, let him forget greatness and ask for truth, and he will find both."

Horace Mann

"The way to right wrongs is to turn the light of truth upon them."

Ida B. Wells

As the proper sourcing of information became a lost art, so did wisdom. Truth is no longer popular. Ulysses S. Grant's quote about how ignorant this country would become without solid education explains why. A WCCrime-infiltrated education system has made us morons.

When I came across his quote online, it was a eureka moment. I felt I had discovered gold. It contained so many answers for how we lost hold of democracy. Yet I felt concerned. I had to confirm they were his words. I had never heard them. I only use facts to back up my exposé about education. I needed to be sure it was authentic.

I found Grant's quote designated as part of his 1875 speech. I still wanted more validation, so I checked Snopes.com, which confirmed its validity. This book aims to connect the public with the truth: dangerous corruption thrives behind the backs of an intelligent citizenry due to a widespread, shameful, covert practice called teacher abuse. There can be no misinformation, only facts.

I am a certified reading specialist. Our training aims to achieve reading and writing literacy. Literacy is more than reading words. That is decoding. One could decode a page of words without knowing what the words meant. To be literate, one must comprehend what they decode and be able to use words to construct meaningful paragraphs.

While earning my degree, we learned very little about media literacy, an expanded concept of literacy that includes accessing and analyzing media messages and creating, reflecting, and taking action using the power of information and communication. We did learn to teach how to access and use correct information. No one is born knowing what encyclopedias do that a letter from your uncle might not. Literacy programs always included learning library skills so one could verify the information.

I earned my Masters in Reading in 1992. By then, there should have been significant mention of media literacy as it pertained to television. There wasn't. Great minds and great schools did not inhabit the world of education, as discussed earlier. It was up to teachers to help students sort out trusted television information.

Older teachers helped, but as time passed, fewer teachers had concerns about where a lack of media literacy would lead. The new crop of teachers was often media illiterate. Had great minds created a needed curriculum on an ongoing basis, media literacy would have grown as media grew. Without those minds, it was inevitable that the internet would run literacy over. Social media became a steamroller of chaos!

Media literacy and character formation experienced similar deaths. The need to teach morals and to know what was factual and meaningful on television flowed from teachers raised when learning to be a person of substance was an automatic part of learning. It had been an expectation in schools.

A quick history of education explains why. Education was a religious endeavor. Teachers had to live with families and weren't permitted to marry. In the nineteenth century, Horace Mann transformed education into public education.

When I started teaching in 1966, we were bound by the proper attire that education's religious profile once demanded. Neither a short skirt or blue jeans, or even pants, for that matter, had a place in our wardrobe. I bought a two-piece dress for interviews and teaching. I rolled up the skirt when I left school, wanting to look stylish.

The expectation that a teacher had a higher moral standard took years to fade but did colossally. It went from lifelong virgins to sex with students. Could the curriculum have made up for the drift from morality? If universities had respected education and stayed on top of cultural trends, it might have.

Older teachers, WCCriminals' enemies, still modeled standards. When WCCrime took hold in the 1980s, they pushed the morally inclined types out. It's been a runaway train, from teachers not permitted to get married to teachers sleeping with students and from teachers wearing dresses covering knees to teachers wearing denim torn at the knees.

I can't verify the exact date that WCCrime made its entry. Kurt Andersen described the evil genius takeover in business in his book *Evil Geniuses* in the 1980s; the parallels align. Plus, my teaching experience in 1970 demonstrated a different mindset.

The principal, who liked to show off our legs, forced teachers to resign after their first year if he disliked anything, including not kicking high enough in his chorus line. (He must have noticed the faces I made. I'm sure that my disguised annoyance was evident.)

I was one of several told that we'd get a good recommendation if we resigned. The principal didn't know I was pregnant and had to leave anyway. But it bothered me that he went after good teachers for no reason, so I contacted the Board. It formed a committee to inquire about these excessive resignations. Other teachers then revealed that they didn't want to resign. The committee determined what he did was wrong. State law mandated teacher continuity. They fired the principal and the superintendent. The Board did its job.

The administrators must have learned that they must control their boards. WCCrime was gradual. It started with shallow administrators not doing their jobs well and then grew to criminality. I have no idea if there was money missing at that school, but I do know that proper leadership was missing.

In time, these incompetent leaders learned to ensure no one knew of their incompetence. The institution became skilled at bigger and better crimes. The temptation to embezzle and take kickbacks grew. And as things went downhill, the media expanded. The internet surfaced in the 1990s. If there had been a goal to tackle media literacy issues, which I doubt, knowing education's cast of characters, they would have trashed it.

Corrupted schools were not focused on properly educating students when the internet surfaced. Analytical leaders would have recognized that an information gap is dangerous to democracy. WCCriminals weren't concerned about building solid citizens. Thus, taking on media literacy could not have earned an iota of thought.

Instead, we created fertile grounds for a society of brainwashable soldiers. This left our not well-educated, not critical-thinking citizens to determine which news was fake. Clever lies finally had a chance.

Disinformation is no accident. It's designed to polarize you and leave an opening for brainwashing citizens. Labeling legitimate news as "fake" became a bonanza for con artists. It took conspiracy theories to new heights. The skyrocketing of inane theories reminds me of an incident that illustrates what led to a life of battling idiotic conspiracy theories.

In 1996, I taught library research skills to my fourth-grade students. No one told me to include that, as no one told me to emphasize learning the multiplication tables. I had had an excellent education, and I knew what was important. Within that statement lies how our country fell apart. Fewer and fewer teachers passed on what they knew, while administrators were abandoning education's purpose.

The assignment was to use encyclopedias to take notes. The lesson was that you must use a trusted source for information, or it could be someone's opinion rather than factual. Also, you must take notes so as not to plagiarize.

One student fooled around. I gave him a "D" on the assignment that deserved an "F" because he was only ten, and I didn't want his mind to close. His mother, an undereducated person, sent him to school the next day with a page from the internet. She insisted he didn't need to learn my ridiculous old-fashioned lesson. Everything you needed to know was online.

My knowledge of the internet at that time was close to zero. Few knew it existed. I instinctively thought: how can you trust "facts" online? I knew that information must have reliable sources. Plus, the parent did the assignment, and since when do parents get to change an assignment to change a grade?

I told the mother that the lesson was based on verified sources and that the internet was not credible. I thought: "Thinking the internet is trustworthy when it could be one uneducated jerk's opinion or a Russian infiltration scheme to divide and destroy our democracy is foolish." I kept that to myself, remaining professional.

Remember, the internet was far less reliable than its current untrustworthy state. This parent's inability to analyze the situation led to a complaint. She reported me to the principal. She won; truth lost. It was what a principal who wanted to get rid of me needed. Worse, the principal had no respect for the lesson.

Thousands of other like-minded principals disregard content and what children need to learn to strip their schools of real teachers. Think about what purging teachers who put real learning first means. Teachers passing down intelligent ways of dealing with information was out. What the principals wanted was in. What a parent wished was only "in" because it helped the principal. It didn't matter if it was dimwitted.

Think more about it. It was 1996. The Wild West of media literacy is taking off with a bang. The lack of teaching intelligent sourcing is one aspect of how we became a nation unable to distinguish between truth and lies. A society of shallow thinkers, i.e., gullible minds, is what our inauthentic schools dumped on this nation.

Disinformation became the new warfare, using clever misinformation to bombard us from within and without this nation. Both foreign countries, such as Russia and the villainous part of the Republican party, are having their way with our brains since most people are without weapons.

A president was able to concoct a proven, big lie to stay in power and to become a presidential candidate again despite his dismal record and anti-democratic behavior because WCCrime has disarmed our ability to think critically, leaving so many of us mentally naked. He has succeeded beyond what's rational because WCCrime put what's rational into a permanent sleep, the way veterinarians euthanize sick animals.

An example of how lost we are surfaced with United States Representative Nancy Mace's recent TV appearances. She had spoken out against rape, explaining it took her twenty-five years to do so due to the shame evolving from not being believed or heard when one is a rape victim.

A reporter asked her how could she endorse Trump, a convicted rapist, given her ordeal with rape, and she accused him of shaming her. Yes, he was shaming her about endorsing a person who, in addition to being a danger to this nation, raped a woman.

A logical mind would think: this is not rape shaming. This is well-deserved you're-ruining-your-country shaming. The fact Trump's a rapist is regrettably not the worst of his qualities. But Mace kept accusing the reporter of shaming her. Since he couldn't define the shame that he directed at her and that she deserved, she dodged it for many watching that encounter.

Plus, she justified Trump's "rape" as only having been a civil, not criminal, charge. So were those twenty-five years she felt shame about stuff being shoved up her vagina with no recourse shame worthy when that guy apparently didn't have any charge at all against him?

Even worse, she attacked E. Jean Carroll for having joked about how she would spend the money she earned in court. She shamed E. Jean Carroll for using humor to deal with rape. If rape is so bad, wouldn't any way of coping be respected? If it's not that bad, and it's okay to shame the way a rape victim deals with it, then why was she so shamed? She lost all sympathy for her shame by rape-shaming Carroll. Had she had genuine shame, she would have had empathy for Carroll.

Or did she have shame but gave it up when she assigned her soul to Trump, as so many have? That would be my guess.

Then, Mace appeared on another TV show, seeking more sympathy for being shamed for endorsing Trump. She spoke about her fourteen-year-old daughter being at the studio when the reporter "shamed" her. She piled on guilt to ensure her misinformation took root.

Those of us with working brains and an ability to dodge manipulative guilt would see being shamed for endorsing a candidate who is a rapist who intends to end our democracy as a good thing. And it was a good thing that her daughter knew that, too. But she insidiously twisted the two other people on this show to somewhat support her phony shame grievance.

In truth, she deserved a boatload of shame. On top of making that obscene endorsement, she showed up on TV as a nauseating hypocrite. She had spoken against Trump for his role in the January 6 insurrection, which included supporting the hanging of his loyal-until-a-criminal-order vice president.

That day elevated Hilary Clinton's use of the word "deplorable" for fans of Trump to understated—some would even say, clairvoyant. Mace had admitted how dangerous he was for our country but suddenly forgot all about that. Was she lying then or lying now? Her devotion to manipulation is unpardonable. Her choice to support him was and is obscene. Well-earned shame ricocheted across pop culture like the smell of rotten eggs from the Salton Sea.

The misinformation she spewed worked on them and likely most of the viewers the way it works on too many people these days. This is why we're in trouble. In a war of disinformation, one must recognize and repel misinformation, the same way the sound of bullets told a soldier to use his gun. Our brains are our only weapons in this new disinformation war, and WCCrime managed to disarm way too many of us.

Many shake their heads, confused about how an inability to discern facts and think critically happened. I look back on that day in 1996 when that parent had her way with the importance of learning truth as the beginning of truth's end. Once teachers could no longer keep truth sacred, one of their most essential duties, disinformation warfare, developed wings.

Do you see the pattern here? WCCrime set free so much of what we counted on schools to hold dear for us—it caused the end of facts, the beginning of school shootings, and our democracy's death spiral. Once the institution we relied on became infested with crime, Trump and what he represents became inevitable.

WCCrime opened doors for profiting with made-up news. Fox News paid almost a billion dollars for the big lie about the election. I doubt they regret it, given how they still own so many minds. In fact, paying less than one billion dollars to catapult their party back into power is a bargain!

And they're still making stuff up. Long after that payout, a Fox News host labeled admiring Taylor Swift as "idolatry" and said *it's a sin*, with a straight face.

Duh, then what is the worship of Donald Trump, which they have promoted incessantly? If idolizing Trump isn't the worship of the Golden Calf, then nothing is. The inability to see through Fox News' disinformation war is one of the clearest examples of failing to teach critical thinking!

When the institution that prepares minds for democracy sold out, alternatives to real news blossomed. As the news became crazier and almost incomprehensible, people like Heather Cox Richardson, a Harvard graduate and history professor, developed a way to help deal with the news. Connecting it to history and facts—the truth—she earned the status of a Substack superstar, demonstrating that an educator's guidance has a vital role in dealing with the media.

Had there been authentic schools, fewer citizens would need her to do the critical thinking she applies to current events. They would have learned and retained history and the thinking skills required to stay on top of the news. Since fewer and fewer people have developed media literacy, she's providing a worthy service.

Her "Letters from an American" emails approach the news with a calm logic to help people cope with the onslaught of disturbing news. She does an admirable job. Yet, in an email, she said, "But it is not just the banking, justice, and military systems MAGA Republicans are undermining. They are sowing distrust of our educational system, claiming that it is not educating students but, rather, indoctrinating them to embrace left-wing ideology."

Playing right into MAGA's hands, she defends education when many know it's corrupt. WCCriminals do use indoctrination to create political divisions that are easier to handle than jail would be. It's never the ideology. They crave the smoke and mirrors that choosing ideologies causes.

We have an education system primed for undermining for reasons unknown to her, or she'd mention that. She became part of the division despite her honorable intentions. This validates why WCCrime must be known. Education exists on a distant island, treasured no matter that it's at the heart of the dysfunction she's trying to calm.

Before women's liberation, our schools worked despite being leaderless because strong-minded, great teachers kept administrators in their place and, in essence, ran the schools. They were the women behind the men's success. WCCrime and women's liberation changed that.

Think about my earlier story about my first year of teaching—1966—when my second-grade class couldn't read because they didn't have the skilled teacher that my next year's class had. It illustrated the stark difference in teaching ability. Great teachers ran schools the way great women used to help create great men behind the scenes. They were powerful, although unrecognized as leaders. Now, hollow men and hollow women rule our schools.

Schools, no longer dedicated to effective teaching, which is teaching that results in learning and learning to become good citizens, eliminated intelligence as a primary guide through life. Ulysses S. Grant's prediction that we'd become an idiotic nation if we failed to educate citizens materialized.

Unsubstantiated conspiracy theories are the new weapons of confusion. WCCrime is a genuine conspiracy—one that foolish conspiracy theories helped hide. It is a secret group involved in criminal activities.

If figuring out a way to end modern civil war isn't enough to get you to read this book about our disastrous schools with their tapestry of subjugation, you have your pick. Think about school shootings, the demise of democracy, stolen tax dollars, or your child in your basement who could have made something of himself had he experienced real schools with real teachers rather than the schools to which WCCrime has given life—I should say death.

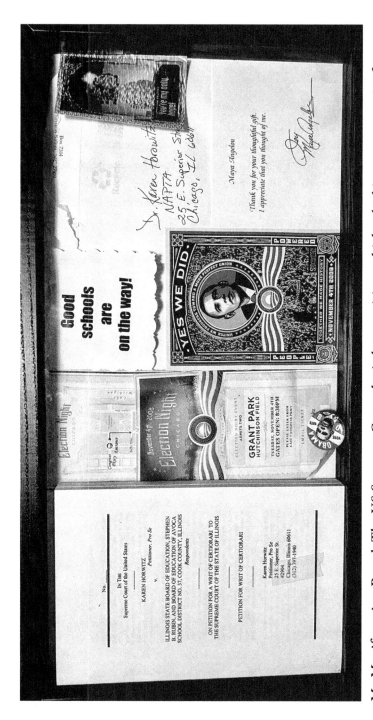

My Manifestation Board. The US Supreme Court denied my petition, which asked it to grant a writ of certiorari in 2007. I went to Grant Park on election night of 2008 with hope. This display includes Maya Angelou's 2010 thank you note plus Jack from Chapter 3's "You're My Only Hope" Valentine.

13
WHAT I DO: MY 1995 MANIFESTO

"Most of the things worth doing in the world had been declared impossible before they were done."

Louis D. Brandeis

"You must be the change you wish to see in the world."

Mahatma Gandhi

"I can accept failure, everyone fails at something. But I can't accept not trying."

Michael Jordan

"Fight till the last gasp."

William Shakespeare

"The way I see it, if you want the rainbow, you gotta put up with the rain."

Dolly Parton

"When something is important enough, you do it even if the odds are not in your favor."

Elon Musk

"What counts is not necessarily the size of the dog in the fight; it's the size of the fight in the dog."

Dwight D. Eisenhower

"Do not follow where the path may lead. Go instead where there is no path, and leave a trail."

Ralph Waldo Emerson

Successful people's wisdom has always inspired me. It provides intellectual footing when traveling in an undeveloped region, such as education. I'm piling on their inspirational thoughts since most people declare that what I do is impossible. I've been speaking truth to power that's been holding its ears since 1995. That's not a reason to stop trying, so I have stayed at it with no intention of giving up as long as I have a working brain. Their wisdom has helped.

Hitler's quote, "It gives me great pleasure that the people don't know what is happening to them," helped too. It gave me another reason to tackle this mission since WCCriminals pretty much model themselves after someone like him. They do everything so you won't know what is happening to you in our schools. I am determined to teach you precisely what is happening in our schools.

And speaking of Hitler, many have heard Trump promise to be a dictator for a day. At one point, Trump cited lyrics from a 1968 song about a snake, saying:

Take me in, for heaven's sake. Take me in, oh tender woman, sighed the snake...But instead of saying thanks, that snake gave her a vicious bite.

He warned his people that a snake is a snake. We can be sure his dictatorship will go on and on. He'll then say, "I told you I would be a dictator, and a dictator is a dictator like a snake is a snake. Vicious."

Many wonder why Trump is admitting this and his plan to end democracy. It seems it would help his opponents. Experts say that Trump's chilling admissions typify authoritarian psychological warfare. They make people believe that a dictatorship is inevitable. They encourage fatalism and acceptance and generate fear to censor those who might otherwise speak out to prevent an authoritarian takeover. His goal is to make people like me not do what I do.

Bullying doesn't work on me, as evidenced by this book. I won't let fear replace civic duty. Robert Reich's article, "Civic Education, Foundational to Democracy,"[24] said: "Once learned, civic virtue must be practiced. As I hope I've made clear, our obligations as citizens go beyond voting, paying taxes, obeying the law, and serving on juries. We owe to one another our time and energies to improve our communities and to protect and strengthen our democracy."

I, too, believe we all need to give back to democracy. Plus, having taught in a WCCrime-infested school, I know a dictatorship up close. Because so few know what I know and could do this work, it had to be me.

Teachers who need to work can't tell you what's in this book. Teachers overburdened with work, a tactic of teacher abuse, do not have time to do this work. Teachers exhausted from the trauma cannot run away fast enough once they retire. Teachers who find earning a degree in education hard can't do what it takes to do this work. It is hard. Thus, I invented a new profession.

One Mother's Day, my twenty-one-year-old daughter, who's now forty, helped me know what I had to do. She told me of a contest she had almost entered for daughters who wanted to see their mothers' dreams come true. She is an expressive writer. She felt she could win a dream for me. So did I.

However, she told me it needed to be a different dream, not my burning desire to expose what is happening in education in our country. She knew that my dream to tell the dirty secret about our schools wouldn't sell to a corporatized America that wants this political nightmare buried deep in the bowels of society. She knew that teachers could not be heard.

I understood. This is material America, and my dream to see good conquer evil is an ideal, not a marketable concept. Dreams have to fit into sound bites. Understanding what is going on in our schools is too complex. Yet, I knew that if I could reveal that WCCrime is erasing education and slaughtering children, the public would demand its end.

Teacher abuse, its chief weapon, is shameful, and what it enables—power mongers looting our schools—would no longer be tolerated. I needed to find a way. I didn't imagine that Trump would come along and I could make lemonade out of him. I know. Excuse me. With him, it has to be orangeade.

Since 1995, I've been building a body of evidence and doing whatever I can so the public will understand what happened to education and what needs to be done. As education's and democracy's BFF, best friend forever, I am providing you with an authentic education landscape. It will help you understand how inevitable losing our democracy is if we don't turn education around. Rather than the hallowed grounds it once was, education is a hollow system that grounded democracy.

Exposing this is what I do. Another way to describe my work is necessary trouble, which the late civil rights activist John Louis coined. He connected it to black justice. It's part of the resistance against any injustice. Because education is the great equalizer, and WCCrime is the great oppressor, WCCrime is a colossal black issue. I detail that in the enhanced ebook, Part Three. I'm sure John Lewis would have lent his term to my work.

The path to education reform is unclouded in my brain. I must do this work to release this haunting truth so I can relax. I cannot stop doing what it takes to get this known. This work turns the release knob on my soul's pressure cooker.

Nothing is more vital for peace than education. Valuing it is in my bones, my heritage. I cannot abandon an orphaned vision entrusted to me. It drives me in a way that's baffling to most—only people with callings could relate. It calms my soul to do this work.

I know our schools are the source of unnecessary suffering. I know the answer to reform. I must pass this on. I have no choice. John Lenin's song Imagine plays in my head as I do this work. We don't need to imagine a better world. We could have one. I know what set us back. I must do this job until it is, or I am, done.

A dictatorial, substandard school system is changing most people as those often referenced boiled frogs that were unaware the water was boiling until it was too late. In time, they feel their souls hardened. Many jump into the arms of an autocratic force. Others lose their deep connection to democracy due to the misery of watching its unfathomable hijacking. They accept the murkiness that took its place, landing in a full-blown depression.

I jumped from that boiling water and retained my deep connection to democracy by doing my work. Rather than earning a salary, I've been spending money doing this work for almost thirty years. The spiritual rewards have made it worthwhile. Three suicidal teachers found me via my website. It educated them about teacher abuse and WCCrime. They let me know that my website made them decide not to commit suicide. To me, saving lives is more valuable than money.

Mary was a teacher that didn't "meet" me. She walked into traffic. She was confident that her hideous death would pull the curtain on her abusive administrators. It didn't. At least one administrator attended her funeral with a school district fruit basket.

Someone who produced a documentary about Mary planned to interview me for it. She was sure that her film would do what a truck's demolishment of Mary didn't do. I told her it wouldn't change things; she became angry and removed me from the script.

I was not invited to the premiere of her film, even though it was in my hometown. That was over a decade ago. You don't know about the film because I was right.

Killing yourself or doing a movie about killing yourself to expose these ruthless administrators sweeps under WCCrime's rug. They have a giant robotic vacuum that never stops vacuuming away the truth. They manage teacher suicides and add them to their list of lies. A suicide is a tree falling in the forest. Abusers rely on the voicelessness of their victims. The only antidote is educating you about WCCrime.

Doing this work is like giving birth. You decide to do it, knowing it's hard and painful but worth it. Something beautiful is possible. To be an activist, you must accept your powerlessness in a world that's not ready to admit its mistakes. Since powerlessness is absolute when being a teacher in a WCCrime school system, you keep wearing the powerlessness. I've done that well.

A superintendent doesn't just earn upwards of 600% more than his teachers; he's an unadmitted king. The lure of power that erased any principles he might have had is potent. There's a possessiveness connected to that power that reared its ugly head during the legal process I initiated when my district took its lawless actions against me.

My attorney was taking numerous depositions for my federal lawsuit at his downtown Chicago office, more than a dozen miles from the suburbs where my school hid its misbehavior and malice. We needed to schedule another day. Someone suggested 9 AM the following Tuesday. I replied that I was not available that day and preferred a time later in the day.

We were drowning in the sound of the elevated train screeching outside my attorney's embarrassing second-floor windows. The second floor in a high-rise is degrading enough. Chicago's well-known elevated train, known as the "el," which zooms around its business section at the second-floor level every five minutes, shattering one's ability to think, revealed that only unimpressive attorneys agree to represent teachers.

His unimpressiveness was not his worst quality. Many months after this costly and disturbing deposition session, he admitted that someone had stolen my precious audio tape of the principal lying from the back seat of his car.

Rather than let me decide if I wanted to pay thousands of dollars to an attorney who couldn't protect my evidence or perhaps did not want to protect my evidence, he waited to tell me until I was well over $50,000 into him and that was after I had spent about that much on the first attorney. (I write about my trauma with her later in this chapter.)

Not wanting another false start, I stayed with him. After he fessed up that he no longer had my original evidence, I called my good friend with a university-level knowledge of astrology. I left a voicemail with my attorney's exact birth time and location. Asking him for that information seemed appropriate after what he had done. He owed me that!

I hadn't spoken with her at all about him. My message was: tell me about an attorney with this chart. The next day, I got a voicemail saying, "Don't hire him. He has several planets indicating he's a liar."

She had no idea it was too late. And my attorney had no idea that I had copies of that tape. Not letting me judge whether I wanted to continue using him after such an incident should have been my decision to make. But again, he was dealing with a powerless teacher. He knew that the way everyone at that school knew that. You can do that to teachers.

I apologize for reminiscing. No, that's too positive a word to describe my lawyer playing me, so I'll call it remembering. As I recounted his less-than-impressive office, memories of his shadiness that matched his office setting took over. I included them to share a day vivid in my mind but unthinkable in most.

Back to that day, I heard my superintendent's teeth make a gritting sound and saw his face turn bright red. My not-so-super superintendent looked like my instant pot during a forced release.

He was infuriated that I was an equal participant in scheduling an appointment. He raged at my power to negotiate despite the comical setting that screamed the truth of my unequal status.

I, this teacher, was in a dump in a city with chic—filled with glass and spectacular views—law offices. His attorney had an impressive upper-floor office with a view of the lake—paid for by you. He could give me the power to choose a time and still lord over me. But he had to hold all the power—all the power.

Teachers were his peasants. Only loyalty earned a share of his power. Without hesitation, the older female board president whisked him away from the table into the hall. Her severe and staid manner had constantly reminded me of Queen Elizabeth. His emotional meltdown had no place in her presence. I could hear her negotiate as a mother warning a toddler of significant losses if he didn't redirect his emotions.

That moment confirmed a few things. Power was his and not to be shared with a teacher. And the queen was running the district. Many wondered why an older woman with grown children had been the board president for nearly a dozen years. I am trying to understand why she wanted that position, but I am sure it wasn't to run an authentic school.

She testified that I was an excellent teacher, but they needed to banish me for insubordination. She had said that the Board would not investigate because that's not what it does—the exact, absurd statement when denying my request for an investigation. "That's not what it does?" Then who ensures a school is safe, functional, and on purpose? The statement admitted the truth—nobody.

I need to let the investigative reporters uncover what motivated her to drive education far from its purpose. But that day, I discovered that the power she had allowed in my administrators' hands was a perk allotted to a mental toddler—in fact, a couple of mental toddlers, given my principal's behavior—and someone needed to alert the public that mental toddlers were leading this nation, not great teachers, or principled educators.

I can't say it was that day that this book became my duty. I had already seen so much outrageous behavior in that district.

But that incident definitely made the top ten reasons why I was sure I ended up at such a ludicrous job.

I was to lead education away from the sinful city of Sodom and Gomorrah. I became called to expose education. I had to keep at it to have any sense of peace. The truth was an albatross. I had to make it go public, or I'd be haunted by the vision in my attorney's decrepit office with these pathetic excuses for public servants forever.

I repeat. I wonder why that older woman wanted to lead that board for many years. However, she was there. She saw his childish behavior and wanted someone who acted like that running the district. That made her more scandalous as a protector of democracy than when she had refused to investigate the wrongdoing I had reported. That made her more outrageous than when she didn't care that her principal made me teach science to get me to quit, knowing that the students could suffer from my lack of science training.

To her, the knowledge that the National Science Foundation recommended that fifth grade, the grade I was to teach, is the level where science teachers should have majored in science made no difference. I know she knew because I had shared that with the Board's deaf ears.

That day, another hollow act brought me back to Sunday School and the thought that education needed King Solomon, not these evil characters. Visions of his tantrum found a permanent place in my head. They made me embrace that a higher power wanted me to complete this job so that sweet pictures of smiling, happy children feeling safe in school could fill that head space rather than a middle-aged man spawning tantrums.

It stays with me because it's so wrong that he ran a district. It's so bad that his clones all over this country are doing the opposite of the public servant thing. A public serpent comes to mind. I saw too much not to do what I do, even though the journey from utter powerlessness to the halls of power is tantrum-worthy if it weren't a calling with spiritual wings.

The seed for my work started blooming when the Illinois State Department of Education told me that education's only watchdogs were you, the voters. That meant there were no watchdogs since no one knows what happens in our schools. And for all the reasons I mentioned earlier, you would never figure these people out. I started documenting. I figured I'd write a book at some point. It took four years of me standing up to them for them to terminate me, so I had four solid years of whistleblowing notes.

I expected a termination. So, I applied to National Louis University's innovative doctorate program that brainstormed school reform. I took several courses toward it. My superintendent ensured the university rejected me from that program, which was detailed earlier. Although I thought that exposing the fraud I named WCCrime seemed most important, I assumed it was local. I thought I had experienced an affluent, cocky district that thought it could do anything. I knew it was a democracy killer. I hadn't made the connection to our democracy imploding yet, thinking it was just that district.

I then met with a renowned leader in gifted education. My success with my gifted students made me think, "I should share the programs I developed, validated by the standardized test, so others could meet gifted needs within a classroom." That scientific affirmation urged me to keep it from fading into obscurity. (Remember, my principal put me on a gifted committee to end a pullout gifted program but never had me share what I did to meet their gifted needs.)

The acclaimed expert in gifted education welcomed me and listened to my thoughts: Should I expose the wrongdoing or develop more gifted programs? I let her know that I needed her advice. She told me that teachers working with gifted students constantly phone her. They are upset that their administrators won't let them use effective materials. She didn't need to say that doing the work to expose the corruption was the right path; she shook her head, knowing I knew.

WCCrime is all about power. If there were an organization that lined up people with buckets to accept their share of power, teachers would be last in that line. I take that back. They would be in their classrooms planning another great lesson.

The people who care about power are the money people, not teachers. We're the idea people. Most teachers live their lives with empty buckets of power, like nuns. Their job and their goals flow spiritually. Using the bell curve to determine power needs, called-to-teach teachers would be as close to Mother Teresa as the Kardashians are to Trump. They're not that close, but close enough to bear a resemblance.

Street smarts also describe power. One end doesn't have it because they don't need it being who they are, and the other end has more than their share to reign or trample over others.

I realized that someone had to figure out a way to shift the excessive power from the self-serving scoundrels who "own" our schools to the loving souls who surrender their ability to educate and protect children. I googled my brain. I remembered what my high school expository writing teacher had taught me about Rachel Carson's 1962 book, *Silent Spring*, being a powerful way to change the world.

I decided to start with a book that would do much of the work an investigative reporter needs to do. I could attract someone who would shame and expose a system that both political parties had corrupted.

I knew it was too long, too detailed, too heavy, and too expensive to be a best seller. I didn't care. I wanted it all spelled out. That was crucial. It had to be a teacher/insider who could endure a time-consuming, unpaid job, know how to write, have a scholarly approach to life, and have an enormous passion for education. The last two qualifications eliminated everyone I knew. I knew my passion was unique, even abnormal to those who don't do life deep.

My goal audience was Oprah, or an investigative reporter, with an emphasis on Oprah. She made it clear that she loved teachers, and whatever she cared about became a powerful force. So, I was okay with selling less than five books as long as those few books rode the change-power route. I nearly succeeded.

Robin, an abused teacher who knew Maya Angelou, delivered my three-pound book, with my letter summarized below, to Angelou's North Carolina home in June 2008:

Dr. Angelou,

Attempting to explain an aspect of our society that is carefully hidden behind tax-subsidized propaganda was not easy. Yet, when I wrote this book, I felt a higher power guiding me. Then, when I "met" Robin in 2006, and she told me she knew you, I knew a higher power was at my back.

If there ever was a situation that needed a voice, this is it. No part of society escapes from White Chalk Crime, the force that has stolen our schools from us. There are few spiritual voices as authoritative as yours. As a mentor to Oprah Winfrey, the giant of our times that has kept me on my spiritual mission to report these crimes, I am in awe. I hope you will read this book and be a hero to the children and the teachers.

Robin is not in the book because when we spoke two years ago, she needed anonymity like most teachers. Otherwise, her story could have been in Lesson #7, where I discuss African-American teachers of great intellect and passion who have been harassed out of their positions. And it could have been in another lesson where I discussed children being allowed to behave outrageously at teachers' expense. It could have been in the lesson that shows how the courts abuse teachers rather than offer them justice, describing how testimony was altered to make her look guilty.

She is one of hundreds of teachers who did not make the book. However, there are enough teachers in the book for you to see that one of the most significant spiritual atrocities is going on behind the backs of an entire society, and we all stand to lose.

WHAT I DO: MY 1995 MANIFESTO

Soon after Robin's purposeful visit, I received a hand-addressed thank you note from Maya Angelou, calling my book a gift. This beautiful soul, one of the most outstanding spiritual leaders whose words dripped with meaning, knew my book was a gift to society. Her taking the time to write and mail this treasured note was better than the celebrity reviews I did not have.

Like my life as a teacher, my book had no home in a society that valued the powerful. In 2010, I received a voicemail from Oprah's researcher, who had my book. I knew how he got it. Maya Angelou famously said, "When someone shows you who they are, believe them." She saw who I was and believed me.

Yet, Oprah knew that being the bearer of the truth about our schools would end her career as it ended mine and all who dared to battle such power. Her researcher listened for a while but didn't call back.

I kept going. Influential people have a lot to lose. I needed a force behind my book so the recipient wouldn't turn me down out of fear as Oprah had. I had to do a simpler book so parents would find out. Once people absorbed what I was communicating, I'd have foiled the power that ensured no one would listen to me.

Since education books are hard to sell, I procrastinated. The 2013 first-grade massacre rattled me. I knew why that happened and needed to get that simpler book published.

I didn't rely on the book route alone. In 2002, while the first book was a pile of notes, I cofounded a website to locate others who could back up what I was saying. As new educators signed up for my group and shared their stories, I became more inspired to keep going. Had I not started the website, I may have given up.

Each new member ensured I didn't and still does that for me. Recently, a group of teachers from Ozark, Missouri, sent me a link to their website. Three whistleblowers in one district is a remarkable sign of progress. It's my fuel. https://www.ozark-teacherabuse.org/ https://www.saveozarkschools.org/ shelly-pettit-story/

205

Our website has provided a panel of whistleblowers ready and willing to appear before Congress or an investigative reporter. Since we can't trust the unions or rely on lawyers, I created a place for the only relief for teachers. I help network members with other members for support and advice. I suggest how best to navigate this treacherous world. Warning them about the legal route is one of my most important duties.

Of all the psychological torture inflicted upon me, having followed my calling to teach, from my days working with brutal harassment and lies about and to me, the worst day of my teaching journey was part of my legal journey. After about six months, my federal attorney and her partner dropped me as a client because my case didn't warrant enough money to make my lawsuit worthwhile. At most, I could win about $100,000.

She decided this, knowing my goals. I had filed it to make the issues go public and expose school corruption, not for money. She knew but suddenly wanted out. She decided this after she had met with three other teachers and me, who wanted legal protection. She knew they feared being part of a lawsuit against these power-mongers. She knew I didn't make this up, having met with the other traumatized colleagues.

After taking at least $50,000, she decided this, causing me to spend close to that again for a new attorney to lose my case. I meant to learn my case, but that was true, too! She offered no refund. It felt like she was working for the district, exhausting my funds and making justice more unreachable.

I did not get out of bed for a few days. This attorney had had a stellar reputation, as did the world of education. Fool me once reverberated in my mind. I heard she became a judge about the same time that Oprah took a pass on helping forlorn teachers and our democracy. I doubt she could pass scrutiny to become a judge had she gone out on an ideological limb. I understood how difficult it is to go up against a mob. I had to accept that most people prioritize financial survival.

That may have been my worst day. However, a story about my psychiatric visit points out how attorneys let teachers down and dump us on a treacherous legal route, the sum total of which measures up to that horrible day.

When my district ordered me to undergo a psychiatric evaluation by their psychiatrist—they denied me a choice—my attorney at that time, the judge's male partner, told me to ask the psychiatrist if I could videotape our session. So I asked. It's been twenty-five years, and I can't remember, but I think I asked before the appointment. We didn't have easy ways to videotape as we do now. But I did have a video camera and could have set it up.

Dr. Fink, the psychiatrist appropriately named and discussed in the Epilogue, said a hard no. I don't have to remember that because he wrote about my asking for a taping of his interrogation of me in his report to the Board about me. Fink found me paranoid based on the request that my attorney told me to make.

I didn't blame my attorney for being naive and helping build a case against me since every attorney is inexperienced with education because of education's low money status and thus clueless about WCCrime. But that attorney also dodged my case soon after I refused the Board's generous financial coverup settlement along with the other attorney who's now a judge—I vote against her every time she's on the ballot since then.

I can't blame him for not knowing the devious ways they treat teachers. I thought I could ask for a videotape of our meeting, which would be appropriate for almost any other worker, not a teacher. First, he wasn't a woman who lived before women's liberation when women were to stay in the kitchen and enjoy their second-class status. Being one gives you insight, but being a teacher goes way beyond that; it puts marginalized women's status on steroids.

Then, what WCCrime added brings the devalued woman state of affairs to an atomic level. Since few people can comprehend WCCrime, including attorneys, I couldn't have expected an attorney to protect me. And my experience with five different attorneys proved they can't.

The first union attorney admitted that the union made her throw teacher cases and that she was glad I was doing what I was doing. Of course, she wouldn't put it in writing, but I can swear an oath that she told me that before she retired. She told me on the day she abandoned a box of documents in my foyer, including the one saying the union was afraid of my attorney husband. They had to tread carefully, meaning I'd get union support, whereas most teachers get none. It meant they'd support a coverup, not real support.

I'd happily do a lie detector test to prove she had spilled the beans. She didn't tell me early on in our relationship. Since I didn't trust the union, I kept reminding her of my work to ensure she knew I was creating a paper trail. I remember telling her that if they made a movie of my book—at that time, it was in story form in my mind—Angela Lansbury would be perfect to play her.

My intention was to make her as paranoid of me as she was of the WCCriminals telling her what to do. My union attorney finally fessed up, partly because she was retiring. Still, I think she did so primarily because she believed I would be heard one day, and she was ashamed of what they had made her do. She had a conscience.

The second union attorney, who tried to manipulate me into holding a replacement hearing, was guilty of something. Either he was trying to save the state board, knowing that my decision was about to be rendered and they wanted to conceal that record. Or, if innocent of that, did nothing about the state board not telling him it was about to be rendered, a legal violation. He should have protected me against a state that unlawfully held that information from him, if they had, causing him to hold that meeting trying to coerce me into a new hearing unnecessarily unless he was on their team—the we-must-hide-the-forged-documents team.

I don't need to mention the attorney who had my sacred evidence "stolen from his car" but failed to tell me in this rundown of my teacher-disappointing attorneys. A judge accused him of possible malpractice regarding my case. I think it was due to his late brief. I'm not sure since he did so many things wrong. Whatever, I have that judge's wisdom in writing.

Then, there was the attorney I hired to appeal my federal case. On the day he did oral arguments, arguing the law and what an attorney is to do for an appeal, he was overwhelmed; my district solely went on a rampage about all the "facts" about my wrongdoing. He and his partner, my sixth attorney if I counted him, left the court rolling their eyes, saying they'd never seen this before. What was supposed to be about the law became another lie-filled teacher attack.

He and his partner weren't alone in their opinion. A good friend who's an attorney and my attorney-husband attended the appeal. Both left the proceedings shocked that what was to be an argument about the law became another teacher torture session. I understand: since they had a personal interest in me, their opinion of how wrong it was only carries a little weight. But they commiserated with my attorneys about what they had just seen as if all had seen Martians. It was unprecedented for all of them. Does that term sound familiar?

I didn't know an appeal was about the law, not another opportunity to bully one's adversary into submission. However, as a layman, I noted at least one of the three judges was either asleep or deep in a daydream and I knew he was not performing his job. None of the judges told the Board's attorney to stick to the law. They seemed to enjoy hearing a teacher being torn apart.

In their misinformed minds, they see teachers deserving of bullying since they're such a burden to their administrators—the usual warped thinking that gives WCCriminals wings.

So one attorney gave Dr Fink ammunition to use against me, and the other four failed me in different ways. Lawyers cannot help teachers much. This is why teachers need citizens to come to their rescue, the goal of the financially unrewarding work I have been doing since 1995.

Discovering and reporting that a just legal path for teachers is missing was a big part of what I did during those years. The legal part of this journey started in 1997 and lasted until April

27, 2007, when the US Supreme Court denied me a hearing. http://www.endteacherabuse.org/PetitionIntro.html

To the extent the court failed to apply the law in the sphere of education and the field of education failed to educate children, our nation lost its ability to remain robust and to compete. That's what put democracy at risk.

Deciding this on my birthday made it even more poignant. I had primarily represented myself. My court memoir, part of which is in this book's Epilogue and all of which is in the enhanced ebook version of this book, details that journey. Still, I missed one particular day because when I wrote that years ago, I didn't know how to include the day I brought my old lady shopping cart to the court without sounding like I was making it up.

It really happened. It was the day I gave my oral argument in court, knowing that the judge would ultimately return all the documents to me. There were a lot. The Board designed an over-the-top record to bowl me over mentally and physically. It did. It needed a cart. No briefcase would do. (There's a picture of it right before Chapter 8.)

Before it was time to load the cart that looked just like the one my teacher friend used to satisfy her devotion to teaching, since her students were worth the principal's mocking—you'll read about her in the Epilogue, I caught the Board's attorney making a colossal mistake. I remembered where in the record I could prove her wrong, so I did just that. My attorney-husband heard me catch them lying. I could see by the look in his eyes that I had scored big.

But the judge, with his already made-up mind, didn't hear it or care. Facts didn't matter at my school. Facts didn't matter in his court. He had his clerk load up my shopping cart to the brim, unconcerned about how I'd get it home from downtown Chicago, happy to rid himself of piles of paper that meant nothing to him.

He was okay with seeing a teacher push a cart like our city's homeless men often did. However, they stole their carts from grocery stores. Mine was the stand-up kind that wouldn't let me have a name that didn't include "old lady."

It didn't fit in a cab or a bus. I walked almost two miles to my home near the Gold Coast area of Chicago, pushing that overloaded cart. I worried a wheel would fly off while thinking that the cart held a few precious altered documents that confirmed the lawlessness they had used on me. It was lawlessness that didn't matter yet. But it would someday. I just knew.

So it justified the embarrassing walk home like it's justifying my work on this book now. Fraud must surface. It's like a painful pimple on one's face that needs to pop to find peace—the analogy is as gross as fraud is disgusting. Embarrassment and hard work become easy when revealing fraud is the purpose, or at least that's always been true for me, even that day.

Meanwhile, my journey through the courts seemed worthwhile, even a victory of truth, since I could help other teachers not take that journey. And that I did with vigor once I had tangible proof that our courts are hopeless for teachers. I will say that it was easier when I believed our courts cared about democracy and would protect its foundation.

In addition to my book and my organization, I worked in as many directions as I could envision—and I still do. I contact influential people as incidents happen, hoping the education/democracy connection will spark their interest. Few respond.

I hear celebrities talk about tweets they saw about their ugly hair and feel bad and wonder how they felt when they saw my tweet about education. It must be avoidance because they proved they do read tweets. I got Ed Schultz, a former MSNBC host, to talk to me. He was concerned but busy. Mostly, I hear nothing back. Believe me, you name them, I contacted them.

One recent example is Matthew McConaughey. I saw him talking about an organization he started, Greenlight Grant Initiative, after the Uvalde massacre. Uvalde is his hometown. He and his wife were so upset they had to get involved. He unearthed that the government had set up grants to help deal with school shootings and discovered that schools were not applying for these grants. He excused their missing applications as busyness and confusion about processing grants.

His organization intended to help with this grant-writing process. I filled out his organization's form, hoping he would expand his thinking about Uvalde. All I need is one celebrity to take on the WCCriminals, and the WCCriminals' pampered life is over. All I received from him was an auto-reply that they received my email and would reply. It's been several months. They did the usual—put me in the circular file. I believe he cares, but not enough to think out of the box.

I had to think this over. I was puzzled at first. Not taking money is not a WCCriminal mode of operating. I bet the administrators not applying for grants to do something about school shootings, are more comfortable embezzling than taking money for a specific goal. There will be follow-ups, and they need to be capable of doing something. They can't support solid teachers. They know they can't do anything.

Their pattern of wrongdoing is a trap. It requires a wall of silence around them, not real teachers. And besides, their crime package is not on the level of the Mafia. They are lawless because it's easy to be in education, not because they have no consciences.

They might feel real guilt and want to dodge it. Taking that money and doing their usual nothing for children may be a step too far. It's dreadful enough that their wrongdoing has led to horrific massacres. To apply for those grants knowing they won't do a thing puts them too close to Charles Manson for comfort.

With years of experience on this topic, I knew that not applying for those grants was fishy. In my email, I indicated that these school shootings are a direct result of lawless administrators running our schools more focused on what's in it for them than protecting our children. I suspect they're afraid to take these grants even though they are a windfall to add to what they've already embezzled. Please let me educate you about WCCrime.

McConaughey's people—I'm sure he's too busy—approached this as almost all approach this most hallowed institution, with unearned trust. My goal is to help the people trying to fix things by substituting the "a" in hallowed for an "o" in hollowed. Only then will they know the problem that needs solving.

WHY DO YOU THINK OUR DEMOCRACY HAS DISAPPEARED BEFORE OUR VERY EYES?

LEARN ABOUT OUR SCHOOLS AND YOU WILL KNOW!

WhiteChalkCrime.com
EndTeacherAbuse.org

/Brochure. c. 2009, . Addendum. 2022

When I contact politicians, I focus on the failure to investigate corrupt schools, a key reason so many citizens mistrust our government. My books document that this is bipartisan—both parties contributed to it and ignored it. My appeal to them is that the party that deals with this will be the trusted party. Many people will see the need for a Trump if neither deals with it.

In 2009, I created pamphlets to pass out at a political event at Roosevelt University entitled "Why Do You Think Democracy Has Disappeared Before Our Eyes?" Most people hadn't given our democracy a thought at that time. Once it dawned on me, I found it inseparable from my work. In the brochure, I pointed out that the party that exposes WCCrime will carve a bipartisan path. It will end much of what divides us.

Then, whenever the ACLU sends a solicitation for money, I enclose that pamphlet in their pre-stamped return envelope, making them pay for their betrayal. Saving democracy has motivated my work long before others had an inkling that it needed saving. The pamphlet is still relevant today. I did not predict Trump. I doubt anyone could have conceived of such a being. Yet, I did then and do now know why he became powerful.

I've contacted hundreds of leaders of all kinds. Michael Moore seemed second to Oprah as a person who might care. One of our members pointed out that he might have ignored my book, which she had sent to him since a local superintendent served on the board of his Traverse City Film Festival.

Almost everyone has a friend or relative who works in education. If their person isn't talking about this, they're hesitant to blow this open and get them upset. They might be a frightened educator who doesn't want to discuss it, or they might be an out-and-out WCCriminal. The person who sent him the book didn't want him to know it was from her even though she knew him. She was afraid. Many others contacted him. Not being one to dodge injustice, he found reason to avoid this injustice.

When I contact people, I focus on one of the many tragedies WCCrime has inflicted on us. School shootings are at the top of that list. I've tried reaching people at Sandy Hook. I spoke with their technology person, the only person I could reach. She had no interest in conveying my message that it's more than guns, as proven by her making no effort to connect me with someone who'd care. I wondered: Does the fear of losing her job motivate her to not want to end school shootings?

I tried reaching activist David Hogg of Parkland. No response. I reached out to Fred Guttenberg, who lost his daughter at Parkland and made activism his life. I expected to hear back in the way I'd expect to win the lottery if I ever bought a lottery ticket. When it's all about who you know, who you don't know doesn't count.

Turns out I heard from Guttenberg. Instead of contacting me and learning why the slaughtering of children occurs, his group invited me to an online meeting with union leader Randi Weingarten, who's gone along to get along with the abuse of the teachers that WCCriminals want to be purged from the system—including teachers who used to keep potential school shooters from going down a dark path.

Ignoring this is par for the course and will remain so until the truth about our schools is known. Weingarten might want to blow the whistle. I suspect she does, given her passion for these teachers. She helps them receive a more generous retirement—I have the receipts proving that. However, she knows she'll end up not being believed and out of a job, just like me. That's why our schools are filled with WCCriminals and people who look the other way.

Guttenberg's response was predictable because this is an issue no one can reduce to a sound bite. The first time someone spoke about what those priests were doing, listeners heard nothing. Sound stops when a recipient's soul cannot hear what they hear.

On 7/25/23, Eugene Robinson, a newspaper columnist, barked, "What is the rot at the heart of this democracy?" I sent him an email with the identity of the rot. He became one of the many influential people who didn't answer me even though he seemed desperate to know.

Each communication I send and each legal step I take has dual potentialities. It either leads to justice or becomes part of a magnificent, meticulous paper trail for an investigation when this issue is ready for prime time.

No step is futile to me since my work is like a scientist's. I trial and error my way to getting this exposed, like a scientist conducting experiments to make a discovery. Knowing I'm right about the "toxin" destroying our nation, nothing discourages me from creating a paper trail that can blow this issue wide open in the same way we uncover all the stubborn problems needing change.

The most challenging aspect of this mission is how little most people know about education. They need to see how dysfunctional it is and help identify why excellent teaching isn't happening or what education could do. It's not just parents that don't know. Professors need to learn. It's an unstudied, intellectually bankrupt discipline, an academic afterthought, unable to shape citizens' minds.

Thus, outsiders need a bridge to grasp what I know as a diligent insider of a scholar-less discipline. I'm building that bridge with solid facts. I'm meticulous about the accuracy of my words. Here's an example of the lengths I go to maintain truthfulness.

I took the position that our elite universities have let education down. While writing this book, I read about Jack Canfield, the author of *Chicken Soup for the Soul*. His history as a successful teacher and author of acclaimed educational how-to teach books made him a person who might understand my work. When I discovered he had attended Harvard, I questioned what I said about prestige universities not educating teachers.

I thought: He's around my age. Harvard had an education department that catapulted him into teaching. Yet, I never knew an education major who had attended Harvard. I never taught with one. I didn't think I was wrong, but the facts in this book must be correct. I had checked Harvard's undergraduate programs and found none in education—only graduate programs. But realized that's now. Maybe they used to have one. How else did he go to Harvard and become a teacher?

I then watched a documentary about his life to get my facts straight. He only pursued teaching after his senior year advisor at Harvard told him how to pursue psychology further, given that he hadn't taken required undergraduate courses. A Master's in psychology was not an option, but he could pursue psychology via education. He didn't have a prestigious education in education. My point remained solid.

Watching that taught me that education, the profession that pays little and offers even less prestige, does have an academic purpose. It can be a back alley for an esteemed discipline. Most likely, the devious nature of education that this illustrated also helped usher in WCCrime. Providing a watered-down version of psychology fits education's shallow nature. Great minds would frown on having the field that holds our democracy together as a back door to another discipline—if education had great minds.

And he didn't remain in teaching. He's made millions selling courses and books despite being a great teacher. He's helping adults find their purpose rather than children. I doubt he knew how substandard our schools are. He switched to a career that makes you wealthy. It's understandable but sad.

He probably is too busy to care about WCCrime, but I'll still try to reach him because he does for adults what I used to do for children—help them find their purpose. And perhaps he'll get how tragic it is that our schools have outlawed that. Or will he prefer to keep things as they are? Good schools will affect his bottom line, while lousy schools have made him wealthy.

I have left no stone unturned writing this book like I never gave up on a student. Figuring them out and helping them grow drove my every move. A teacher must work on a mission like this since it parallels running a successful classroom.

Teachers help students grow, not expecting to see them change but having faith that they will. A teacher is built for this seemingly not-going-anywhere job. I created a paper trail, trusting it would succeed like I had helped my students grow. I knew I wouldn't see them as successful citizens, but I was confident that I helped them build their bridges to good lives.

The rewards of teaching are intangible and profound. Being an activist feels similar. The only negative aspect of this job is that it exists. To think we have an entire nation of people clueless about education and about our schools is depressing. Since this needs to change, or we'll lose democracy, it's a worthy job. That counters the depression and keeps me proud to do it regardless of how long it takes.

Horace Mann shifted education to a public venture without concern it would become a system of opportunists rather than public servants. This mirrors our nation's fiasco in not having anticipated a criminal might become president.

I aim to shift education to a respected ideal by constructing a protection framework from fraud and fraudulent public servants—what Mann failed to do. I want to succeed in my lifetime, for everyone's sake. I'm confident someone will discover my paper trail when this nation is ready to face this, which may be when it needs to dig itself out from under a cruel dictator. I built a trail of facts officials can avoid but not deny, confident a grandchild or great-grandchild will carry the torch if need be.

My work isn't static. The recent craziness about not teaching black history occurred after my last book. Had I addressed that in the lesson on racial issues, I would have pointed out that administrators welcome controversies to distract from their wrongdoing. Plus, teachers most likely to stand up against not teaching proper history are the ones they want to push out. Controversy helps them purge great teachers, and indulging right-wing parents makes them appear to support parents.

Their primary objective is to distract you from WCCrime. Those enraged about questionable left-wing happenings in our schools, such as teaching pronouns to primary students, are in the same bamboozle boat. WCCriminals perform acts to distract you from their wrongdoing. They don't care about pronouns or covering up slavery. I know because they wouldn't take teachers like me away from you if they cared about what's suitable for children.

They set political fires to get you to hate each other, just as they prohibit teachers from telling you the truth to make you mad at the teachers. It's a political game. WCCriminals play political ping pong. The issue isn't the issue.

They are more astute at politics than some of the brightest minds. A case in point is Bill Maher of HBO's *Real Time*. His comment the other night earned him a place in this book, as a 2008 comment earned him one in my first book.

At that time, I included him discussing the lies that keep WCCrime booming. On top of that list is the falsity that firing a bad teacher is impossible. You can find that lesson in the enhanced ebook or the need for that lesson on Bill Maher's reruns since he says it a lot, unaware he's servicing fraudsters.

Recently, when he said, "Thousands of schools won't tell you if your kid is transitioning," I wanted to transition the channel on my TV. Hearing an intelligent guy like him operating like a marionette for the people who have destroyed democracy is more upsetting than when a nonthinking type parrots WCCrime falsities or even Trump's lies. We have an intelligence famine, and educrats are focused on transgenders. Really? He doesn't get it.

Since WCCrime is a house of cards, it needs serious screens to hide behind. Political issues that put you into an emotional blender keep you from discovering what WCCriminals are doing, such as embezzling, and what they aren't doing, educating.

If any administrators are really doing that, not telling you about your child transitioning is about as offensive as it gets. It makes no sense other than to make you mad—to disable your brain. That's the game. Get you angry at political issues. Get you mad at teachers. They harness your anger as far from their houses of cards as possible.

A description of the 2014 book *Serious Repercussions* by Pennsylvania teacher Sallie Montanye said the death of a child was of no public significance. The author's story is here: http://www.endteacherabuse.org/Montanye.html.

I know I mentioned her story before, but I had to include it again. Do you really think they care about supporting a student's transition if they don't care if a child is suicidal? Plus, thousands of districts are allowing the banning of books. They don't care about your child transitioning. They don't care about offensive books. The only thing they care about is you never finding out about WCCrime.

The proof that this is true is our schools are failing at the issue delegated to them: educating children. And children are being massacred, but they're expending energy on trans rights, erasing black history, and banning books as if those issues were theirs to solve while they're not applying for grants to help them solve the school shooting problem?

Earlier in this chapter, I spoke about how a movie star was making excuses for why schools weren't applying for free money to solve school shootings. Now, here's a TV celebrity thinking they care about trans rights. WCCriminals may have failed at educating children, but they have excelled at making people dumb.

219

Why is Maher focused on administrators' ridiculous decisions instead of what's wrong with our schools that we have such foolish administrators? Why would people who are failing at educating their students embrace a controversial issue unrelated to their duties? It's called diversion. Their skill with diversionary tactics is outstanding. I would say that Maher's lack of critical thinking regarding our schools highlights how lost people are. However, in this case, it's a lack of knowing what's really going on since no one has been able to make the facts in this book public, ever. No one can think critically without the real facts! Keeping this truth hidden makes a lot of people seem stupid.

Until people, courts, and government officials become educated about our schools, they will be like the laborers who carried heavy stones up hills to build sturdy pyramids, except they'll be building sturdy walls to hide WCCriminals' houses of cards.

Sorry to repeat, but repetition is needed when prior knowledge is non-existent. I'm building those scaffolds needed for learning something shockingly new. Educrats do not care about gay rights. They don't care about inappropriate books. They don't care about woke issues. They don't care about right-wing issues. They don't care about offensive books. They care about preserving WCCrime.

They use these issues like a bullfighter uses a red cape to steer a bull away from his body. Once you and celebrities like Bill Maher understand that you are the bull administrators are manipulating, you'll have that aha moment to empower you to be part of a movement to take back our schools. You'll want to get off the team that helps these charlatans.

Bill Maher has been an unwitting member of the team for at least sixteen years. If he reads this book, I'm confident that he'll switch teams as one in favor of a democracy. If you know him, send him a copy. He's too smart to be okay with serving WCCriminals. He'll appreciate it.

As the *Wizard of Oz* had his way until someone pulled the curtain and showed him for what he was, WCCriminals operate behind a curtain that this book draws open for you, something no one has done in such detail before. Whether liberal or conservative, you want and need good, safe schools.

Your rage is now in WCCriminals' hands, and you are their puppets while your children and our democracy are their victims. The divide between these tribes that they helped forge and now perpetuate is a WCCrime safety net filled with misery for all of us.

When the tribes learn to direct the rage at the villains, not each other, we will find the compromise a democracy offers. As it is, a political division is a kill-three-bird-winner for them. Many teachers have been doing what they can to remain in the profession they love but will find these political issues challenging. These acts that push teachers to the end of their spirits might cause them to speak out or resign. But only a few!

Unlike most, I view these issues, as I did Betsy DeVos, as a horror to many, yet inconsequential to me. I know that our schools are so fraudulent that these inequities and their inequity-inducing leaders are icing on an already poisoned cake.

Also, I read a lot. I devoured education books before I wrote mine and continue reading new books and articles. Over a decade ago, I read Laurie H. Roger's 2011 book *Betrayed: How the Education Establishment Has Betrayed America and What You Can Do About It*. I skimmed through it again to see if I should mention it in this book.

I checked her blog, which was an active, passionate one at one time. It started in 2008 as a blog for parents frustrated with administrators. It appears abandoned since 2014. Nevertheless, I found a few gems on her blog. John said, "My point in writing is that I knew several graduate students who enrolled at XXXXX [university name redacted by John] to attempt to invoke change in our failed academic system. Everyone was either compelled to alter the research focus or was blackballed."

His comments, which paralleled my experience with National Louis University, confirmed that our universities have locked education in a closet, hoping it won't scream. We can't know how much they focus on pleasing the criminals or avoiding the discipline that makes them bear the dunce cap. Either way, his comments prove that universities assist WCCriminals and maintain a status quo that crime, not productive research, requires.

Rogers, the author of this book, who has a degree in mass communications, not education, said what I'm saying but did not notice that WCCrime is fueling their bad decisions. She referred to conspiracy theories. That's as close as Rogers came to WCCrime. She did not realize that they practice a different business model—education as a front, not their purpose. She captured what's wrong with education but not why. She described WCCrime as the "Network." She said,

> That dishonor goes to The Network, a moniker I've given to the conglomeration of corporate and government interests (and their allies) that have seized control of America's classrooms. The Network is huge—containing most of the K-12 education mob, plus its allies in the Department of Education; colleges of education; unions; media; government agencies, associations, and legal teams; foundations; corporations; legislatures; fundraising groups; colleges and universities; business; and even the courts. The Network prefers to operate quietly, promoting supposedly good intentions. Its hallmark phrase: 'It's all about the kids.' But try opposing The Network on behalf of a child—yours or anyone else's. If you can't be put off, persuaded, ignored, bullied, or bought out, The Network has no problem getting nasty. The more honest and honorable you are, the nastier The Network becomes.

She confirmed my bipartisan stance on WCCrime when she said:

> This isn't about left or right, Democrat or Republican. It's about 'in' and 'out'; money and power; agenda and ideology. The Network spends much taxpayer money growing itself, feeding itself, and shielding itself from accountability. The bigger it is, the more power it has. The more power it has, the more friends it gains. The more friends it gains, the more

money it gets. The more money it gets, the bigger it grows—even as it completely fails our children. Allies of all stripes play along.

I agree, but I have to add that it's more than a network. I've seen the crime. I'm curious how many articulate people on her blog are now behind Trump. Every passionate educator who writes a book speaks about administrators, exasperated; they are unaware of what must be done. That's where I differ. I know we're dealing with sociopaths or sycophants not focused on education's purpose or who lack the brain power to do the job.

I reread Roger's book with a pit in my stomach, aware of how much effort she had put into writing her detailed book. Her authenticity as a public servant, coupled with her naivety about the state of affairs in education, made reading it painful. I felt her anguish while visualizing a manufacturing belt where ardent workers shaped the people on her blog into MAGA worshippers, preparing them for a life of fighting the system that let them down.

We have a nation of good people knocking their heads into walls, thinking education is lost rather than owned by thugs. The most significant part of my anguish was knowing that people like her end up deciding we need anyone but the establishment running this country.

I don't know that this is her truth. But based on how NAPTA's membership tanked, I suspect Trump as the solution may be her thing. I tried to reach her, but she's done with that blog and unreachable. As I read each page, I kept visualizing more and more Trump voters, hearing what called them while also understanding they were making the same mistake made in 1930's Germany. The problems were so significant that Hitler's charisma and determination blinded them to who he was and the awful things he would do.

I don't know Roger's political leanings. What I do know is how the education system's utter ridiculousness drives many to lose faith in the establishment while convincing them a deep state has taken over when I know it's unchecked fraud and a system left adrift for close to two hundred years. The state may be profoundly ignorant or deeply in denial. However, allowing crooks to sabotage education has left our leaders gasping for democratic breath while crooks pocket the spoils.

The advantage is not our government's. So why would they just let this crooked world be, other than out of ignorance? A deep state contrives to keep an advantage. There's no advantage in allowing a bunch of low-IQ thugs to steal our education system. It's as it is because this neglected institution has little value and few critically thinking minds watching over it since powerless teachers are voiceless.

As mentioned, Rogers called the power that kept real education from happening "The Network." She described it as an impossible force that blocked practical ideas from taking place. To her, this was our democratic government messing up. That conclusion is understandable. She had a degree in mass communication. She hadn't taught. She didn't have access to the fraud the way I did. She didn't realize how the discipline of education had no respect, no solid leadership, and how intellectual lightweights and thieves had overtaken it.

I view what happened as equal parts of stupidity and fraud. Since education has yet to have an intellectual powerhouse leading it since Horace Mann died in 1859, there's been no one of substance telling the government what it needed. We cannot expect a president to know everything. We can only expect him to listen to leaders in each field whose job is to keep that area functioning. That lack of competent leadership allowed education to become a world of greed.

On Roger's blog, she spoke about interviewing superintendents ignorant of various math series, who reminded me of my superintendent. She mentioned Secretary of Education Margaret Spelling's inaccurate analysis of student progress. To her, it was frustration. To me, it's WCCrime. In Part Three of the enhanced ebook, you can read about how Margaret Spelling acquired that top job after participating in an education scandal.

Rogers performed a much more thorough investigation of all the foolish things in education than most teachers' books do. Still, she missed WCCrime and education's intellectual lack. It's the latter that brought us to today. The thieves would not have had an easy home in a world of great minds.

We are losing our democracy because education, the one thing that could have held it together, is a facade. And it has as many people mad as it has people ignorant. It has our courts and public officials clueless and thus appears to be a deep state, but is actually a dumb state.

So when I visit a blog like this, I see people like the people who stormed the capital on January 6. They're right to be mad about education but wrong about why it's so messed up. And they're craving a self-serving autocrat in the same way the starving people of Germany became Hitler's fodder. Knowing this has catapulted me over the obstacles of doing this work. I've been at this for twenty-nine years. Rogers gave up at ten years. Unless we get education right, our democracy stands little chance for success. So, I keep reading.

Sometimes, I miss a book like 2015's *The Teacher Wars* by Dana Goldstein. I just read it and discovered one more book that missed WCCrime. She traced the history of education, but her only mention of WCCrime was the notorious Atlanta cheating scandal and suspicious erasures on Washington DC test results, which are a deviation from the norm to most.

I found her statement, "It's hard to know what to make of teachers," interesting. It tells me she doesn't get it. She recognizes education's chaos, not the WCCrime that causes it. Thus, she fails to identify the reason for teachers' peculiar state. A reviewer demonstrated the same loss of understanding:

> It's hard to know what to make of teachers. In the news and in the movies, they are sometimes vampires sucking off public goodwill and sometimes saviors of America's children. In this totally surprising book, Dana Goldstein—who has always been Slate's sharpest writer on education—explains

how teachers have always been at the center of controversy. At once poetic and practical, *The Teacher Wars* will make school seem like the most exciting place on earth."—Hanna Rosin, author of *The End of Men.*

Keeping teachers at the center of controversy is a strategy to keep power from them. Goldstein mentioned Superintendent John Deasy's purchase of 600,000 iPads with no hint of scrutiny, overlooking a 2014 scandal detailed in the article, "LA Schools' $1 Billion iPad Fiasco Ends After Corruption Revelations."[25] She also missed disreputable exits reported in another article, "Infamous John Deasy Resigned under Suspicious Circumstances Again,"[26] by Thomas Ultican, who said:

> The Stockton Unified School District (SUSD) board accepted John Deasy's letter of resignation effective June 15, 2020. His quitting mid-contract marked the third straight superintendent position he ended similarly. All three time[s], the resignation came with ethical charges and legal suspicions.

Ultican cited those shady departures as 2001 and 2004, long before Goldstein's book that let that administrator off the hook.

More disappointing were some endorsements written about Goldstein's book: "Anyone who wants to be a combatant in or commentator on the teacher wars has to read *The Teacher Wars.*"— Chris Hayes, host of MSNBC's *All In with Chris Hayes.* Wrong! Chris Hayes needs to read my book.

And, "Dana Goldstein proves to be as skilled an education historian as she is an astute observer of the contemporary state of the teaching profession. May policymakers take heed," Randi Weingarten, President, AFT. Weingarten didn't take heed and respond to my emails about teacher abuse.

Journalists need to know WCCrime to do their job in education. *The New York Times*'s acclaimed journalist Nicholas D. Kristof recently said, "So maybe I was wrong. I used to consider health care our greatest national shame,...Yet I'm coming to think that our No. 1 priority actually must be education." If he reads this book, he will know that to be true!

Actually, their reporting is worse than useless. It perpetuates the Educrats' agenda—the coverup of WCCrime.

The name Deasy rang a WCCrime bell in my brain. Janice Howes, the teacher who wrote the marvelous 2005 book *The Black Hole in the Blueprint*, worked for a scandalous thug in California. I thought it might be him. Upon checking, her bully turned out to be Alan Bersin, a star of Part Three's Lesson Eight. I got my thugs mixed up.

It turns out that after wrecking the San Diego schools, Bersin won a top job at Homeland Security. A 2015 newswire mentioned that a whistleblower reported Bersin as amongst those responsible for violence, corruption, and dysfunction at CBP [Border Control],[27] just as Howes had conveyed he had done to the San Diego United School District. Her reporting didn't work. WCCriminals live to corrupt another day, in this case, in another arena.

Reading inspires me to carry on. I count watching informative videos or documentaries in the same category. Often, what I watch is about as inviting as a kale salad. It's good for you, so you eat it even though you prefer to take a pass. Education as a topic, or even education when you're a child, and even most adults, is like kale.

I always disliked school, but I did what I had to do to graduate. Only a few people like it. That is why exposing WCCrime is so hard. You must eat kale to learn what the bad guys are doing. They are confident you won't.

Bad tasting, healthful eating came to mind since a NAPTA member sent me a YouTube of his nefarious Missouri school district's meeting. I started watching it and felt like I agreed to watch an algebra class. A group of concerned citizens, with a principal mission of being a watchdog of the district, known as the Ozark Schools Support Team, gave a lesson on how school boards become corrupt.

It didn't take long to switch from "another boring video" to Wow, I just learned something. The speaker explained that there's a state board organization that boards and vendors join—MSBA. They pay over $13,000 a year. It instructs them on how to dodge rules. Each state has one. I needed to learn more about this organization. It should have been in my 2008 book, Lesson Thirteen.

I woke up in the middle of the night, disturbed that I had missed it. The next day, I found out why. A courageous board member had told the truth—something that rarely occurs.

He revealed that they have lawyers and advisors that purposefully teach districts how to avoid rules and laws, i.e., commit WCCrime. He gave an example. According to the law, every matter, with only a few exceptions, should be discussed in open meetings with parents. They can tell parents a particular matter will be addressed privately, and it becomes accepted as legal.

He pointed out that board members are to listen to constituents about issues. Still, they advise them to only discuss issues at meetings. They have a routine that frightens them into submission, deeming the superintendent all-powerful.

I knew someone turned board members into robots, closer to the pod people from the cult movie *Invasion of the Body Snatchers*, but now I know who. He said, "Once they receive the MSBA indoctrination, it is impossible to reach them anymore unless they ALREADY knew the training was full of lies and propaganda. If we can reach them FIRST, we can help them see the falsehoods in what the MSBA tells them."

After years of activism, I marveled at this plan, hearing it for the first time. I recalled how my school board behaved, even the ones who supported me. Unlike this brave board member, they never told me. I suspect they bought into it like a child entering a strange car because the predator told them, "Mom sent me." Board members traveling with predators do not know what they do not know.

My board had not listened to me. I recall a high-rise memory, towering over my hellish years in the school district. I had prepared an elaborate presentation for the Board, detailing the constant abusive things my principal had done to me. I presented it on Martin Luther King's birthday. I hoped the arc of justice would knock sense into them.

A few days later, I received a letter saying that investigation is not what they do. Now, knowing about the ISBA, Illinois' law-evading organization, it makes sense. Someone made them think that's not their job when it's their reason for existing.

The MSBA explainer went on about an excessive teacher turnover rate without explaining it. That made me think about my job with the "I'm not afraid to hire smart teachers" principal, who was fired when I blew the whistle on how he made teachers pretend they wanted to resign. That was 1970. I figured things changed because administrators got smart. Now, I'm still determining.

Most don't seem like they ever could get smart. The brains behind committing WCCrime and getting away with it must have been the state board association. WCCrime began to blossom around 1980. I had mentioned the ISBA's financial fraud in my 2008 book but missed that they secured absolute power for superintendents. They belong on the accomplice's list, and as far as I know, they're the only accomplice that evaded it.

He relayed that A/C suppliers, architects, lawyers, etc., paid yearly fees to be members, and guess who got the jobs at the various districts? That explains why a district would hire an architect who knew nothing about libraries to design a library. I thought they might have hired someone unfit for the job because he was a friend. Now, I suspect no skilled architects were in the state association's membership. I wasn't wrong that it was a corrupt move. I just needed to learn more about how their corruption flows.

I have to admit I marveled at my superintendent's guts for crossing out a line on a parent's letter. The line said he gets what he wants, not what the children need. He folded the page; part of his marker's cross-out line still showed. He submitted it to the legal record. And the state tried to "lose" the entire record, so I'd never get my hands on that altered document..(Document at the beginning of Chapter 6.)

As explained, a reporter scared them, and they did "find" the record and "find" the hearing officer, and I have that document. But it still has yet to matter since the year 2000. So, they did get away with it. At least so far.

It wasn't courage that inspired all this. It most likely was our state board association empowering them. After watching the MSBA explainer,[28] it made sense. I get why most people have better things to do than watch a video that feels like school. But if we lose democracy, we will lose doing what we enjoy. What the fascist government has in store—Project 2025—will be our lives. If we spend time learning this and help to end it, we can return to doing what we enjoy.

I'm not saying the following is their plan, nor can we know it isn't their plan. I watched a Netflix documentary called "*Ordinary Men*," which showed how, before they devised gas chambers to do genocide more efficiently, ordinary German men living in an autocratic country were asked to shoot Jews at close range, face to face, during World War II. Most of them went along because people find it uncomfortable when they don't go along with others.

Authoritarian Trump has promised to end democracy, and it will then be his choice as to how we enjoy or not enjoy life. Since he cannot tolerate looking at people maimed in war[29] and ugly women are not his type, or an illness might make any of us look not up to his standards, he might order us to wear burkas—maybe men too?

If so, they'll be red, with MAGA emblazoned on them. And we'd have to pay for them. An autocrat is the determiner. That, coupled with his position that a celebrity can do whatever he wants to women, seems like a lot of us will want to leave this country. Just saying.

Taking the time to learn a complex issue, such as what went wrong in education, is like doing well in school to have an easier life. You did it, even when you really didn't like school. You need to study something again for an easier life. It's much shorter than a semester and worth millions of hours of freedom.

Even if you think murdering people sounds like fun, as some of them did, according to the documentary, there will be things you won't like when you give up your former democratic life, such as the television stations Trump allows us to watch. He plans to end the ones he doesn't like.

Education geek that I am, the YouTube presentation thrilled me. This was a pivotal missing puzzle piece that even I had missed. The presenter clarified that their goal was to return MSBA's power to the people without taking sides in the culture wars. People with different beliefs needed to play a role in expressing their concerns. Schools are like the military. They don't get involved in politics. So when they do, be suspicious. WCCriminals care about money and power, not the culture wars. So when they promote either side of those wars, it's for money and power.

Authentic educators know their job is to maintain a democracy, as military leaders know their job is to safeguard the country. Neither would consider siding politically since they work for the entire nation. Someone like Glenn Youngkin, helping parents get their political views stamped on their schools, is vying for votes while not being true to what education is intended to be.

Administrators supporting culture wars are playing the distraction game. Look over there while I'm arranging a kickback, which makes a fight over book banning advantageous. Intentional political battlegrounds, under which they hide organized crime, guarantee people won't see past the surface.

They inflict extreme practices on our schools to ensure that the community obsesses over that practice, not on WCCrime. We must run schools based on research, not fads. We need honest research and academic knowledge to lead, something discussed in more detail in the next chapter. We must rely on verified knowledge. We cannot rely on the whims of parents, such as the one who insisted the 1996 internet was all her son needed to do research.

Here's an example of why academic research must take center stage in decision-making. Education leader Carl Washburne, who died in 1968, determined that teaching reading should start in first grade. That's when most children are ready to learn to read. He found that discouragement occurred with earlier attempts with students who were not ready. Discouragement could result in a mental set against reading lasting for years and hampering success at school. Many children learn to read earlier. But as a whole, many are ready after age six or seven.

We don't want to create a segment of scarred children when it is not necessary. I taught second grade. I observed that the children who came into second grade with fluent reading left second grade at the same level as those who learned fluency in second grade. Thus, teaching reading early had no advantage. Granted, some children enjoy reading earlier, but schools must take a democratic approach and do what leads to better learning for most.

Schools started pushing academics in kindergarten, which is harmful to some children. Administrators may have wanted their schools to seem advanced. Parents may have pressured schools into fast-tracking their children.

The schools need to be the experts and avoid acts that harm children. Only individual children ready to read early should learn to read early. Parents know the downfall of toilet training too early. When it comes to literacy, research must take the lead. Plus, even more importantly, kindergarten is a time for character development and socialization, the lack of which has compromised democracy.

There is a black hole of missing knowledge facing anyone who hasn't experienced WCCrime firsthand. I gave you specific examples to help you understand how authentic educators think. Unlimited opportunities for administrators to take advantage of their power exist. That black hole is mammoth. It remains in place for a few years before teachers begin to get what's going on. And some never get it. It is both shocking and complex.

I'm working hard to build needed bridges to cross that divide. Some of you will find a bridge early on in this book and not need to read the rest. These bridges will materialize once learning happens. I keep seeking new ways to explain this by keeping up with anything on television related to education or corruption.

Many friends stopped watching TV, sickened by Trump news. I watch it to find a possible gap where interest in my work might fit. I look for public officials and celebrities that are worth contacting. Since our celebrity culture, with our schools missing in action, played a prominent role in evaporating our democracy, I keep up with it.

Recently, I heard that the American Bar Association formed a task force to help save democracy. I am working on reaching someone there. No one else has put this million-piece puzzle together yet, and that task force will spin more wheels due to the black hole of ignorance. They know schools are bad and teachers are essential, with little depth to their understanding. I expect the usual rejection born from this is too hard to grasp.

I scour the internet. I came across a teacher story, "'Corrupt' school offers money to' shut teacher up' (part 1)."[30] It had all the elements of WCCrime—covering up safety issues, harassing dedicated teachers out of teaching, and buying loyalty. It's more recent than the stories on our site. It proves WCCrime has not stopped, though I stopped adding stories due to budget restraints.

This superintendent wants to cover up a safety issue, so this caring teacher needs to go. He even took the time to intimidate this teacher in person. There are hundreds of stories on our site. Teachers hope you'll read them and make noise. Since suicides aren't enough and stories aren't enough, I push on.

I will continue contacting people with power to help me start an investigation. One of my last contact attempts before publishing this was Liz Cheney. Her dedication to democracy has elevated her and her family above the mistakes many think they made.

Her father was Vice President when President Bush promoted WCCriminals into the Department of Education, as documented in my prior books and in the enhanced ebook. Her sacrifices, similar to mine in education, demonstrate her sincerity. Because

Liz understands democracy and Trump so well, I hope she will embrace my work.

I do not believe there is "losing" in what I do. It is only discovery and something upon which to build the next direction. Feeling like a victim is a place where nothing happens. I keep it happening.

Recently, my husband asked if I had ever watched the television program "Abbott Elementary". I said no, thinking, "I'm not sure why. It won awards. It's a topic dear to my heart. But I never watched it." Later that day, I saw an ad for it. I looked at the picture and knew. Schools feel like the home that broke its promise—a home that abandoned me. It was my soul's home. The sadness never goes away. Teaching became a wound. I feel happy doing this work because it's essential that people like me, who belong in a classroom, will one day be in a classroom. I don't feel happy watching a school that's oblivious to WCCrime.

For me, the classroom was magical. Taylor Swift's acceptance comments about her 2024 Emmy seemed torn from my teacher brain. I felt the same way teaching as she does writing music. What I'm doing now is work. Teaching was a joy.

I've reached out to so many but heard back from so few. An important person responded and agreed to look at my work this year for the first time. I won't mention the person's name because the forces that do not want WCCrime to end will hound that person to ensure there's no investigation.

The truth in this book must explode on a level that won't allow anyone to push it back into the nasty vampire vault in which it has subsided. Sounding an unstoppable alarm is this book's goal. My heart is much lighter than it's been for the past 29 years since I believe the student is ready. I end this chapter with what I've done symbolically since 1999.

Every time I get a pedicure, I have rhinestones put on my big toes. If this truth remains a secret, I plan to be buried with them. Here's why: During my final teaching year, my administrators had battered me, so my doctor ordered me to take two weeks off. My attorney submitted the doctor's letter, which resulted in an order to see their psychiatrist.

When I was ready to re-enter the war zone, they ordered me to stay home and told my students that I was sick. It was a very depressing time for me. After several weeks, I went for a manicure and pedicure to cheer me up. Rhinestone flowers on my toes were a statement: they would not steal my joy. My students loved it—well, not the boys. I made sure they had other things to love. It became my trademark. I ran a joyful classroom.

A random parent recognized a teacher enjoying the day when I should be at school and reported me for being at a nail salon. Since they had lied about me being sick, they could not reveal that they had ordered me not to come to work. Nor had they imposed restrictions on me.

The rhinestone flowers became symbolic because they were described in detail in their legal brief, trying to humiliate me for being frivolous. In the same brief, the board president said I was too dedicated. How do the rhinestones fit with the too-dedicated remark?

Their obscene treatment did not break my spirit. Rhinestones represent what they did to teachers like me in New York. There, they ordered their political prisoners to report to the Rubber Room, named that because teachers felt like bouncing off the walls. They kept these teachers there to get parents mad, thinking they were paying teachers not to teach because of the unions when it was a ploy to anger parents.

My district was small. It didn't have a rubber room. So, they created a virtual rubber room for me. That parent's report was perfect for them. It fulfilled their goal, making teachers, not the criminals, the problem with our schools.

Then, on a lovely Sunday at an outdoor mall, someone spotted me and reported me for shopping. I didn't have a bag. I didn't shop. Yet, a parent accused me of shopping. Neither reporting parent was a parent of my students. They knew my value. Of the students in my class the prior year, over half requested me for a second year. Almost all had signed a petition on my behalf, asking the Board to listen to me, which they didn't do.

The Board thought it had ownership of me and my weekends, too. My husband had insisted we go to the mall and enjoy nature as if he were escorting a mental patient for a cheer-up event. I was on medication for depression that had caused an allergic reaction, as well as six new cavities in my teeth. I was downhearted. It was a nice day.

All I had left from teaching were sparkling flowers on my two big toes. I keep those sparkling flowers to remind me that you cannot destroy a great teacher. My spirit is still sparkling, and I am determined to teach this nation about its failure to provide real schools. That's what I do. And that's what I'll continue doing—as long as we're still a democracy.

14

I KNEW WE'D LOSE IT BACK THEN

"Teachers are more than any other class the guardians of civilization."

Bertrand Russell

"Education makes a people easy to lead but difficult to drive; easy to govern, but impossible to enslave."

Peter Brougham

"If you want to live a happy life, tie it to a goal, not to people or things."

Albert Einstein.

Teaching was never just a job for me. It was a passion that seeped into every fiber of my being. The injustices I witnessed in the education system didn't just haunt my thoughts; they became a part of me. They found a home in my mind or perhaps in my soul. The two are so intertwined that I can't tell where one ends and the other begins. But what's important is that I know WCCrime and can help you know it too.

When I wrote my first book in 2008 to expose it, I knew schools had a role in our democracy, but like most, I took democracy for granted. Or at least I thought I had taken it for granted until 2016 when I reread my book *White Chalk Crime™: The Real Reason Schools Fail*. I reread it because "you know who" turned our world upside down, and it became clear that the world, once governed by reason and logic, was no longer. The following passage, found online, made sense to me:

> Whatever the reason, it's been a dispiriting experience for anyone who grew up with expectations of living out one's life in a decent country, with decent neighbors, in decent communities, only to be forced to face the reality that at this point in time, nearly half of the voting American population, statistically, is positively reveling in the destruction being wrought by Trump, having rationalized it, justified it to themselves or otherwise made their peace with it.[31]

I knew why. Corrupted schools produce undereducated citizens—a culture of media illiterates who mix conspiracy and reality. And, if they teach history—remember the teacher that didn't like science, so didn't teach it—they do so without teaching the skills to apply it. That, combined with resentment toward those who allowed such horrid schools, is a lethal package.

Had my book gone viral, we could have reformed our schools, ended, or at least reduced, school shootings, shored up the middle class, and dodged an army of conned souls who want to elect an indecent establishment disruptor. This book offers a second chance to solve what led us to Trump.

Education is the foundation for a nation's ideals, which in America is democracy. A criminalized foundation is to a democracy what a termite-infested foundation is to a building.

Our democracy gave way to a con artist. Jon Meacham's 2018 book, *The Soul of America: The Battle for Our Better Angels*, quoted Franklin D. Roosevelt, "The presidency is not merely an administrative office. That's the least of it. It is more than an engineering job, efficient or inefficient. It is preeminently a place of moral leadership."

He's got that right. Citizens pass down values from generation to generation. Our once-hallowed schools planted deep values. No more! A superficial education guarantees value impermanence—democracy's extinction. Other issues may appear more pressing, but nothing is graver than the need to dismantle the time bomb eroding America. We chose a hollow soul with no use for democracy. Our fraud-filled foundation attracted a leader who is a bombastic promoter of hate, fear, and division.

Hitler said, "Whoever has the youth has the future." He was spot on, too. The power to restore our democracy lies in fixing its foundation, which cannot happen without knowledge of what caused its collapse.

My teaching experience mirrored what we endured under Trump's profiteering regime: lawlessness, self-serving acts, lies, employment of grifters, cover-ups, destruction of revered institutions and mores, vice as a virtue, all about money, disregard for others' needs, celebrity over substance agenda. A regime that has been a shock to most is a déjà vu to me. Abraham Lincoln predicted this when he said, "The philosophy of the school room in one generation, will be the philosophy of government in the next."

Teaching has become a world of upside-down ideals. The disgust you feel trapped in a deplorable reality show will help you understand what drove me to write my 2008 book in which I all but predicted a President Trump. Passages from it show democracy was always my purpose. They warned of his coming, in theory.

I wrote these passages in 2008, but I knew them in 1995. It was 1995 when I found out there were no watchdogs. It became clear that expertise was no longer welcome in education. Dumb people and crooks were in charge. It bothered me. I knew you couldn't have idiotic schools like this and not expect this country to fall apart.

At that time, I didn't know Ulysses S. Grant's quote about the importance of people becoming intelligent. Still, I knew schools like the one where I taught would not make that happen. Dumb and crooked policies and people who don't care about or have any idea how to achieve intellectual muscle could not create an intelligent nation. Yet, somehow, Grant's prediction was in my brain. The only thing I knew about Ulysses S. Grant then was from an old Groucho Marx show where one of his favorite questions was, "Who was buried in Grant's tomb?" When contestants got it wrong, his gotcha moment made people laugh. He gave the last name of a president, but they got it wrong. How stupid.

He enjoyed mocking people's lack of intelligence. Now I'm wondering: could Grant's quote about stupidity be why Groucho always asked that question? Perhaps Groucho was more brilliant than I thought!

Whatever, I knew our schools were a danger to society as I knew who was buried in Grant's tomb. And I've had to live with that knowing for way too many years, so figuring out how to share it with you has been an obsession, with which I've had to deal so I could sleep at night.

I've done well at that. Most people who know me will be surprised when they read this book since I've kept this knowledge in my brain, knowing there's a time and place for everything, and the world wasn't ready to know what I learned.

Then Trump came along, and I saw him as "Miracle-Gro" for the truth about our schools. Those flowers I used that product on became huge, reminding me that we have the power to adjust nature's plan! Remember, I was born to teach—to be a teacher. I know when learners are ready and what makes them ready. That was my gift.

Plus, finding a positive aspect of Trump is a gift I offer those who want to put him in charge of our destinies. I hope that offering will be enough for many to love him in a different way that won't destroy our country.

My point is what I wrote in 2008 that you're about to read had been brewing in my brain for thirteen years. Now it's twenty-nine years. When I learned that it took thirty years until the truth about what the priests were doing became learnable, I saw Trump as an opportunity, a sign from above that I could finally teach you what's been gnawing at my brain.

I must point out that it's not like the worm in Robert F. Kennedy, Jr.'s brain making him run for president at such a treacherous time as if he's trying to erase all the good his family gave this country. It's more like a light of wisdom I've had to store until the learner is ready.

Knowing I have a purpose has given me a sense of peace. However, I must admit preparing a lesson dealing with a person as petulant as Trump is an unprecedented challenge, even for me.

I've said it takes a book. In this case, it took a few books. Please read these passages I wrote in 2008 so you'll realize I am not making up the fact that I knew what our schools would do to our country long ago.

I said then:

> Schools are organized crime, stunning in their audacity to violate laws. Ignoring these truths, EducRAT$ have replaced our ticket to freedom with a shell game. We are all losers. We all live in a lesser world, within a declining empire, because when education fails any of us, it fails all.

I say now:

> The well-educated and privileged must read this book.

I said then:

> God had a plan to create loving, patient people, whose qualities complement the needs of children and who can educate them for success: devoted teachers. With those running our schools methodically disposing of those who were called to teach with a deep love for their work, and who could turn

241

their students' lives around, our entire nation has begun to collapse.

I say now:

I am called to teach why we're losing our democracy.

I said then:

Wise people know that a little perjury, a little lying, and a little altering of documents is always bad. Any lying under oath must be considered serious. Laws are societal agreements, and those who pick and choose are enemies of society. Even when an act against the law appears harmless, failing to attach consequences permits others to do the same, with chaos as the end product.

Once the public connects these not-so-little lies to EducRAT$'s ability to seize teachers' power and create schools that promote EducRAT agendas rather than meet the children's needs, they will realize they are far from "little." Once the public grasps that the puppet society that is our schools is one of the largest all-time swindles in our nation, the public will insist on tethering EducRAT$ to the laws of the land.

I say now:

Trump's ways fit with our corrupted schools.

I said then:

I am sure if they investigated, they would know that any institution this corrupt, this filled with terrorized souls knowing they cannot anticipate any help from the media, the courts, the public, or the unions, could spawn characters that behaved as though they had descended into Sodom and Gomorrah, because they have.

I say now:

I described Trump and his sycophants before I even knew them!

I said then:

This workforce of people who just follow orders within a system that was intended to be dedicated to children is a levee about to burst and devastate our nation. Hollow schools will not hold up a democracy!

I say now:

The levee broke. All we hold dear is rushing away.

I said then:

If the portion of the public that cares about its children and about its freedom will learn the truth about our schools and stand up for just this one shattered aspect of our society, the education that will evolve will raise a new generation who will carry the ball of democracy and protect us all from electing future ruinous governments. It is crucial that our nation restore its backbone.

I say now:

I, along with the majority of Americans, believe that we have elected a ruinous government.

I said then:

> Education is the backbone of our culture. The America about which I signed up to teach no longer exists. We now have a country obsessed with power, ignorant of history's lessons, deserving of ridicule and enmity. Most people are too busy or too preoccupied with celebrities, gossip, and material desires, and thus unconsciously facilitate dictatorial rule by default.

I say now:

> If we dislike what Trump's doing to our country, we must be honest. We must admit that smaller versions of "democracy destruction" angered enough people to vote for anything but the establishment. We went from imperfect to a dumpster fire. My 2008 book documents much of that imperfection. Leaders must fess up.

I said then:

> Thomas Jefferson's: "Education is the anvil upon which democracy is forged." He and America's Founding Fathers knew that an uneducated populace could not sustain a thriving democracy. Without good schools, at best, we have a mere appearance of a democracy, not a solid democracy.

I say now:

> Thus, we have made it far easier for a scoundrel to shift our beloved experiment of democracy into an autocracy, his now-admitted goal.

I said then:

> People have abandoned trying to change things and have turned to hollow lives because the powers that be have made it so futile to stand up to their vast power.

I KNEW WE'D LOSE IT BACK THEN

I say now:

> Another Trump term offers little hope our democracy will last. Trump admires Putin, the democracy hater who poisons his adversaries. Love of Putin is a danger sign that our under-educated nation has missed.

I said then:

> I wrote this because I live in America, the home of the free and the brave, and in America, we cannot tolerate an education system run by a few who've grabbed our power. The present system and a vision for a free country are mutually exclusive.

I say now:

> Trump and his Republican sycophants destroying our institutions and ideals prove this to be true.

I said then:

> I can show you that in the education arena, we have trashed the Constitution and that those who hold power in education hold it above and beyond the Constitution.

I say now:

> You are now seeing our government do what administrators do—lawless acts with quislings ready to do whatever it takes for power.

I said then:

> We need people of courage to insist that education remain subject to the laws of this land and that the judicial system

ensures that the whims of those in power do not erase the foundation of our nation.

I say now:

Even if brought to justice, the vacuum that brought us Trump will continue to devour all that we hold dear if those in power ignore what is in this book.

I said then:

A society without dedicated teachers is open to uncivilized rage.

I say now:

Rage will spiral if leaders ignore my contribution to save our democracy.

I said then:

Until truth scales the mountain of propaganda and special interest that EducRAT$ have erected to keep their GAME going and penetrates the minds and hearts of we the people, education and all that it impacts will remain grim. We, the people, must get involved and force those in power to dismantle WCCrime.

I say now:

No president will improve our democracy and its institutions without ending WCCrime. Nothing can change if the opportunists controlling our schools keep it hidden by keeping people like me silenced.

I've included quotes from my 2008 book to show you what we could have fixed a long time ago. We have another chance. We need someone bold who'll admit we've messed up in education, listen to those who know what learning is, and lead us from WCCrime. We need citizens to read this book and join a movement to make that happen and defend democracy. Please help me give Trump lovers a reason not to need him.

Allowing fraudsters to hijack education is one primary reason many see a need for a strongman. They're right! We need a strong person to end this theft of education. Unfortunately, a con man was the only "strongman" available.

These shares from my 2008 book also serve as a portfolio of my future predicting abilities. In the next chapter, I share my visions for what schools could be and that could make up for an almost two-century failure to move education forward.

I have just proven my visions are worth taking seriously.

15

VISIONS - FOR VISIONARY SCHOOLS

"Where there is no vision, there is no hope."

George Washington Carver

"There's no use talking about the problem unless you talk about the solution."

Betty Williams, Peace Activist

"Patience and perseverance have a magical effect before which difficulties disappear and obstacles vanish."

John Quincy Adams

In addition to my on-target predictions in the last chapter, I have more than my share of hope and ideas for reforming education. The psychiatrist who helped me deal with the physical rape I had experienced when in educational film marketing diagnosed me as living life with rose-colored glasses. That diagnosis, coming from a doctor who fell asleep during sessions, seemed logical.

He was not called to help; he did his job with his glasses off. My positive outlook is why I have education solutions worthy of consideration to solve our democracy problem. I'm as confident about what needs to be done to reform education as I was when I put together a plan for each of my student's success. We know that great teachers make a difference in a child's life. This teacher plans to make a big difference in reforming education and restoring democracy. It's time visionary people led education.

Despite the current uncivil behavior, there are pockets of old-fashioned, devoted teaching. During Teacher Appreciation Week, the TV show The View featured a teacher celebrated for what she has done over forty years. Past students showed up to praise her in a "This is Your Life" style presentation. She's a stepping-stone teacher. I bet no child in her classrooms ever felt enough anger to shoot up a school. Rage had no home in her classrooms. I watched, moved by what she did, saddened by what I didn't get to do.

These teachers are nearly extinct. They only exist in schools with authentic administrators. As long as there are any left, and there are, as she proved, we can multiply them. That is my first goal. I would achieve that by exposing WCCrime, causing the self-serving to flee.

As dozens of actresses testified against Harvey Weinstein once an investigation occurred, thousands of teachers will come forth. Most will be like her but with less positive teaching experiences. It will send selfish administrators running. Teachers will finally have the autonomy to do the "called-to-teach" thing, and the profession will blossom. Fewer teachers will quit. More people will want to teach.

Except for those who become teachers only to become administrators, you won't find many people who choose to teach but find children annoying any more than you find veterinarians who dislike animals. Some employ a severe approach to control a classroom. Still, it is harshness emanating from a lack of training rather than a dislike of children.

Many, captured by such an evil system, become bitter and unloving. Ending WCCrime and putting dedicated teachers in leadership roles will erase that. Teachers do not need to be great intellectuals as long as they love children. Right now, an incredible intellectual mind has no place in this field despite that's what we need leading education. That needs to change.

What happened with Whole Language, the teaching of literacy in the 1990s, illustrates why education needs great academic minds. Whole language, considered a fantastic thing by some and a disaster by others, became a new way of teaching reading and writing. It was intended to bottle what outstanding teachers had been doing for years. Its biggest problem: it required spontaneous decision-making and banked knowledge.

Most teachers operating with loyalty over competence agendas were either not that smart or doing the survival dance. Traditional skills-based, literacy teaching guaranteed the learning of reading. It didn't take great intellect. You follow a manual. Whole language, which tries to copy natural talent, requires a thorough understanding of learning needs. It guarantees failure for less intellectual teachers. If leaders had understood Whole Language and WCCrime, they would have shelved it.

Whole Language relies on: children learn to speak naturally and can learn to read similarly. Watch and guide them as they self-learn. Traditional reading is teaching skills step by step until the student learns to read. Detailed teacher manuals, written by reading experts, provide sequential lessons. Follow the lessons, and students become readers.

Whole language experts believe that many students waste time learning step by step. They can skip steps and become readers. So, the burden is on the teacher to determine if the student can skip a step. It requires spontaneous observation and deep knowledge of necessary skills—scholarly teachers, the enemies of WCCriminals.

Outstanding teachers used traditional manuals that assured learning. They'd plug in creative lessons such as a class play, newspaper, or class story. They'd run a three-ring circus, with children learning at their own pace. Researchers tried to figure out a way everyone could do that.

It was an admirable but unrealistic goal. Without step-by-step manuals, many teachers substituted the fun parts as if they were teaching reading. Teachers must recognize missing skills and teach them, which takes more work, brain power, and spontaneity. Thus, teachers began to fail at teaching reading.

Reading specialists take dozens of courses to become experts at teaching reading. Other teachers take one course. Most teachers need more training to help students find their way. If only great minds at the universities who came up with Whole Language knew who would teach it. If only great minds at universities would recognize the need to know this before letting it take over.

Whole language is a beautiful way to teach reading for those who get it, but it is a disaster for those who don't. And with no leadership to figure out who would get it or who we have in our classrooms, it brought down scores. This sloppy pattern needs to change.

A proficient curriculum will lead to success in all subject areas. Democracy teaching must be lodged in a thought-out curriculum rather than left to teachers. The example of Whole Language and how it brought down reading scores when widely used illustrates the need for a step-by-step teachers' manual for every subject. That way, less academic-minded teachers will not skip important lessons as many do now. Once proficient, teachers can operate less from manuals and more from insights. Yet, some will always need manuals. An authentic principal needs to distinguish.

Education will change once we banish WCCrime and ensure competent teachers hold curriculum power. They know what works. Curriculum decisions must reach down to grade levels, which I address later.

The second thing I'd do is turn teaching into a profession. It's called a profession by those who have never had a teaching job or by WCCriminals luring teachers into a web of deceit. It's a pretense offered to compensate for low pay. I'm not alone in this thinking. In "When we fail education, we fail democracy," at

Edsource.org, teacher Bill Conrad said,[32] "While there are many outstanding educators, there are not enough highly qualified professionals to turn teaching and administration into a real profession yet."

Rather than an opinion, here's a definition: "Core characteristics of professionalism are Competence, Knowledge, Integrity, Respect, Conscientiousness, Emotional Intelligence, Appropriateness, and Confidence."

These qualities grow no roots among administrators who lack morals or teachers who operate like puppets. Most teachers would follow orders that make no sense in a heartbeat. And if they had emotional intelligence, they would find a new career once they discovered the psychological battlefield. Professionalism cannot exist in a world of predators and prey. A field that needs to measure up more to warrant proper research or a solid connection with our nation's esteemed universities is no profession.

In the 1800s, Horace Mann made our schools pillars of democracy. One of his main principles was that well-trained, professional teachers must provide education. Society has changed. Women's liberation, computers, social media, and less fear of religion reign, but education hasn't changed.

Administrators once allowed spirited teachers to perform their magic, which compensated for the administrators who couldn't. These teachers led, although not on paper. They were like the "woman behind the man" model that dominated most marriages. Now that dynamic women choose actual professions—equal partnerships too—and WCCriminals purge the few called-to-teach teachers from their fiefdoms, only the "know little about how children learn" administrators shape democracy's foundation.

Plus, the fear of going to hell seems to be a thing of the past. Whether antiquated religious threats are admirable, they kept many people obeying laws. Churches should modernize and point out that hell is not an elevator with a 15-person limit. Instead, it has those invisible boundaries that work for dogs, and this generation's hell will be expansive. I don't plan to find out personally, but it makes sense if hell ever made sense.

No modern education leader has recognized the need to fortify these pillars based on these changes. All education leaders since Mann have proven they aren't capable. They have yet to notice societal changes. They have not seen WCCrime, or worse, noticed and did nothing about it. The leader must be an educator. A called-to-teach person must lead, not a business person or anyone who did not choose education.

I am curious to know how Horace Mann took the reins. I wonder if the people he worked among were as hollow as the ones leading education now. That includes all Department of Education secretaries, especially the ones who secured that job after being involved with false dropout rates during the Bush administration. We need a leader to do what needs to be done in modern times—to elevate education and provide guardrails against it slipping backward.

Making teaching a profession and connecting it with prestigious universities are steps two and three. Fourth, I'd create a teaching position that requires the completion of a to-be-invented scholarly degree with a salary and ranking commensurate with administrators and cease giving administrators 552%-766% more than a starting teacher as they do in Missouri.[33] These typical salary discrepancies make no sense when great teachers are the rainmakers.

I'd add these graduates at each grade level, making one teacher responsible for that grade level's curriculum, thus creating a master teaching position. This position would pay like other respected professions. It would solve the problem of inappropriate and deficient curriculum while carving a teacher/scholar path comparable to other professional paths, such as graduating from law school.

A master's degree in education, as it is, is not enough for these master teachers. I taught with a teacher with a master's degree who didn't know what the word "prose" meant. I'm suggesting a more scholarly track that attracts the best minds to a more sophisticated education undergraduate program and a more challenging master's degree. There is a need to revamp teacher education to upgrade teaching into a profession that attracts those who could and should lead, such as the teacher you'll meet in the next chapter.

There will always be tiers of teaching ability. We need a way to designate and appropriately reward these tiers. An entirely different teaching position would solve this problem in a way that performance bonuses never could.

Offering bonuses to teachers amid WCCrime is a joke. If they cared about performance, they would never have terminated teachers like so many of the NAPTA teachers who gave their hearts and souls to the job! However, performance bonuses for principals who attract and keep called-to-teach teachers, which they then share with these teachers, make a lot of sense when crime is no longer the way of life in education.

Since, in my vision for reform, principal salaries will be much closer to teaching salaries to discourage opportunists from becoming principals, performance bonuses based on excellent teaching under their watch make sense.

Having a university counselor say I was too dynamic to stay in the classroom speaks volumes about what's wrong in education. It confirms that teaching is not a profession. Children need dynamic teachers. Why would a person like me, a kid whisperer, ever want not to be with children? Was she thinking I'm too dynamic to accept the salary, so I'd want to go into administration? Probably.

Teachers like me never want to go into administration. We enjoy performing our magic with children. The classroom has to be dynamic for us to stay. And, above all, that means no incompetent warlord bossing us around. We must treat those who know how to make learning happen like artists who need creative space to accomplish things that administrators could not. Leadership must also originate from excellent teachers, not from administrative types with limited experience in the classroom telling teachers what to do.

The way it is now, we have teachers who don't like teaching science, who don't bother to teach science—more on that later—and new issues like media literacy needing emergency development. What the master teacher figures out for her class, she shares with her team. That way, teachers who are great with children but struggle intellectually have academic guidance.

Further, a great principal must learn more about the curriculum to provide sufficient intellectual guidance. There is a curriculum director who does that without input from the teachers. That is a higher-paid position that I would integrate into the master teaching position, so the intellectual aspect, the grade-level know-how, and the money are part of a master teacher profile.

We must apply intellectual analysis to determine what and who is teaching it at each grade level. By creating a new position like this, the nature of education will attract authentic professionals.

Also, knowing how learning works is essential to good teaching. The grade-level leader would learn brain-based research, apply it when making curriculum decisions, and teach it to the team. This leader would also consult with the grade below to develop continuity. And would not allow effective programs, such as the vocabulary program I invented, to slip through the cracks. It's decades later, and no other teacher has ever learned what worked magnificently. Teacher leaders need to have equal power to principals.

An experience I had with sex education shows flaws in the curriculum this would correct. When they moved me to fifth grade, I was to teach sex education for the first time. I inquired about specifics from my peers and received vague references to the content of the curriculum. They told me to write down the children's questions and that we would answer them after a field trip on this subject. There needed to be a written curriculum. There wasn't one.

Soon after the year started, my teammates shared a film to preview for use with this unit. At one point in the educational movie, it showed a married couple standing next to a bed with a narrator saying that sexual intercourse usually takes place in the bedroom between married couples. Although the principal had given this film to the team to preview, and the others had felt it worthy of consideration, I had a problem with the word "usually." Maybe it was because I was a parent, and none of the others, including the principal, were.

I suspected that a student might ask, "Where else does it happen? Who else does it?" leading to discussions of pornographic films, teenagers in cars, or topics inappropriate to discuss. I relayed my discomfort with the film; the film evaporated.

What didn't evaporate was the contents of the film and the name of what I was to teach. It led me to believe that teaching about sexual intercourse was part of the curriculum. As my students asked questions, I wrote them down as instructed.

To my surprise, when the field trip took place, the discussion dealt only with body changes, taught to the boys and girls in separate rooms. This was precisely what I had learned in fifth grade. It was puzzling. There was no mention of how a baby was formed, simply how bodies changed in puberty. Why had they considered that film? I now had a list of questions I would have to avoid and a longer list of questions of my own about the curriculum. Why wasn't there a written curriculum on something this important?

New teachers join grade levels, but only teachers new to the school receive mentors to help with materials and methods. I, a teacher who taught for four years at another grade level, had no information on the topic. She assigned no one to help me, although the others helped when I asked.

Wasn't that the principal's job to ensure I correctly taught a controversial subject? Parents expect caution. Why did they circulate a film discussing sexual intercourse to include in a curriculum that didn't mention sexual intercourse? This irresponsible handling of such a delicate topic was disturbing.

Since principals prioritize building false cases against teachers they don't want around, regardless of their talent, principals are too busy playing politics. They don't worry about the welfare of the children, even in an arena as controversial as sex education. They do not see their job as a duty to the children, parents, or society. They see their job with opportunistic eyes.

They play games rather than think, create reality, or live in integrity. This is scary to those of us who have viewed this negligence and lack of concern for children up close. A Russian Roulette-like curriculum thrives while fear blankets the mountains to the outside world with thick clouds.

In hindsight, I removed a bullet of harm aimed at our children. It was rare that they heeded my analysis of things like that film, and especially that it did not come back to bite me. I suspect the topic was too controversial to stir something up against me. They let me be the child protector I was and still am. Each grade level needs a teacher like me in charge of the curriculum to safeguard what is taught and not taught.

The sex education example shows a door opened to an unsuitable discussion in a value-laden province. To this day, what occurred mystifies me. The principal suggested adding a film about sexual intercourse, not knowing that our sex education curriculum didn't include sexual intercourse. Having taught the curriculum, the teachers knew the film was inappropriate but apparently didn't want to anger the principal. They were unwilling to tell me that the curriculum did not teach that. It might make the principal mad. How much more dysfunctional does it get?

I know one of these teachers was bright. Fear, a product of a harsh top-down education system, made her a dummy. How can we educate the public when fear rather than critical thinking drives the system? How can adults, behaving like children, mold the next generation? Teachers acting like battered wives cannot lead anyone to a worthwhile place. Think what this implies when it comes to school shootings. Terrified teachers can't be proactive. Looking the other way is the safe way.

A curriculum must be smooth and effective, not sloppy. Material that's part of the curriculum but omitted is another issue grade-level leadership would prevent.

The principal moved me from fourth to fifth grade and ordered me to teach two science classes, hoping I would quit. For two years, I had many of the same students, as well as a few students from the other three fourth-grade classes. The day they opened their science texts, I pointed out that the book was like last year's edition, and several hands waved. Each had Mrs. T the previous year. In unison, they said, "We didn't have science last year. Mrs T doesn't like science. We had self-esteem instead."

I am not making this up. Not only had that teacher, a favorite of the principal who would have earned the performance bonus had one existed, neglected to teach the curriculum, but she replaced it with a topic that deserves another book. There's too much praise on the self regardless of what the self achieves. This is another reason why we have self-centered creatures rather than citizens.

Once you understand WCCrime, you will realize that focusing on self-esteem rather than achievement was no accident. It diminished the gifted and future leaders. It equalized critical thinking into worthlessness. Great students and teachers needed leveling since not-so-great students composed the WCCrime leadership. Intelligence became a threat when corruption without consequence became the game.

The principal did not care what Mrs. T did as long as she had the proper level of fealty and helped leadership push out quality teachers. Her curriculum choice was a delightful substitution now that schools are about what works for the criminals running them.

And suppose you doubt the manipulative nature of assigning honor to each child regardless of their scholarship. In that case, I'll help change your mind. They didn't put lousy athletes on teams to make them feel good about their bodies or students lacking social skills in leadership roles to feel good about their lack. They equalized scholarship to diminish the mind's importance. WCCriminals need us dumb. With limited minds dumbing down schools, intellectuals can't monopolize power. Based on society today, they did great at that!

My principal proved that she didn't care about science. She switched me from fourth to fifth grade, so I would have to teach a sophisticated fifth-grade science course to two classes. She should have inquired about my background in science. My last college course in science was thirty years prior. I had a Master's in reading and had focused my studies on language.

The principal had surprised me with this assignment in front of my fourth-grade team. I saw through her and responded, "That's great. I had a good aptitude in science." That was true. Remember, I outwitted the rocket scientists in my advanced high school chemistry class? However, I didn't choose to pursue it and needed more current knowledge. Shocked that her ploy backfired, an unguarded response slipped. "Oh, that's great. I couldn't teach science. I don't know what I would do if I had to teach it."

We had the same certification, and she couldn't handle science. Her response revealed that she assigned this complicated lab course to me, hoping I couldn't cope. Children as pawns, why not, was her mantra. She likely knew Mrs. T didn't teach science and factored that in when she ordered me to teach it. I bet she thought, "Teachers don't like science. What a grenade I hold in my hands!»

To bolster my science knowledge, I visited a local organization that sponsored our scientific field trips. The person in charge asked me for my primary area of concentration in science. I explained that I didn't major in science, and she responded, "Aren't the parents furious about not having a proper science teacher in such an affluent district?"

The woman knew how wrong this was. I guess I was to fabricate an area of focus and run out of the building. I did not know what a Stepford teacher was to do in that situation. But I knew that telling the truth was not it! I had researched the National Science Foundation's recommendation for science teachers. They recommended having a science specialty starting in the fifth grade, the grade I was to teach. "Why would the NSF count if the law didn't?" I thought.

I conveyed the unprincipled principal's quote about science to the Board, pleading with them to listen to what the principal was doing. At my hearing, a witness confirmed that the principal said she couldn't teach science and acted surprised that I could.

The Board didn't care, and the hearing officer didn't care. In time, I proved nobody cared.

Later, when the hearing officer, Harvard graduate Rubin, decided my dismissal case, he declared that the teacher must "save face." He deemed me unprofessional for telling a parent the truth about my lack of science skills when the parent inquired. He found it even worse that I told a student to ask the other science teacher, who had a science background, a question the student had posed to me. Every fifth grader had Mr. B as the science teacher for years. This year, the disposing of me took center stage, not science, not the children.

I was to not tell them, to cover up, lie, and deceive. Real teachers believe in the Golden Rule: "Do unto others what you would want done unto you." We want to know the truth about the schools where we send our children. We would be angry if our children's teachers covered up information. This belief guides how we practice our profession.

In his opinion, I was to cover up in the same way an HMO doctor is to pretend you don't need to see the cancer specialist when it costs too much. He opined that a teacher's duty is public relations and saving face, not to ensure schools are run in the best interest of students. Most doctors are miserable practicing medicine this way. Most teachers submit. Why? Are teachers less ethical than doctors? No. The reason is TEACHER ABUSE.

A doctor can leave an HMO and still be employable. But they smear teachers who speak the truth. They defame and cleanse them from the profession. Few believe them; their career is over. The predatory administrators and sycophant hearing officers have a magic wand to make teachers go away. As sex abusers know their victims will not be believed, administrators know they're safe. It is time we took those wands away.

This Harvard graduate's decision said, "Teachers are obligated to lie to make their superiors look good. Karen Horwitz is unprofessional for refusing to hide embarrassing information from parents." He operated from the premise that education is a business that belongs to those in charge, not a public service.

My vision is not about "saving face." It is about "revealing face." The goal is to get enough teachers to speak out so the public believes us. Then, exile the scoundrels from this profession so we provide a solid education and create prepared citizens, thus fortifying democracy.

Harvard proved its failure to uphold and value the discipline of education, thus our democracy, via one of its shameful graduates. To Rubin, education is about something other than doing what is suitable for children. It is about politics. To him, those of us with integrity, who will not sell out children, are the cancer that must be stopped. With the flare of a flamingo dancer, Rubin waved WCCrime into the court.

New special education regulations made hiding teacher backgrounds from parents unlawful the following year. I was not the only person who thought parents had rights. I was the only person who seemed to care about the school's purpose. But, this is another law they'll ignore.

"Called-to-teach" teacher power is the key to success. Some teachers must be elevated from the bottom of the hierarchy. This new master position needs to be year-round so that these teachers can focus on students during the school year while gathering information to enhance the curriculum over the summer. The extra months of work would warrant a pay increase in addition to a pay increase reflecting the higher level of this position.

This plan to elevate teachers within grade levels by melding curriculum responsibilities into their jobs would attract the best and the brightest. It would encourage prestigious universities to alter education's stepchild status. They would have a greater purpose in welcoming education as research-worthy as they educate these more scholarly students.

You can count famous education leaders on one finger, and it's been centuries since that one became well-known. John Dewey, a philosopher and psychologist, and others have impacted the direction of instruction from outside the field of education. No educator has shined a light on education's basic structure or leadership as it has deteriorated over the years.

School choice surrenders Mann's vision for a healthy democracy by diluting public education with no plan to fix it. The business minds that believe competition will cause the public schools to improve are wrong for reasons beyond WCCrime. Education is an ideal that thrives in people's minds and spirits. It gets lost when monetized. It needs great thinkers and believers who are not focused on money. The business world misunderstands education. Their attempts to lead education into a world of competition energized rather than eradicated WCCrime.

Current "leaders" focus on policy issues rather than on WCCrime. They either act as if crime disappears without law enforcement or indulge in it upon discovery. I Googled a list of current education "leaders." I have contacted many about WCCrime and have rarely heard back. They lead as they led the remodeling of the deck of the Titanic without considering a structural problem. Since Mann, we've not had a leader with the depth to visualize the moral cancer lurking deep within education.

This was not a need in Mann's time. Teachers were religious figures eager to give their lives for the ideal of education. Education was a sacred practice—a sanctuary. When our country transitioned to a trickle-down economy in 1980, opportunists in the education world saw education as a business opportunity. As with all unregulated businesses, a free-for-all took place, allowing white-collar crime to trickle down, too.

If we create this needed grade-level master position, we will kill many birds with one stone. It includes turning teaching into a profession, connecting to prestigious universities, providing a solid education and citizens, and fortifying democracy. Whole language would flourish within this structure. Teachers would not fail to teach a subject they didn't like, with grade-level leaders guiding the curriculum. This would elevate the profession. Leadership would emanate from academically inclined, loving teachers rather than ambitious, self-centered administrators.

The fifth step deals with parents, the other beneficiaries of children who become productive citizens. Due to WCCrime's divide, parents feel the need to use social power. Efforts to reunite them must take place. The PTA is a mainstay in schools. WCCrime impacts this, too. Parents report abusive treatment if they do not go along with administrators' sketchy ideas.

The parent who joined my group, thrilled to discover why teachers had been so unhelpful and uncaring—thinking they were Satan—reverberates in my mind. Her seeing teachers in such a mistaken way says that WCCriminals have succeeded so well at turning parents against teachers that had their goal been authentic schools, they could have been great. Or could they? They were good at promoting hate, just the opposite of what good teachers promote.

Our schools need administrators with teacher's hearts. Administrators must rise from dedicated teaching. Now, they endure teaching for a short time to obtain power. We need to lengthen that time! Once we eliminate WCCrime and put public servants in charge of this, this fifth step—uniting parents and teachers—will fall into place. You can count on that.

My sixth step is a revamping of salaries. We must reward those worth the most. Great teachers are the key to a thriving democracy. Yet, we pay principals two to three times more and superintendents way more. Administrators who attract and retain a staff of hero teachers would be worth many times a teacher's salary. Now, a WCCrime principal cannot trash a hero teacher quickly enough.

And deficient principals feed their egos, going after gifted teachers. Most principals taught only a few years before they rose in status. Few were excellent teachers, which is why they earned their administrative certification. Power explodes in their brains. They treat teachers in a way that comforts their egos rather than benefits society.

Many teachers become administrators because their big egos make them bad teachers. Hero teachers don't have big egos; that's what allows them to put children first! We currently pay people with big egos way more than those who benefit society. Whether this stems from the historical male domination model or ignorance, it needs to change in education.

Lower salaries for inexperienced teachers are appropriate; they should increase with experience. The exception is the new crop of innovative teachers that top schools educate to become grade-level masters. They will remain in the classroom as leaders. We need to establish a new track for an entirely new leadership role. Some of these leaders will switch to administration, but only after training an equally qualified replacement.

This means leaders of substance will make decisions. Their salaries will start out much higher. They will be worth the higher salaries now wasted on shallow administrators. These master teachers will also integrate needed lessons in democracy and citizenship. As the keepers of democracy, a role not before visualized, these teachers will become education's gold.

Thinking through how to reform education without understanding the realities of WCCrime and the lack of intellectualism is foolish. Business minds are not going to get it right. An MBA lacks knowledge of education's needs. It requires inside experience, success, and an understanding of the wrong direction education has taken. Education leaders must understand the "called-to-teach" soul and why this profile no longer fits in most of our schools. The wisest route would be to draw wisdom from the teachers who did not fit in our corrupted schools. They must pass their knowledge on.

I cannot stress enough how important it is to attract good students to education. We must make teaching an attractive career. During my last year earning my elementary education degree at the University of Illinois, a dorm-mate kept complaining about an education class we both had. I said, "It's so easy. I don't get why you're so upset." In a high-pitched retort, eyes teary, she said, "Karen, you don't understand because you're smart."

The education classes were so easy that I struggled to understand what smart had to do with it. I had to spend time doing things like making a papier-mâché pig mask, but nothing challenged my brain. I got that other required courses were sometimes challenging. The education courses all ranged from easy to ridiculously easy.

Once I knew that my college friend found simple courses hard, I surmised that many teachers must be like her. Yet the system, as it is, values us all as the same. That needs to change. We're not attracting bright people when we don't know or appreciate the difference. Those struggling, whiny types forge their way to leadership and often take revenge on competent teachers as they surpass them in power.

One reason education is so dysfunctional is some of the dumbest amongst us rise to the top with power plays, not smarts. They spend the rest of their lives making society pay for how bad they felt being the not-so-smart student. Their playbook of shutting out and shutting up the intelligent people in education lies at the core of what happened to democracy. They've woven throughout education like hair on a never-cleaned hairbrush.

By shifting power and money around, we'll protect against WCCrime returning. Intellectual teachers will provide fortification against wrongdoing that the weaker types accept. They will connect our schools to our universities. Administrators need to come from successful grade-level leaders. Then, we will no longer have power seekers in the lead.

The knowledge of why we need education must never slip away again. Improper acts will melt away once we fill education with bright, moral leaders. Hero administrators and successful teachers will lead, rather than teachers as loyal foot soldiers for administrators. Schools need to restart teaching democratic knowledge and mold character. They must operate like a democracy while modeling democracy for students to absorb starting in kindergarten.

A seventh step is to protect teachers' efforts in addressing students' unique needs, including mental health issues. When administrators closely shine a light on teachers, the opportunity for abuse escalates. Students with special needs must be "written up" to address their needs. Teachers whisper, "Don't write up a student if you want to teach in peace."

Much of the brutal harassment inflicted upon me evolved from the special needs committee. It included the blacklisting of me for helping my student opt out of remedial reading. He didn't need it. They didn't care.

I remember when the special education director boiled over in anger and blurted out with a spray of unwanted moisture, "You are always so full of facts. It's so absolutely frustrating dealing with you." He hurled more accusations like an eight-year-old boy screaming and pounding his feet, saying, "You never let me go anywhere." It was hard to decipher what infuriated him the most—my astute responses or that they came from a woman who reduced a middle-aged man to a petulant child. Likely, it was inexperience dealing with a teacher who dared to use her brain, an outlawed act.

There is a silent agreement. Teachers must treat administrators the way wives used to treat their husbands, who owned the marriages. Women were to idolize whatever idiotic words left their mouths, with no hint of judgment. Marriages were for the men and their egos, and women were to submit. Teachers have adopted that mantle in their relationships with their administrators. They allow what is right for the children to fade away. To him, facts offered to solve problems are bullets to dodge, not solutions to weigh. He was right. I never stopped using facts to solve problems.

This has to stop for the sake of children in general. We must stop breeding school shooters. WCCrime is like "Miracle-Gro" for troubled students. The special services department must provide insightful, empathetic counselors to help deal with challenged children. Insight on what to do with them unfolds from the "facts" he strongly condemned. Empathy emerges from an open heart, unlike his with a double bolt.

The enabler social worker at my last job was empathetic at one time. Our ruthless principal taught her that you go along with her or suffer. She changed from a warm colleague to someone with no business helping children. She should have been there to help me help my students. Instead, she took on pleasing the administrators who drove me out of teaching. She had no concern for what this did to my students. I recommend training counselors about WCCrime and having them work with grade-level leaders.

Hero teachers are incompatible with WCCrime. This is at the core of the school shooting problem, as discussed. However, having all educators rise to be heroes is ideal but unrealistic. A counselor's entire purpose is to help children with their emotions. So, it's even more detrimental when counselors betray students. To re-establish trust, we need hero social workers, not advantage-seeking social workers. We have created a twisted culture. It will take years for children to trust educators who sold out. Grade-level master teachers in charge of counselors would be a needed safeguard.

My eighth step would be placing strong, intellectual leaders on a vision committee. They need to add to the ideas I have suggested and have some teaching experience. Based on the people who join our online group, many great minds are ready and willing to lead. I would want them to develop a public relations agenda to help recruit better students to teach. They'd also contact universities to get on board with education as the democracy upholder it is to be.

Once revealed, investigated, and ended, there will be a learning curve for outsiders to understand WCCrime. They'll need to learn what happened to education and what needs to happen. These university connections must be based on ideals rather than money. The connection has to become more than doing what the powerful want.

My ninth step would be to educate all educators about WCCrime and the work ahead of us in moving on from it, a plan the vision committee would put together.

My tenth step, which would occur with step one, would be to get apologies and a plan for addressing the unions' capitulation to WCCrime. I have data showing what they did. I accept that the unions had no choice. So many people ignored me, from Oprah to you name it. This is a horrible can of worms. I get it. But what happened to our democracy is a barrel of poisonous snakes, so we have to open this can.

The unions need to admit that they succumbed to WCCrime. In detail, my first union attorney admitted that the union was corrupt. She wouldn't put it in writing, but she thanked me for doing what I was doing. She acknowledged the union forced her to throw teachers' cases. She said she had no choice but to keep telling me they couldn't find the hearing officer—a lie. And I am not sorry for repeating this. This is at the core of our problem!

She dropped off a box of correspondence that included a document with an admission. It showed that the local uni-serve director was on top of my situation because my husband was "a powerful corporate attorney." The union couldn't blow me off as usual; they did what they could to bury me.

Here's a recap of the Top Ten Steps for Reforming Education :

1. End WCCrime

2. Make teaching a profession

3. Connect education with prestigious universities

4. Create a leadership position at each grade level

5. Unite parents and teachers

6. Revamp salaries

7. Teaching experts address student welfare and special needs

8. Place strong, intellectual leaders on a vision committee

9. Educate all educators about WCCrime

10. Admissions and apologies from both unions

Data that validates success in education must guide us. Adam Grant's 2024 book, *Hidden Potential: The Science of Achieving Greater Things*, has just that. Despite finishing this chapter, I read his book to see if I missed anything. I did not find much, but I would add an idea from his book: looping, or having children stay with the same teacher for several grade levels.

I agree that's an effective practice, having had at least half of my class two years in a row when my principal ordered me to move from fourth to fifth grade. It's more demanding for a teacher to learn multiple curriculums. However, it reduces the time required to get to know students, making a teacher much more effective. My idea of grade-level leaders, my fourth step, would facilitate looping.

His book validates my visions even though he is amongst many intellects with no clue about WCCrime. High on the validation list is the importance of character development, which he says sets the ceiling to success since it prioritizes values over instincts.

I mentioned that teachers with depth mold students and help them develop character skills. Marginalized teachers, operating in fear, cannot. My teacher-as-influencer concept matches what he suggests for success. He claims having an effective teacher in kindergarten affects future salaries and that a "joyful illiterate kindergarten" should be our goal. He points out regretfully that in America, kindergarten is more like first grade. Earlier, I also pointed out the perils of early literacy.

Skilled teachers are education's bedrock, and their absence is its demise. Effective kindergarten teachers know that teaching academics too early is problematic beyond the readiness issue. He says that the most critical lesson in kindergarten is learning is fun. It fosters a love of learning and better character skills. Teaching academics too early displaces a needed focus on character development, which he credits above all for success.

"Children learn as they play. Most importantly, in play, children learn how to learn." O. Fred Donaldson. "Rushing children's development is a formula for turning them into who they are not. Letting them play is a kind means of meeting them where they are and encouraging their authentic unfolding." Vince Gowmon. Professional teachers would know this and plan lessons based on what they know rather than what administrators force on them.

Grant touts extra grading time so teachers don't "burn out." Actually, burning teachers out is a WCCrime agenda. He also mentions the importance of student welfare teams. These teams would spot troubled children if they relied on teacher wisdom rather than administrative whims. Currently, teachers live in fear of upsetting their bosses rather than in fear of enabling a student massacre.

He features Finland's education practices that made them number one in 2003—teachers as trusted professionals and principals involved in teaching. Both are part of my vision. He says that teaching is Finland's most admired profession. This is what reforming education in the ways mentioned herein would accomplish in our nation. He conveys Finland's motto: we can't afford to waste a brain. My motto: we can't afford to have social influencers controlling our children's brains!

He mentions that Finland's scores began to slip in 2009 and that they attributed it to the need to read more books. The internet is a challenge. Teachers must work hard to cultivate the reading of books as they are the gateway to opportunity.

Finland's slippage demonstrates that more than great schools are needed. I would now add a focus on media literacy to my top ten list. We must help students understand where and how to find truth and why reading books is crucial for success. Given such stark data, it's too important to be off my list! I had envisioned this as part of education's better university connections—better research and curriculums. I now think it needs to be mentioned. My reading his book is a perfect lesson in why we all must read books to succeed!

He discusses the lattice system for ideas, pointing out that top-down organizations often fail at problem-solving. He details how teamwork saved mineworkers in Chile in a way one would not see in the top-down education system that existed even before WCCrime.

My ending exclusive administrative control of teaching and structuring equal power for the academic-minded in education accomplishes a lattice rather than a top-down system. Collective teamwork, with teachers having the autonomy they have in Finland, ensures effective problem-solving. A culture that encourages students to thrive intellectually must value intellect in its teachers.

However, as I read his thoughts about how difficult it is to develop a student's hidden potential and pondered the title of his book, I kept thinking: potential is not that hidden for me. I've always seen it in my students. I know this is true for many of our NAPTA members. I know this is a gift that those of us called to teach possess, and that's why we've been so frustrated that we have no home in education.

Grant is an organizational psychologist. He has much to offer the world of education. However, those born to teach offer more. Until the world of education has a structure that can include people like us in a leadership capacity, student potential will remain a hidden challenge. Education leaders must own the gifts needed to help children soar so they can share them with others.

Administrators cannot again be so powerful that unions bend to them. Quality teacher leaders need power so that their interests have power. Education has to warrant more university participation. It cannot create a fraudulent world again. It must be an honored powerhouse. It must start producing great leaders.

Forty suggestions for federal and local change:

1. Create a panel of teacher/educator whistleblowers (Panel) to describe good administrators. Form a committee to create a lesson plan for educating about WCCrime: Why Education Reform Couldn't Have Happened but Can and Will Now;

2. Create a report detailing professional, as opposed to criminal WCCrime, i.e., acts that suppress good teaching and undermine a democratic atmosphere. Use it to create committees, federal and within school districts, to enforce it;

3. Find a leader of the caliber of Horace Mann from amongst whistleblowers;

4. The Panel must approve committee members; leader will determine the roles of the Panel v. committees;

5. Conduct congressional inquiry about WCCrime using this Panel and their publication;

6. Encourage cable news to interview Panels to educate the public;

7. Work with the FBI to allow WCCriminals to resign and lose their certification to avoid jail. There are too many to prosecute. Create a dollar amount after which they must charge;

8. With the Panel's guidance, the US Department of Education must help states establish teacher abuse hotlines to investigate complaints without identifying sources. Use this data to end WCCrime;

9. The committee will set up a plan that may include allowing those accused of WCCrime to return to classroom teaching for five years before reevaluating whether they can resume leadership roles;

10. Panel and/or committees decide policy regarding former WCCriminals. Forgiveness of administrators and accomplices that fess up on a case-by-case basis;

11. Education about WCCrime with suggested changes for the Department of Education, unions, lawyers, courts, and state education boards;

12. Required education about WCCrime for all educators;

13. Report any new WCCrime, criminal or civil wrongdoing. Deal with professional wrongdoing as per #2 above. Nip it in the bud;

14. Principals and grade level leaders equal power, salary— power balance to counter the administrative tendency toward greed;

15. Special services and guidance counselors—under both grade level leaders and principals;

16. Superintendents and assistant superintendents lower salaries—money shared with grade-level leaders;

17. Administrators must teach for ten years and have achieved grade level status for at least two years to qualify for leadership;

18. The committee determines bonuses for superintendents based on their ability to run a democratic system and uses teacher input rather than top-down dictatorships;

19. Use only standardized achievement tests that include student IQ's to evaluate teacher effectiveness and connect bonuses to effectiveness to avoid punishing teachers for low-level students;

20. Teacher leaders equal with administrators to board members;

21. Increase teacher salaries as appropriate; increase classroom funds to ensure that teachers do not need to use their salaries;

22. Empathetic counselor/social worker responsible for keeping tabs on troubled children—no forgotten children, especially those with hopeless parents. Assistance and protection for home visits;

23. Curriculum leader rising from grade level leader-answering to board equal to superintendent—avoid power disconnected from the classroom—curriculum protection;

24. Curriculum leader with research skills and connection to universities;

25. Curriculum leader/democracy expert; on top of social media education; develops solid democracy curriculum that includes strategies to meet diversified needs.

26. Regular teacher evaluations of leaders;

27. PTA meetings with leaders and principals for parents to express concerns; establish PTA for secondary and higher education;

28. Federal funds partially based on compliance with reform;

29. Too dynamic for classroom thinking must end;

30. Each state's superintendent association must be investigated and regulated as they appear to be a primary source of WCCrime;

31. The Department of Education must establish a network with top universities to encourage the development of advanced teacher training programs and enhanced teacher abuse research as part of the initial investigation of WCCrime;

32. Elevate university status via school districts; develop academic connections rather than only business connections;

33. The Department of Education must file a lawsuit to rid itself of WCCrime if discovered; no more assuming administrators are public servants;

34. Education about WCCrime available through PTA to help parents understand the adjustments being made; it will take time for teachers to get over fear and be candid with parents;

35. Create a K-12 committee (possibly universities) to educate and advise to prevent school shootings using advice from whistleblowers who know how WCCrime made protecting children impossible. Ending WCCrime is the primary solution to end school shootings. Establish a program to identify troubled children and give them hope, the cure for their rage;

36. The Panel needs to get involved with and help choose new leadership. Choose leadership from those who opposed WCCrime and acknowledge that the union or current leaders who have not worked to end WCCrime cannot take a leadership role.

37. Education must undergo a shift comparable to the 1800s when Horace Mann turned religious-oriented schools into a public education system without concern it would become a system of opportunists rather than public servants. It must shift to a system that protects public service by admitting the inundation of WCCrime and elevating scholarship to attract educators of substance;

38. States now control education. Our nation will become more harmonious once we have authentic schools. Then, have discussions about altering state control somewhat so the eradication and prevention of WCCrime remains nationwide;

39. The ultimate goal is to elevate education status in this nation in terms of scholarship and trust. It will then attract the best and the brightest. WCCrime has filled it with the exact opposite types. Start this reform ASAP to create a more informed electorate for the 2024 elections;

40. Use the Enterprise theory cited on p. 52 of former FBI Acting Director Andrew McCabe's 2019 book, *The Threat*. It allows investigators to structure their understanding of crimes that are too vast to comprehend. It is perfect for WCCrime, which vandalized our democracy because it was so hard to grasp.

Outlawing WCCrime will shift leadership from selfish to service-minded types. It will feel like someone waved a magic wand. The union president who perjured herself at my hearing saved her career at more than my expense. She did it at democracy's expense, too. The librarian, who went to an attorney with me and two other teachers for protection from age discrimination, did likewise. She signed an affidavit saying she didn't see any age discrimination at our school when she sought relief from age discrimination the previous year.

I'm sure they and the teachers who stared at ceilings in shame will welcome the end of WCCrime so they can apologize. They were decent people who had to endure an indecent system. They sacrificed their moral compasses to survive. They were not fraudulent public servants like those who led our district. They were victims, too.

It's a minority of people that benefit from it. Many do their best to limit wrongdoing to the extent they can. They go along just enough to stay employed. Trying to restrict WCCrime means settling for unsuccessful schools that they think could be worse and, in time, will be worse. Being a little lawless is like being a little pregnant. Both stay "a little" only for a while.

The majority will rejoice to have real schools. And as disappointing as the union was, they will welcome freedom from WCCrime's oppression. Many years after participating in that fraudulent hearing, the union president sent me a Facebook friend request. Had her use of her power to destroy my career haunted her? The "friend" request lingered for over a year, then disappeared.

Was maintaining the lies getting to her? I chose to ignore it, knowing nothing had changed. I couldn't forgive what she had done in the past, as it was still taking apart our schools. Plus, by the time of the "friendship" request, Trump had entered our lives. I kept thinking: she helped make that happen.

WCCriminals are submerged in power; the rest comply. The latter are realists. My replacement union lawyer told me, "No one will ever get anywhere doing what you're doing." The world of education counts on that and behaves accordingly.

For that reason, exposing and ending WCCrime will feel magical. With WCCrime, schools will never, ever change. Without it, schools will miraculously change. Teachers chose their careers to serve the public. A handful of educrats seized power and created their very own mob-like environment. It's not an entire system of gangsters on board for an easy life.

Once WCCrime ends, it will feel like we freed concentration camps. Powerless teachers let WCCrime rather than their ideals guide them. They feel shame. They will eagerly put enabling behind them. This is unique corruption. Most educators want to serve the public. A few figured out how easy it is to control teachers and break the law. Figuring this out is hard. Exposing it is hard. Ending it will be easy.

We need enough people to demand an end to WCCrime. I want to do what the Kardashians do—influence people. I do this work so democracy won't end, but school shootings will.

We need teachers to be heroes again. Teachers must matter! I'm not writing this book for money. It is easier to get rich by buying a lottery ticket. If you think I am doing this for anything other than public service, I failed to educate you about the bell curve—how people are different. Or your soul is too close to Charles Manson's, incapable of knowing an idealist. If you have otherness in your soul, it will connect to mine as mine does to yours.

WCCriminals don't have otherness. A 2008 article, "The Smearing of Armand Fusco,"[34] reported that Dr. Armand Fusco, the 2005 WCCrime warrior, finally became a target. For years, he remained unscathed despite having exposed school corruption. In time, educrats accused him of "dreaming up corruption to sell books." It's logical that materialists project fixation with money on others with values foreign to theirs. Yet, they're wrong about the profitability of books. The article said:

> Rather than embrace the retiree's warnings and proposed reforms as vital tools that would surely be useful to rebuild taxpayers' faltering faith in government schools, educrats' first reaction was to pretend Fusco didn't exist. His offer to conduct corruption-fighting workshops for the Connecticut Association of Boards of Education and Connecticut Association of Public School Superintendents was ignored...

When shunning didn't work—when it became clear that Fusco was finding an audience with members of the media, elected officials, and good-government activists—the monopoly attacked…Last month, in a memo distributed to all Connecticut superintendents and board of education chairs, the executive directors of [Connecticut Association of Boards of Education and Connecticut Association of Public School Superintendents] claimed his' attacks' on government schools' are so far removed from the reality of public schools that we see no common ground to even have a conversation on this subject.' (Translation: We're afraid to debate him.)

It detailed WCCrime that occurred after Fusco's 2005 book:

In 2006, according to the *New Haven Register*, the West Haven Board of Education not only let friends and relatives of the board chairman and a school principal off the hook for essentially stealing services to which they weren't entitled, it has effectively lent them, interest-free, the money that they need to cover their misdeeds.' An investigation is reportedly underway into whether the New Haven School District exaggerated the number of projected students for a new school to inflate state subsidies. And a grade-changing scandal is swirling in the Windham School District…But as more officials and advocates solicit his aid—and more citizens grow concerned about the way waste and mismanagement in Connecticut school districts surely drive the state's runaway property taxes—the indefatigable reformer's credibility will only grow.

This authenticates the premise of this book. Materialists, who cannot lead with what they do not know, cannot grasp, and cannot respect, have a stranglehold on our schools. They control all the information about our schools. They have harnessed our society to unprincipled values and shut principled people out. They know Fusco isn't profiteering. He would have indulged in WCCrime if he were one of them! Instead, he devoted his retirement to exposing it.

Folks, WCCriminals are brazen. Educrats commit WCCrime confident that the public will never figure this out. They cover it up with arrogant statements such as the above. They think people are naive and too stupid to know that making money by self-publishing a book is rare.

Only best-selling books earn profits. Education books by unknown authors are never best sellers! Those of us who value ideas over spending money to publish books do this to be heard over what the cash-obsessed do to stigmatize and silence us. They will lie about anything to continue their profitable activities at the public's expense. Accusing Fusco of profit-seeking is laughable.

My educrats needed to terminate me on false and contrived grounds. Aware that a due process hearing would expose WCCrime, they offered a large settlement in exchange for my resignation. I turned them down, determined to create a paper trail of WCCrime. I spent over $300,000 on legal fees before giving up on lawyers and over $6,000 on court costs to take my case to the US Supreme Court.

I paid for courses on website creation and writing to create and maintain a website for 22 years. I paid to run a non-profit organization so I could locate abused teachers and like-minded citizens. I worked at this for almost three decades with no salary. Even if this book becomes a best seller, I will only recoup a small portion of what I spent out of pocket to stop these thieves from robbing us of our freedom. It has never been about money for those of us trying to expose WCCrime; it has been all about money for those partaking in it.

Alexandria Robbins' 2023 book, *The Teachers: A Year Inside America's Most Vulnerable, Important Profession*, captured what teaching is today. Please go to Amazon and read the book reviews to hear teachers' candid thoughts. They're a chorus of heartwarming and heart-wrenching emotions. Her book talks about what WCCrime does to a school without mentioning WCCrime. It confirms the unprofessional and chaotic world of education.

The reviews include a teacher whose teaching experience has been positive. Why didn't she mention her district if that's true? Another reads like a public relations bulletin from administrative staff, not uttering the "great" school district's name. It sounds like educrats performing damage control after Robbin's illustrative book.

However, almost all express gratitude for this honest book, with its rarely-told descriptions of teachers' lives. Most loved her book. One did not. She felt it sugarcoated the horrors teachers face. That reviewer wished Robbins had interviewed her so she could relay all that administrators don't want to be known—like what's in this book.

Her reviews provide data supporting the unprofessional nature of teaching that I decry. Having read this far, you know the why behind this dysfunction. They also confirm the deep natures of teachers. Almost every reviewer expressed passion for the job along with disappointment. They made it evident that teachers are a unique breed. You hear teachers who love teaching but struggle to find the light to thrive in this dismal "profession."

Teachers are the valuable gift we've returned. They are special people dealing with an obstacle course rather than a profession. Throughout, they mention demanding parents without the truth behind that—administrators set up parents to abuse teachers. Remember the parent who thought teachers were Satan before she found our website? Administrators force teachers to operate with their hands tied behind their backs so parents will despise and disrespect them. Manufactured hate protects WCCriminals. All lose in a system rigged for the powerful.

The book *The Teachers* presents a robust case for the reform I've proposed. Teachers are a force of nature. Administrators treat them as their abandonable toys when they are a spiritual phenomenon. Lack of appreciation and understanding of a great teacher is the root issue that needs reform. Teachers cannot thrive and do the things that make them who they are when immersed in WCCrime's toxic plastic rather than in the rich soil of respect.

I know a teacher's unique, magical nature is real because I have been a teacher and a parent. I accomplished wonders in the classroom while struggling as a parent. The charts that worked on my students became piles of rubble when used at home. Behavior modification ideas that sent my students soaring evaporated before my parental eyes.

It seemed my children fought me with greater intensity because they knew of my power to influence. They were determined to stop me from using it on them. And for the most part, they succeeded. (There's another book in me on that topic that I will never write! Writing books is not my thing. I would not have written this one if it were not for how dreadful our society has become. You can thank Donald J. Trump for this book.)

Teachers hold extraordinary God-given power. It became clear that this endowed power was only to teach other people's children, not to raise my own. That was nature's plan, which leaderless education smothered with WCCrime. The teachers' reactions to Robbins' insightful book reveal how our society treats this treasure—gasping for breath. WCCrime has almost eliminated this incredible power. It has been stealing it from society and forcing us to increasingly deal with social influencers educating our children.

Now that I have shared my vision for schools that will hold up our democracy, your homework assignment is to read about the Republican vision for us. I ask you to Google Project 2025 and learn what the end of democracy will look like. It ends the Department of Education. Currently, we have inept education leaders and those who have caved to WCCrime. According to this plan, Trump's cronies will run education.

WCCrime will allow for an easy transition. The only change will be that the administrators now taking advantage of all of us and the unions helping them do that will hand over their power and perks to Trump's cronies and become losers like the rest of us. WCCrime has taken us to a point where many citizens will accept Project 2025 as frogs in slowly heated water meet their fate.

This could not have happened had we had authentic schools. This won't happen if enough citizens vote out the party about to end democracy in the House of Representatives, the Senate, and the presidency, sending a message that democracy matters.

The question is: can or will the members of a society filled with students that our schools failed to educate appropriately be able to jump from the menacing water and assist in implementing this blueprint for democracy's future—attracting and supporting called-to-teach teachers, a needed counter-vision to protect us from the authoritarian plan for us—Project 2025? Or are we so hardened that we're okay with Project 2025, a real-life version of *The Handmaid's Tale*, and letting the guy who separated children from their parents to solve immigration issues handle education issues? In November, we'll know the answer.

The truth about WCCrime must scale mountains of propaganda and special interest that those holding power over our schools have erected to keep their game going. Truth must penetrate the minds and hearts of us, the people. We must demand an end to this corrupt system that is destroying our education and our future. It's time for us to stand up and fight for real, authentic schools. Otherwise, the future of education and what it impacts will remain grim.

Once we bring back the intelligent women Horace Mann could never have visualized as a pillar that education would, in time, lack, this stupidity takeover will end. Since he could not have imagined that women would become equal citizens one day and no other great leader who recognized education's importance would replace him, nothing was ever done about this monumental problem.

We must get involved and force those in power to dismantle WCCrime. It's time for us to stand up and fight for real, authentic schools. Without investigation of WCCrime, our democracy, now under siege, belongs to the highest power bidder, which, believe it or not, will get worse.

16
MEET THE FUTURE - AFTER WCCRIME

"The principal goal of education in the schools should be creating men and women who are capable of doing new things, not simply repeating what other generations have done."

Jean Piaget

"The secret in education lies in respecting the student."

Ralph Waldo Emerson

"If I were given one hour to save the planet, I would spend 59 minutes defining the problem and one minute resolving it."

Albert Einstein

I've defined the problem. However, it took more than 59 minutes. I appreciate you remaining with me. We can resolve it in one minute, however. End WCCrime. Then, upgrading the profession with those it has held captive will be easy.

I often think about how people with mediocre brains lead our schools when the intellect is at the core of what education needs to nurture. Suppose we were to fill our sports teams with coaches with mediocre athletic prowess. Imagine watching sports if we paid no regard to athletic ability. It would be unwatchable. That's the paradigm we now have in our schools.

You will not find many education graduates more talented than the NAPTA teachers WCCriminals cleansed from the system. They have college transcripts and awards to prove it. We have the wrong kind of minds leading. The people molding brains have yet to learn what a brain needs.

Mediocrity created a powerful vacuum that welcomed WCCrime. By making peace with mediocrity, educators have participated in the demise of democracy. It's as essential to bring back intellect as it is to eliminate WCCrime.

Our universities failed to recognize how sacred K-12 education is in a democracy. Now that women's liberation changed education forever, they need to make teacher education a valued curriculum. They need to ensure that dynamic people can remain in classrooms. They must encourage research rather than let significant studies on teacher abuse disappear into the black hole of disrespect. They need to connect with practicing teachers, not just power-seeking administrators.

They have let us down by doing none of the above. They are as guilty as the unions that went along to get along and helped teachers like me retire to please the powers that be. They are as guilty as public officials who ignored our pleas to investigate this. They are as guilty as the courts that rule based on an assumption that those running our schools are doing so for the benefit of our children and democracy. They are as guilty as the media, which did the same.

The January 2024 article, "40 Years After 'A Nation At Risk,' Key Lessons For Reinvigorating America's Teacher Workforce," is another "scholarly" article that fails to note WCCrime. These authors ignore the disposing of teachers who threatened lawless administrators during those years.

It said: "Both the quality of current teachers and the quantity of available talent to fill teaching roles in schools were sorely deficient, and prioritizing quality will limit the number of people who can meet the higher expectations." These "experts" had no clue that ending WCCrime would allow quality teachers to fit in. Encountering another group of experts operating with ignorance, I repeat ad nauseam: WCCriminals don't want quality teachers.

One comment highlighted how lost they are: "To address both teacher quality and quantity simultaneously would be a Herculean feat." Getting anything right is a Herculean feat where WCCrime freely flows. As long as teachers are human piñatas scheduled to burst into uselessness, he's correct. Once we make teachers leaders rather than education's roadkill, successful schools will be so easy that it will embarrass those who think like this!

In a 2023 article titled "Stop Bleeding and Start Leading: Dispelling Teaching's Greatest Myth is the First Step Towards Educational Reform," Chris Edwards, Ed.D, said, "The current American educational system de facto exists primarily for administrators, and educates students only to the degree necessary to maintain the administrative structure."

He has that right! He goes on: "The lesson is simple: a corrupt bureaucratic system will mask its bureaucratic corruption right up to the point where it collapses and takes everything else with it…Instead, reform must be built upon new ideas presented by teachers. Teachers themselves need to stop bleeding and start leading."

Yes, teachers must lead. However, that can only happen by ending WCCrime. Its ruthless teacher abuse renders teachers impotent. Plus, it's a system dependent on attracting people who accept marginalization since that's what women did before women's liberation. Given that the education structure was male-dominated until it became WCCrime-dominated, teachers cannot lead.

Edwards chose a perfect word when he said teachers must stop the bleeding. It implies violence, which is precisely what so many teachers face. However, it's psychological violence. They're more than afraid to suggest better programs. They know to pretend not to notice potential school shooters. Ask teacher Ed Cobin how he felt being criminally indicted for telling the police that a student brought guns to school. To administrators, teachers with opinions are enemies. Innovators' careers in WCCrime schools bleed to death.

The fact that Edwards has been allowed to break free from the Stepford mold suggests he is one of the lucky few who works at a school that cares about education. He's on the right track. Teachers must lead. That will only happen once it's recognized that it's more than a bulging bureaucracy. It's a mafia-like system working against the job of shoring up our democracy. It's unlawful and threatening for teachers. They can't survive fighting it. Administrators have way too much to lose, giving up this cash cow. Plus, jail threatens them once their corruption is known. And the unions are right there with them in the coverup.

He's right about what we need to do but wrong that it can be done without the power of government behind us. Until we expose WCCrime, nothing will change except the democracy that relies on real schools. That we will lose.

Assigning guilt will not solve this problem either. We need great teachers taking over leadership positions with minds capable of leading us away from this mess. We need 2024 to be the year education moved from the archaic system that thought becoming public was enough. Horace Mann led us to a place of stagnancy.

No great leader has recognized how stuck in a rut of ignorance we have become, how technology and women's liberation changed society, and how we lost so many great teacher minds due to it. These lacks welcomed WCCrime.

Rather than dwell on the mess these losses allowed, I want to show you that we don't need to create the kind of people who could turn education around. They exist. We need to attract them to a career in education so they can inspire others to be like them.

I want to introduce you to someone who could be the next Horace Mann but won't because he's leaving this profession after two years. Great minds like him will not remain in a vacant shell feigning to be a profession. There's no point. He knows he can only serve the public if he's connected to power.

In high school, he made a brilliant documentary on education. He described its hollowness without knowing its source. Throughout his documentary, he wove a yearning for education to make sense, to start working. He earned a Master's degree to teach, thinking he'd find that lost field of purpose in our schools. His vision showed a future leader. Yet he's moving on. He shared why with me:

On the surface, my story is a classic case of teacher burnout. A passionate young man feels a calling to become a teacher. It aligns well with his talents and his desire to contribute to a better world. He goes to school and becomes fascinated with teaching as both a science and a human art form; he's deeply inspired by the writings of John Dewey, Maria Montessori, Rudolf Steiner, and Paulo Freire. He begins working, and at first, it is exhausting but thrilling. Then, slowly but surely, the reality of the job sets in. The idealism and intellectual zeal that brought him into the profession begin to thin and fade. After a couple of years, he reaches a critical point where he must decide if this career is going to be healthy to stick with in the long run. Ultimately, he decides to leave.

Why are young teachers burning out and leaving the profession at what seems like a faster rate than ever? I only have my perspective to share. Many of my reasons are personal; for example, I'm becoming a father this year and will soon have many more responsibilities. I feel a stronger sense of urgency to find a higher ceiling of income, autonomy, and flexibility in my career.

Beyond the personal, there are many structural problems in schools—problems that are largely outside my control, and with which I know I can't continue to abide. I could write at length, for example, about the embarrassingly low expectations students are held to in reading and how that has ripple effects across every dimension of school. I could write about the "school-to-pharma" pipeline, where students are increasingly conditioned to pathologize and medicate away their personalities to conform to school cultures.

But out of all the structural issues I could expand on, I want to focus on junk services. The education industry today is flooded with junky, low-quality, plug-and-play technology and services that only solve superficial problems while deeply exacerbating others. Thanks to these junk services, many students, maybe a majority, are not being truly educated. They are being McEducated—sitting in front of cheaply made laptops and performing highly abstract, repetitive tasks which, in a Pavlovian fashion, gradually move them from one standardized benchmark to the next. Rather than learning through authentic experience, challenge, and mentorship, rather than building character and pursuing complex goals, students are clicking through online modules, patching ideas together with little substance or critical thought, and demonstrating their understanding through simplistic digital assessments.

This has the effect of demoting teachers from chefs to line cooks. As a new teacher, traditionally you are trained in curriculum development, class management, and educational psychology. Then, you would be thrown head-first into the job. After grinding through the early years, eventually, you would come out "the other side" as a seasoned teacher with a curriculum that you had built, tailored, and perfected for yourself over the years. Now, thanks to the glut of junk services either suggested or required by school districts, new teachers never get the opportunity to do this. The content of lessons, and even many aspects of how those lessons are delivered, is simply outside the scope of many teachers' jobs today.

The writing is on the wall: if you truly love teaching as a human science and art form, if you want autonomy and creative control over your classrooms, if it makes your skin crawl to watch a generation of students subjected to superficial, technology-based McEducation all around you, then this profession is not for you.

This is the key realization that is pushing me out of the field. It's not that I've burned out as an educator, or that I enjoy teaching less than I thought I would. It's that, despite all the time, money, and hard work I've dedicated, there are vanishingly few opportunities for me to thrive and grow in this profession. As the years go on, I can either become a McEducator and wait for my pension to kick in, or I can show myself the door. Given how much I truly love teaching, the choice is clear.

His explanation of why he's moving on adds color to my account of WCCrime, the force that watered education down the drain. He may have no idea why education is what it is today—most people don't—but he nailed what WCCrime has done—ended character development.

I loved his from-chef-to-line-cook analogy. It says it all. I would add "to-butcher" after the order taker line cook since the creativity that called-to-teach teachers possess deep within must be cut out of their souls, or they cannot be part of the WCCrime education era.

His fast food analogy brilliantly describes the education world. I, too, described education as food. I focused on education as the healthy food in life that has become desserts and addictive sugar. He took it further, labeling it as fast food—addictive sugar and chemicals disguised as healthy food. His analogy is better than mine since WCCriminals disguise everything!

Most of all, without realizing it, when describing all the junk technology and tools, he arrived at the heart of WCCrime and its focus on buying things. Kickbacks and under-the-table deals thrive around financial opportunities. Accessing money via buying stuff is the WCCriminal's scheme. He saw all the inferior equipment as junk academic choices. I see them as vehicles for productive embezzling.

The school that ended my career had a ton of tech equipment that just sat there because they didn't have people to teach how to use it. Many questioned why they would buy it to leave it sitting around. There were rumors. I didn't know what was true. I was too busy fighting off abuse to deal with more. But I do know that the Board let it happen, and they would want to avoid a person like me around with bandwidth available to look into it.

When he was seventeen, this teacher, who shared his thoughts with us, recognized that education made no sense. This teacher thought he could make it make sense by trying to teach. No teacher can. This book has explained why. Teachers are human piñatas scheduled to burst into uselessness. I repeated that vivid, accurate descriptor, hoping it would remain in your minds long enough to get you to want to make this book go viral. We could change that and perhaps hold onto him if we accomplish that!

This young man's intellect earned him a free ride at a well-thought-of university. His refusal to accept mediocrity left him with no option but to find a new career. There are many more like him leaving education. Great minds cannot tolerate the mindlessness at its core. Teachers who can play the needed politics to stay on top of this discipline soon realize they'll become outcasts to the malfeasants making such bad decisions. Intellectuals care about their profession, which gets in the way of those who do not. It doesn't have to be this way. We can make great teachers into leaders rather than into education's roadkill.

All we need are voices educated about what happened to education to speak out with me to resurrect real education. Do your share to make this happen. Share this book. Get these truths known. Show this young man there is a place for him as a leader in education. Stop our threatening future that will erase democracy and so many of our freedoms from happening.

Opportunists, not humanitarians, scammers, not visionaries, lead in the world of education. This will only change if the discipline becomes respected and attracts excellent minds. If a place opens up for called-to-teach, brilliant souls like him to remain in education and serve our democracy, we can all move out of this darkness. Let's make education part of the prestige world and close the door on WCCrime.

17

DEEP STATE OR DUMB STATE?

*"Education is the most powerful weapon which you
can use to change the world."*

Nelson Mandela

*"The further a society drifts from the truth, the more
it will hate those who speak it."*

George Orwell

*"Government, even in its best state, is but a necessary evil;
in its worst state, an intolerable one."*

Thomas Paine

You must know by now that I see great teachers as a Kardashian antidote. I believe in a free market, and what the Kardashians sell has its place. Our problem is that great teachers lost theirs. I want to create a balance between them. When we lost our balance, democracy toppled.

Mom Kardashian is a great marketer. Her daughters are, too. I'm different. Money didn't call me. I have two daughters who each found a slot doing work to make this a better world—one in public health and one managing charity donations. Both needed meaningful work; money is secondary to them.

Neither made the education mistake, though. Even if my daughters hadn't seen how the education world had treated me, they knew better. They knew meaningful work in education was a thing of the past and our nation's root problem. Nevertheless, letting authentic education rest in peace with dial telephones and handwritten thank-you notes is not okay. It was our stability. It was our sure thing.

It may be hard to believe that intelligent people once led it. When I attended my daughters' college graduations, especially the daughter who earned a Ph.D. at Yale, it was clear that no one in their scholar-filled lives was anywhere near education. If I had to find one thing that took education down, it's the lack of great minds choosing it.

When I say what education needs, I'm not talking about good brains alone. I'm talking about smarts with depth of character— being born on the side of the bell curve that makes a person have to make a positive difference in this world.

Education leaders need to be people like you met in the last chapter: people who find learning easy and are passionate about making this a better world for others. Once called-to-teach souls hold power, a democracy birthed and nurtured by loving souls will replace our wayward democracy. These are people who appear as suckers to Trump. They are so opposite that they can only be ships passing at night.

Smarts are essential, but more is needed. An intelligent person created Teach for America and made lots of money while adding some cement to WCCrime's foundation. We need intellectual idealists who can grow the heart of education to lead it away from its stupid place and make it work, not intelligent people who use it as a stepping stone to make money.

Don't look to any current education or union leader to change what they've held in place for years. Their having held WCCrime in place for decades is all you need to know—they're the problem, not the solution.

Chapter 15 shows how I'd change the structure so it could and would thrive. The key to that working is attracting and keeping the right people in leadership. They must be intelligent and have attended good colleges, but that isn't enough. There's a list of names in Congress who fit that profile, such as Ted Cruz and Elise Stefanik, to name a few, who should be far from our schools.

Keeping education salaries on the lower side was protection against opportunists like them. We still need that protection. That's why I suggested spreading out the high salaries that administrators now earn so they reward real success while adding only a little money to the big picture. Education needs to pay a decent wage and become a respected discipline to attract the people it needs. It has to welcome called-to-teach types. They need to lead.

That will happen with minimal money added as long as schools reward competence. Please reread Chapter 16 if you still need to absorb the profile of a called-to-teach teacher. He moved on over wrong policies and wrong opportunities, not money. He rejected the brainless ways he knew would lead nowhere positive for him. And besides, WCCriminals have stolen so much money, ending it might provide all the funds we'll need.

I've shared my life so you can see the people we need in education. The great thing about a democracy is that we are all different. Still, we fit together like a giant puzzle that produces a beautiful picture. Our schools help us find our place in that picture.

As hard as it is to believe, there was even a place in this giant people puzzle for Trump. Had more of the pieces of this puzzle had a solid education, they would have remained in place rather than have allowed him to grab seventy-million of them and put them into a giant, jumbled wad, now saturated with his super glue-like hate. A solid education teaches us who we are and where we belong. If enough people know that, we can carry the burden of those who don't.

Decades ago, we started becoming lost because our schools began deteriorating. We can no longer see the once gifted, extraordinarily peaceful picture of all types of people living in harmony on that puzzle. We see chaos. People living together were to be as beautiful as nature. The same force created both. That force also provided the teachers with the tools to make it happen. All you need to do is look at a beautiful sunset, our majestic mountains, or all other awe-inducing natural landscapes. You know, the source of all that must have given us something to make the people's lives on this blessed earth a blessing also.

For several decades, we've rejected those special teachers gifted to us. We've allowed other-center types to make selfish wads with every puzzle piece they can grab—each person—rather than letting these undereducated or unfulfilled souls find their place in this intended-to-be exquisite picture. Trump took wadding to new heights. WCCrime provided that opportunity.

We must take that opportunity away from him or any other self-centered creature lurking in our future. To take it away, we must understand it. Helping you understand what WCCrime did is the sole purpose of my work and this book since it opened the door to Project 2025, not just Trump. Whereas authentic education was intended to and would have elevated all lives, Project 2025 intends to permanently disempower the individual to simplify the lives of the wealthy and powerful. We must stop Project 2025.

Nevertheless, as I explained earlier, I know WCCrime requires a lot of work to grasp. I understood it even more when I tried using artificial intelligence (AI) writing tools while writing this book. I heard so much about how they clarify writing that I gave it a try at improving a few paragraphs. It didn't get WCCrime. It got it as corruption, but not how it turned education into a system of uselessness with its firing and muzzling of great teachers. And it didn't get the connection to democracy. It took me longer to fix the paragraph it wrote for me than to write it myself.

Since AI can't figure this out, it told me neither can the best minds in government. To me, that was more proof that we live in a lost, dumb rather than wicked, deep state. It confirmed my three-decade thought that WCCrime needs a book.

Over and above that, not knowing my gender, it referred to me as "he," assuming only a man does thinking in education. That was the cherry on top of knowing AI is useless for teaching WCCrime. There was no man with a great brain anywhere I taught. I take that back. The male science teacher at the school where the principal had the female teachers showing off their legs led the protest against that principal for forcing good teachers to resign. Because of him, I went to the Board and reported that principal.

I gave AI a second chance to prove its worth. I increased my submission. I used Chapter 3 about my student, which no one could figure out before they placed him in my fifth-grade class. I asked it to summarize that short chapter. Here's its summary:

> The text above is a bold account of a teacher who refused to give up on a struggling student, even when others had written him off. Through a meticulous analysis of the situation and a deep understanding of the student's needs, the teacher was able to identify and eliminate the obstacles preventing the student from learning. Her decision to remove an unhelpful assistant and offer extra time and support to the student was a clear demonstration of her unwavering commitment to her students' success. This story is a testament to the power of determined and assertive teaching and the significant impact it can have on a child's future.

Even though I had mentioned how twisted things were at my school, including how they violated laws, it ignored that and focused only on my helping the boy rather than my working against all odds. It missed my paragraph that explained why I told you about this boy. It missed the following, which was the end of the first draft of my chapter. That had said:

> WCCrime twisted everything about this incident. Special education law, the boy's success, and what the parents wanted were meaningless to my administrators. Their goal was

DEEP STATE OR DUMB STATE?

getting rid of teaching that showed how unsuccessful they were—one of the worst aspects of WCCrime. Their shameful mission to thwart my attempt to help this boy shows exactly how WCCrime has ended teacher influencing. Based on testimony from thousands of teachers who've joined my group, this is happening nationwide. You need to know this.

I had used the word "twisted" when describing what went on with Jack, mentioned WCCrime, and cited their obscene goal, but there was no reference to any of it.

Since AI missed the point, I added a couple more paragraphs to wake it up. I recalled what I learned about brain-based learning—a learner needs scaffolding to learn something new. Without prior knowledge, the learner cannot understand.

I scaffolded my lesson for AI as if to build a revered museum. I described how the union went after me—one of its members—while helping the special education teacher who hadn't joined the union. That indeed pointed out a hotbed of corruption, wouldn't you think?

Another sturdy ladder to the truth was my mention of how they treated this boy's parents. I conveyed that the Board accused the parents of supporting my teaching because they had to spend time doing their son's schoolwork before I entered the picture. They may even have used the word "lazy" when labeling these parents. Actually, I heard them use it. I don't remember if they used it on paper.

How could this be happening? I turned this boy into a student, and the powers at my school preferred him to be a needy, incompetent person. And AI missed that, too?

I had added the union's complicity and the Board insulting the parents—their typical way of achieving submission. It still wasn't enough for the so-called most intelligent force ever to comprehend the idea of this paragraph, much less this book. Despite adding this, AI's new summary still said nothing about it. It was so similar to the first one I didn't bother to share it. It felt like the same wall I've encountered for decades.

297

Please go back and reread Chapter 3. It's a short one—not as short as before my scientific AI experiment, but less than seven pages. The added paragraph that AI still did not grasp when doing its second summary begins, "This incident highlights the inferior teaching in our WCCrime schools. Get this."

What does this mean about the future of AI? I'll let the AI experts figure that out. I know what it means about WCCrime. It's an unfathomable concept. That's why it has prevailed in its takeover of education and will continue until someone makes it fathomable, my goal.

AI did accomplish something positive, however. I had not mentioned something significant when discussing this incident. AI's failure is making me include an essential piece of information now: the Jack issue is on the audiotape my district fired me over—for not returning all copies.

I left the audiotape out partly because I was trying to keep that chapter short. I had said enough about WCCrime. I added Chapter 3 when the book was nearly done so you would profoundly understand what excellent teaching looks like. I wrote it to convey how a solid teacher can help a child if the powers permit.

I had promised you a trip with a full view of my teaching life and I realized I missed an important site. What's been going on in education is no easy lesson. This was my career, not yours. We had spent too much time driving around the school. I needed to take you deep inside, so I circled back to take you there.

I added this new chapter near the beginning, accepting the burden of changing lots of chapter numbers, feeling like I had driven you through the ghetto during a storm with a broken windshield wiper on the passenger side. I wanted to share an unforgettable moment of teaching—perhaps my most unforgettable moment of teaching.

Understanding my motive for adding this chapter helps you understand why I didn't add the bombshell audiotape. Yet, in the second draft of Chapter 3, I did add more wrongdoing thinking: it was so perverse that the union helped the nonunion member and not me, a union member, and that the Board put down the parents. I decided that these facts deserved a place in this chapter. However, I must admit that the impelling reason I added them was to see if AI could get this right with more detailed WCCrime information.

AI set me on a course to prove its unworthiness for problem-solving and changed my purpose for that chapter. It was projected smartness—accidental intelligence. Because it failed, it made me smarter. Nevertheless, I am adding the audiotape connection here rather than in Chapter 3. I'm not giving AI another chance, but you must know this.

Here goes. I had mentioned that my district terminated me over an audiotape at the beginning of the book—in the "About the Author" section. I kept the audiotape because it proves how the team ganged up on me while foiling Jack's progress. The tape catches the principal lying about special education laws. It has the parents praising me. It's a reality show on steroids. It's not Survivor since I didn't survive. It's closer to Trump's "I can do anything I want" soliloquy when exiting the infamous bus. The details would disgust any listener.

And it was only a short time after that audiotaped meeting that those WCCriminals commenced their expert damage control. They ordered me to stay home. For all I know, they had Mrs. O back in the classroom, convincing Jack that his brilliant ideas were wrong. I know that I never got to say goodbye to Jack or any of my other students.

Then consider this. That was the audiotape allegedly stolen from my attorney's car, the attorney my astrologer said not to hire due to his planets showing he was truth-challenged. I didn't need the tape to "disappear" to know the tape's or my astrologer's value!

They were going to terminate me one way or another. This way, I'd have what everyone now calls the receipts. By the way, the descriptor "receipts" does not measure up to this audiotape that proves that our schools are a hot mess and that this country needs to listen to me. It's closer to a jaw-dropper. This paragraph from my first draft of Chapter 3 adds a lot to why they didn't want me to have that tape:

> This district, which also accused me of violating special education law for sharing issues about this boy with board members, had a fourth-grade teacher, no longer at our district, become involved in this issue so she could testify against me. They shared all the information with her, a non-employee, yet I was wrong to share it with board members, whose job is to protect the community.

In that paragraph, I referred to sharing issues with board members without the details to keep the chapter short. AI had this information for their first faulty summary and ignored it, not once, but twice, just as WCCriminals hope you'll do now. They hope you'll ignore me telling you more about that audiotape. I hope you'll read on with sleuth-hound ears.

Before that meeting, knowing that the principal was on the warpath, I asked the Board to have a representative attend. They refused. I then asked the parents for permission to tape it. The mom said she would tape it if I didn't, so I taped it.

I was so disturbed by the principal's misrepresentations about special education law and her attempts to turn the parents against me during that meeting that I asked two of the board members to come to my home. I played the audiotape for them so they could do their duty—stop these WCCriminals.

The Board decided that my sharing it with them had violated special education law that requires confidentiality of a student's Individual Education Plan (IEP). Yet, the Board didn't think that they broke that law by transmitting this confidential information to a teacher no longer employed at their district. Pretty crazy, huh? However, it's not crazier than their thinking board members have no duty to safeguard students from evil administrators!

These meetings were not ordinarily taped, and they were not a school record. However, the hearing officer decided they became a school record because I played them for two board members. I decided they belong in a fireproof box, which is where they have been there since 1999 until this nation recognizes WCCriminals for what they are.

AI proved that more intelligence is needed to solve our nation's problems. It only knows what is common knowledge. It does not think critically the way all inventors and leaders have. It did add value, however. It proved me right when I said that WCCrime is too hard to grasp. Plus, it got me to add an audiotape that proves this story about Jack and gets to the heart of what's wrong with our schools.

But beware. Only you can solve this problem. Great minds have not solved education problems for years because inferior minds have pushed them away. Whether their inferiority stemmed from their inability to fathom WCCrime or from their being in a position too challenging for their intellect or wallets, the results are the same—failure.

We cannot expect brilliant people who have not studied education to understand how it went wrong. Our presidents have not had someone with vision and profound knowledge of this field consulting them for years. That's why they're lost.

However, we cannot expect brilliant people who have studied education to understand how it went wrong, either! Diane Ravitch, one of the most admired present-day educators/activists, could have been an exception had she not failed to see WCCrime. I've admired her insights about education, yet she seems to overlook WCCrime and has cut too much slack for leaders who are obvious WCCriminals.

One example was a New York superintendent who rose to power due to outstanding success with his district's reading scores. He secured a better position in a California district, where reading scores plummeted under his watch. It turned out that his "success" in NY was different from his claim. Due to gentrification, his district suddenly went from lower to upper middle class. It had become desirable geographically, and families changed from poor and struggling to those with financial stability and a love of education.

In one of her books, she described his phony "success" that secured his new position without judging him as a WCCrime problem. He had used that success to rise in leadership. If he didn't know it was due to gentrification, he's not very smart. If he knew, he's not very ethical. He sold success that wasn't a success either due to shallow values or shallow thinking. Either is different from the leadership education needs, yet the only kind it has.

This story gets worse. This administrator's wife, also an education leader, was the very person who put a stellar teacher, a member of our group, into New York's infamous "Rubber Room." The union assisted in her retirement rather than helping this superior teacher remain in teaching. Ravitch spoke about this man in one of her books, as she spoke about the union in many of her books—as if neither were the problem. The theme from the "Twilight Zone" played in my head while reading her book, which had nothing bad to say about the union.

This is a failure to put these pieces of the education puzzle together. Ravitch has a brilliant mind and an admirable career trajectory. I wondered why she hadn't figured out WCCrime. Her friendships with union leaders and other education leaders may blind her, or she's too idealistic to consider it.

I don't know why I figured it out. Was it growing up beside gangsters? I don't know, but the union is corrupt based on what it did to many of our members and me. I know social connections can muddle truth. Whatever the case, Diane Ravitch operates with WCCrime blinders. Rather than going along to get along, she may be among the educators who go along because getting WCCrime is not in their wheelhouse. Maybe they're too close to Mother Teresa to even consider it. I must be far enough away to know evil when I see it.

Even as I write about Ravitch, I grow. I had difficulty speaking critically about her because she is brilliant and courageous. Her heart is in education. I came close to not adding my dismay that she missed WCCrime. I said it with the same reluctance that makes me want to apologize to all my teacher readers trapped in education's slimy, dead-end cul-de-sac. Education is challenging for anyone with good intentions.

I remember the person at National Louis University who was designated to tell me that they turned me down for their Ph.D. program. She sounded horrified. She had encouraged me to sign up for it, and now had to pretend I didn't belong in it, and pretend that she hadn't misled me. This is the price most have to pay to stay in education. I hope they will read this book knowing I don't blame them. We need to pull off this dirty tablecloth, dishes, and all. I understand why so many went along, but that needs to end so our democracy won't.

I thought: Ravitch knows Randi Weingarten personally. I know Randi Weingarten is intelligent and caring. She helps abused teachers. What Weingarten didn't do was speak out and insist these outstanding teachers remain employed. She was on email chains with me and didn't bother to support what I was doing. She pretended not to know me. I bet Ravitch had the same hard time finding fault with Weingarten as I did with Ravitch.

The autocratic system that forces people like Weingarten to go along needs changing. It's unrealistic to expect people to do what I did. I've spent thirty years earning nothing while spending money. They know that well-situated power gets its way. They do the only realistic thing one can do when a system is rigged. We need to free them from that! And I'm saying that despite the unsavory things the union did to me from the local to the top of the NEA.

I've had many heart-to-heart talks with my teacher colleagues. They always speak about teachers' golden handcuffs. Usually, teachers starting a different career need to start over as if they never went to college. A teaching degree is less than worthless in business. It suggests you'll be wrong for business. When teaching jobs became scarce, I had to work as a secretary for a few years as if I never went to college. Starting over is not a welcome choice.

In addition to their financial needs, they believe they should continue teaching and do what they can. They tell me that they remain silent to do that. They do their best to deal with these incompetent leaders. As years pass, these workarounds dig a deeper hole, leaving well-intentioned educators trapped and the world of education barren.

Most teachers have big hearts but are out of their league dealing with WCCrime. Many administrators mean well, too. Bringing a school down doesn't take a slew of sinister people. One rotten lemon, left in a bag of lemons, soon makes the entire bag worthless.

It is overwhelming to deal with so many good people trapped with only a few taking advantage of education's loophole of opportunity. However, if we don't state the problem, we can't solve it. WCCrime is so organized that ending it demands the calling out of all enablers, not because they're as bad as those leading this crime but because they're empowering it.

Doing this work wouldn't be in my comfort zone if the problem and solution weren't so clear to me. Someone needs to lead lost educators, and who could lead became obvious to me. It needed someone who didn't need to make a living to do it.

I also cut slack for the presidents who have overlooked this. I get why they missed it. It's not that they were too close to the selfish side of the curve; it's that they were too far from the facts.

Education is complex. Most have yet to study it. Schools that once turned out real intelligence now serve polluted intelligence. Artificial intelligence can't seem to help. That's why we need WCCrime-free schools that produce solid citizens. Presidents rely on advisers. And since no one in their circle of cronies has figured out WCCrime, no one can advise what to do about it. The great minds in education are stuck in WCCrime's quicksand, leaving no competent advisors at hand.

Since the choice is quicksand or exit the area, great minds do the latter. Reread Chapter 16 about the excellent minds that education lost as a reminder of why they left. Is it any wonder that no one advises our government about what's wrong with education? They either leave before they find out, leave when they find out, or oblige it. Whistleblowers are as scarce as women willing to frame Harvey Weinstein were for decades. It took only one to solve that problem. I'm hoping to be the one to solve this problem.

The government and AI have their limits. Since all who have led in government missed WCCrime or became vessels for it, it's a we-the-people dilemma with some mighty, solid evidence.

We can restore this broken community. We can see that giant puzzle of people appearing like our most beautiful sites—our magnificent mountains and awe-inspiring shores. None are perfect if you look closely, but none are as ugly as democracy has become. President Biden told us he wants to lead with a vision for democracy's future. He can learn what to do by reading this book. Woodrow Wilson said: "The ear of the leader must ring with the voices of the people." Let's make that our goal.

You now know the leaders that education needs. A deep state would not want to know them. A lost state would welcome knowing them. If we spread the word about WCCrime and watch what this country does, we'll know what we have.

"The illiterate of the 21st century will not be those who cannot read and write, but those who cannot learn, unlearn, and relearn."

Alvin Toffler

18

MAKE SCHOOLS RIGHT TO MAKE OUR NATION RIGHT

"When the People Lead, the Leaders Will Follow."

Mahatma Gandhi

"That these dead shall not have died in vain–that this nation, under God, shall have a new birth of freedom and that government of the people, by the people, for the people, shall not perish from the earth"

President Abraham Lincoln, (The Gettysburg Address)

Thank you for still being with me. Hopefully, that means you care about our democracy. If you're still with me because you're a parent dreading having to lie to your children by telling them they're safe when they go to school, I appreciate that, too. We both want that lie to become a truth. Thus, I need you to play a role in getting our schools back from WCCriminals.

I wrote an email about this soon-to-be-published book to my over 2200 members of NAPTA, the National Association for Prevention of Teacher Abuse, aware that more than half of them have chosen Trump as the solution to this messed-up democracy. Even though we disagree on the solution for this country, we agree on our schools—how wrong they are. I asked them to put aside our different political solutions for this country and help get this book read.

Pundits ask: what extraordinary conversation will prod the rule of law into wakefulness and repair this democracy? Those who know the truth about our schools see the answer: an admission that those in power allowed democracy's foundation, our schools, to career into nothingness.

Unlike most opposing Trump, I know our schools, so I understand why so many chose him. While he makes no sense to those who see him for who he is, he makes perfect sense to me for what our country has become due to our schools. My book intends for him to no longer make sense by helping those in power see where they went wrong. I'm confident that most who have joined our group are connected in our love for good schools and can come together to turn them around by electing a president who hears us. So far, none have heard us.

Recently, Robert F. Kennedy sent an email also promising to be a sledgehammer for change, mentioning everything but education. Since he doesn't recognize the problem, he won't solve it either. Instead, he might help elect a person who'll end democracy—a dictator—by dividing the votes of those against a dictator.

Democracy leans toward taking a generous position toward others until proven wrong. My book has traced how our schools have exhausted that generosity toward the establishment and caused a collapse in moral and ethical values. Our poorly educated nation has become desperate.

Most of us are drowning in despair over Trump or our disagreement with those who've chosen him. This is an intolerable state of affairs for anyone who believes there's a duty to help our fellow man. Teachers chose a career to do the latter, yet our lack of real schools preordained abandoning that duty.

Since we have marginalized teachers, we have caused the collapse of the moral and ethical glue that used to hold us together. Once people understand that the marginalization started with WCCrime, they'll realize how easy solving this problem will be. The seeds for coming together to solve this problem exist in our mutual love for education. Therefore, I have asked NAPTA members, some of whom joined over twenty years ago, to help get this book read regardless of their politics. We connect in a more critical place. We connect where democracy lives or dies. We need you to connect, too.

The first thing you can do is easy. Whether you're an educator or citizen, sign up as a National Association for Prevention of Teacher Abuse member. You can join here: http://www.endteacherabuse.org/MemForm/MembershipForm.html. Now that I have explained further how much teachers need you, I hope you will become a member of NAPTA.

It's free. It's easy. It will make a difference by creating a significant voice against WCCrime. The press listens to numbers. This is how we'll get an investigative reporter or *The Boston Globe*—the newspaper that exposed abusive priests—to take on WCCrime.

I've taken care of the proof. I have the forged documents my district used to get rid of me and lots more. Other group members have sent me all kinds of receipts. I have TV news videos that report scandals, and I even have a video of a Florida teacher's coerced psychiatric visit. (Her predators were not as skilled as mine, who outlawed videotaping and used my request for it against me!)

I didn't detail my proof since it is so voluminous. It would take another book. Rest assured, an investigative reporter can nail these criminals. But do not rest assured that they will without your insistence. Despite decades of books and desperate phone calls, they have yet to listen to any teacher whistleblower! Visit: https://www.whitechalkcrime.com/#vid and listen to the teachers with bags on their heads reporting their outrageous charter school in

NY. Hear them describe devious administrators and how they manipulate parents. They tell how their principal refers to some students as "retarded," a word no longer considered decent.

Listen to the podcast of Five Whistleblowers at: https://soundcloud.com/karen-horwitz/how wegottrumped?ref=clipboard&p=i&c=1

http://protectschoolchildren.com/ is a website I developed around the time of Sandy Hook. Because everyone is focused on guns rather than on the creation of the shooters, I decided to wait to develop it once citizens understood the main reason for school shootings. I hope this book will accomplish that.

The most important thing we can do is figure out how to get our president to read this book. (Past presidents and other public officials reading it would be good, too!) President Kennedy made Rachel Carson's dream of doing something about pesticides come true after he read *The New Yorker* magazine's serialization of *Silent Spring*, her watershed work.

If you or anyone you know has contact with *The New Yorker* or any magazine that might care about democracy and ending school massacres, please get this book to them. What President Kennedy did was democracy at its best. He listened to the people. The state was not too deep for him to access important information. And information did not get lost in the swamp then either. Let's make this history repeat itself, not Hitler history!

We can make school reform happen by making sure those in power know or have to know the truth about education. It will be more than fixing our schools. It will be repairing our foundation. Getting to the core of why education has failed us and promising to do something about it can and must be the counter-vision to Project 2025.

A president listening to its citizens will offer democracy a lifesaving shot in the arm. We must stop pretending our schools are okay so we can begin to win. Fixing our schools is much easier than dealing with a tyrant running our lives—what we can expect if we don't. I can promise you this: even if we dodge Trump, we are doomed with the schools we have. Our choice is to do nothing and surrender our freedom to Project 2025's authoritarian plan for us or really make America great again.

The war against expertise and ethics started in our schools when limited, selfish minds took them over. It will only end when brilliant, generous citizens take our schools back. I hope you will help make that happen.

AN ADDITIONAL DOSE
OF INSIGHT

I finished my book and sent in the final manuscript, and then the following happened. Its lessons were too potent to leave unsaid. Fortunately, I was able to add it.

◆ ◆ ◆ ◆ ◆ ◆

I was listening to my 2008 speech at the Washington, DC, mall. Someone had paid all the costs—as much as $20,000—to hold this protest event that attracted only a handful of teachers for reasons explained at http://www.end-teacherabuse.org/epic.html

I was surprised to hear myself speak about how WCCrime would bring down our democracy. I thought I hadn't been that specific about democracy back then, even though what our schools would wreck was always on my mind. Hearing my speech reminded me that my predictions were indeed spot on.

My superstar hero, Former Connecticut Superintendent Dr. Armand Fusco, in his NAPTA t-shirt, waiting to speak after me.

I could see Dr. Armand Fusco standing behind me, waiting to speak. I admired him so much. He was one of my favorite education activists. Being a superintendent who spoke truth to power made him a superstar to me. He hadn't responded to my emails for a few years. He was substantially older, and you can guess where my mind went. I decided to Google him and see if I was right. I knew it would make me sad, but there was no other explanation for having lost touch. We were united about our schools!

I was wrong. Armand was alive and well and had just published a terrific-sounding book pointing out that our schools are unsafe. I thought: "That supports my position on school shootings, and I need to read it while wondering why he hadn't told me. He knew I had a chapter in my first book on that topic. Why hadn't he contacted me?"

Then I found a recent hour-plus interview he did. The mystery of why he hadn't returned my emails unfolded like a Grisham novel. Listening to him, my happiness exited like a slow leak in a pool float. At approximately thirty minutes, I went from thrilled to "Oh no." However, having watched only ten minutes of the interview before having to leave for an event made this new realization even more dramatic.

My thoughts were still in the past. I became certain that Armand's email had changed, so we lost connection. I found his telephone number on the way to my granddaughter's birthday party. I planned to text him the next day. I spent much of the day excited, thinking I'd reconnect with this wonderful man soon and that he'd be happy to hear about my upcoming book.

When I was back home watching the video, it took time to discover I was wrong because he was still describing WCCrime with his vivid descriptions of law-breaking that I remembered well. He spoke of an administrator who ignored the law about having to compile a public safety plan. That official didn't bother to assemble a committee to arrive at a plan. Instead, he listed a social worker as the committee—what Armand noted as a ridiculous one-person committee. He described that administrator as a man running the district like a king who answered only to himself.

I was elated. I thought: "Armand was alive; we were on the same page, and he had more evidence." But that soon changed. Our affinity began to fray when he connected the dots to "It's the woke unions connected to the Democrats that are ruining our schools." He angrily spoke about this king-like Connecticut superintendent, suddenly blaming radicalization, not WCCrime.

I've repeatedly pointed out that WCCriminals use politics to attain power. It's their cover. It's the WCCriminals' lawbreaking that says who WCCriminals are. They operate outside the democratic system and are the enemy of democracy. I described this in detail in Chapter 13, where I pointed out that they harness your anger as far as possible from their schools, which are mere houses of cards. But that was this book, not the 2008 book, which brought us together. And politics have gotten much more polarized. So instead of the corrupt force that WCCriminals are, he was judging this education thief as a political force.

For every superintendent using extreme left-wing Democratic beliefs, there's a superintendent banning books and pushing extreme right-wing Republican beliefs. Using politics to divert attention from their wrongdoing works like a charm, but I had thought it wouldn't with Armand. He wrote the book about their corruption. He knew the real problem.

I now knew otherwise. My good friend Armand had fallen for their convenient cover-up for WCCrime. Diverting people so they're tangled up in politics is an ingenious way of keeping their house of WCCrime cards safe. They make people fight over politics to give their corrupt way of life—ignoring laws and ignoring their purpose to maintain democracy—a cover.

WCCriminals do not indulge in corrupt acts to promote ideology. They care about power and money, not ideology. They want to keep their wrongdoing going while eliminating any threat of jail.

You can bet that this superintendent that Armand condemned for being blanketed in fighting racism has no concern for the issue of racism. In fact, he could be a racist, given that he's turning people against the problem by taking racism to extremes and making people angry.

I heard frustration coming from deep inside Armand and his interviewer. They both care about the plight of black people. They've worked hard to help black people. They aren't at all racist, yet this superintendent is making them feel like everyone is racist. Thus, doing something about unwarranted racism became Armand's sole focus. By adopting the ideas of a black extremist, Armand's local administrator had placed himself in a tent of safety.

This administrator manipulated Armand so he'd focus on radicalized education, redirecting him from what he used to be focused on—corruption in education. Discussing our schools, these two men shifted their concerns from WCCrime to political radicalization.

Go to https://tinyurl.com/mvdfsmbf and listen to Armand, obsessed with what he sees as an unwarranted battle of racism his local administrator undertook while almost dismissing that superintendent's failure to create an authentic school safety plan. He pointed out that this administrator's only concern was his image, period, and that school shootings are too "negative" for him to consider. He described him and others like him as failing to do their job. Yet, the racism issue became THE issue.

WCCriminals grift their way to the top by concocting a shield of offensive politics. Our schools were to be where democracy blossomed. By adding politics, which has no place in our schools, democracy dies.

The interview awakened me to why Armand stopped responding to my emails. He saw my 2019 book describing how we ended up with a dangerous con man as president glaring on its cover and saw it as political. I have no idea how he feels about Trump. Still, a good guess is he thinks he's a necessary evil to conquer the Democrats and the unions. So many think that.

Like so many others, he missed the point. The enemies we must fight are the WCCriminals who do anything to maintain power. As with so many teachers, the unions have commiserated with WCCriminals because they have no choice. WCCrime is too powerful. No one has been able to expose it, and the few who have tried are voiceless pariahs.

The Democrat party, like the Republican Party, includes honest, caring people as well as self-serving types. For every Republican who has adopted Trump's unlawful ways, there's likely a Democrat who has adopted WCCrime's corrupt ways. Actually, there are so many Republicans supporting Trump that the ratio is probably way off

Our problem is that so few of us have a voice due to the absolute power of WCCriminals, who use polarization to cleverly disempower us. Each side wraps itself in a political rather than a critically thought-out battle, which I have proposed in this book and what Armand sought until that administrator used politics to capture his mind.

Our schools are supposed to be as far from politics as practicing medicine. Doctors do what it takes to keep people alive, with their patients' politics bearing no weight. Rather than see his superintendent's acts as a manipulation to maintain power, Armand fell for it.

He saw my disgust with Trump as me being a Democrat. I could be, and I could not be. My battle to save democracy is about democracy, not politics. There's Liz Chaney and Adam Kissinger, definite conservatives who feel the same way about Trump.

This is why our society is lost. When schools became political instruments rather than the preservers of democracy, there was no longer an institution to ensure that politics stopped at democracy's door.

Armand's interviewer expressed angst that a social activist teacher told his daughter the Bible is a fairy tale. A teacher must keep her political or religious views to herself and help children learn. That a teacher was saying that reflects how lost education is.

Democracy means people with different views figuring out how to compromise and live together. When the institution that is to safeguard democracy does the opposite, we're in trouble.

I admire Armand for his dedication to education. His book on school corruption underpinned my work and helped keep me on this mission. But when he started pushing Moms for Liberty, I realized even he had crossed over into political quicksand.

This is not a left-versus-right battle. I dislike policies from both extremes, and I agree with some. Our schools were meant to be places where people learned to deal with our differences, not where they were taught to choose one side.

A superintendent who embraces politics is a red flag that waves WCCrime. We must respect other political views in a democracy. We cannot let different views make us enemies. Watching a wonderful man get this all wrong proved this isn't a war of good versus bad people. This war is happening because too many bad people are in positions of power. They make us fight over politics so they can reap the benefits of WCCrime while democracy falls apart.

Armand may be right that a person is making millions pushing his extreme theory of racism. The WCCriminal embraced it for selfish reasons, too. The solution for ending selfishness is real schools.

Everyone has political views, but only some want to find a way to live harmoniously. Our schools were to teach us how to do that. Our focus must be on bringing them back to that agenda, away from the rotten politics we now have because our schools lost their way. It's not the conservative or liberal values that are bad. It's our inability to negotiate values, having lost the institution that was supposed to teach that.

The people who use our differences to make us hate rather than learn to live together are democracy's core problem. We must focus on WCCriminals breaking laws and purging great teachers; we cannot let the tricks they use to get us off track undermine democracy.

Armand made a great case against this superintendent's violations of laws. Still, he then fell into the superintendent's clever political rabbit hole. We can work out differences in a democracy. We must keep our eyes on restoring democracy, or we'll end up living in an autocracy, having to follow one selfish man's beliefs.

Education has had to cope with vultures rather than leaders. For over a century, education hasn't had a leader who can bring it back to its purpose by implementing policies for the good of democracy. That will only happen in a place outside the realm of politics where a called-to-teach leader takes the reins.

Right after writing this, I turned on the television. I saw Randi Weingarten, president of one of the teachers' unions, pretending to be democracy's savior. She was responding to a Republican having called her the biggest danger to democracy. I can defend her. She's not the biggest danger. WCCrime is. However, her refusal to admit that she's more of a hostage than a leader makes her dangerous. People like her need to come clean for the sake of democracy.

She bragged about supplying books to students, a minor act compared to not keeping dedicated teachers in the classroom. She didn't care about protecting great teachers—she had ignored me and my organization. She helps get rid of boat-rockers. She does only what WCCriminals allow her to do. Providing banned books helps keep the focus on politics where WCCriminals want it. She does what they allow, what keeps them alive.

I understand why she's afraid to admit what's happening. I am confident she knows I am right about what's wrong in education as she goes along to get along with the status quo. She's too smart and too caring not to know.

I am holding on tightly to the reins of truth, awaiting a genuine leader. This book will attract a solid leader once the government puts education in a safe place and implements safeguards to protect democracy from the forces of selfish people.

Democracy depends on an informed and critical-thinking electorate that will not fall for WCCriminals' political ploys. No one invested in having their way politically, religiously, or financially can or will create such an electorate. We need a leader who focuses on what education is intended to be.

Armand stated that his local superintendent was breaking laws. However, his superintendent's political stance became the most important issue to Armand. When Armand shifted to "I need to protect our nation from the Democrats" and began advocating for parents to join right-wing groups, he became lost in the incivility of our times. Incivility is what schools were to prevent. Not doing their job has subjected us to a graver danger than anyone can imagine.

This was a sad moment in my journey. I discovered that ninety-one-year-old Dr. Armand Fusco, a good man and a devoted public servant at one time, is now lost in the uncivil world that imposter schools have created. That's why he stopped responding to me.

EPILOGUE:

COURT-ASSISTED, END OF A TEACHER STORY

The following is the beginning of my memoir about the end of my teaching career and my journey through the courts. The complete memoir is in the enhanced ebook version of this book.

My principal's tactical dishonesty in the fall of 1995 launches an abusive journey that the Board compounds with a brutal legal process lasting through 2007. One valiant board member votes against terminating me, one plays both sides and abstains, but my superintendent has the votes in his pocket for a political assassination to happen despite the cost, financially or otherwise. To them, power over children is an entitlement.

So what if purging great teachers threatens democracy. On April 21, 1999, while most feel horror over what happened at Columbine the previous day, a vengeance-filled superintendent sends me a notice recommending my termination. Neither sleet nor snow nor Columbine fazes him or the Board.

I do my best to succeed at making a record that ends up proving that no court will consider teacher abuse. I learn that I need to shame our country via the court of public opinion. I keep a diary to do that.

In the spring of 1993, a talented principal hired me to teach fourth grade at a school in an affluent Illinois district. I felt I had won the lottery. My dream, literally, had come true. The visionary principal resigned that June. It became a nightmare that turned into a vision to expose the truth about our schools.

Working under a limited, ruthless principal who, at the age of 29, had only taught fourth grade for a few years set into motion the torpedoing of my career. In her first year, she terminated two older teachers up for tenure and angered the community. She then ousted the over-forty-year-old librarian from her position and made her into a floating substitute.

The Board had to maintain her $70,000 salary contractually, so she was earning big bucks to sub. They relied on two favorite educrat ploys: overpaying to get parents mad at teachers and humiliating teachers to get them to resign. Unhappy about her treatment of three veteran teachers, many parents warned the district that they would watch what they did with me. They felt the principal didn't want what they wanted: experienced teachers.

The following year, she gave me tenure with one hand while harassing, bullying, and accusing me of false charges with the other. As a resident of a nearby district that fed into the same renowned high school, they knew I was not working for survival. They expected me to quit. They were wrong.

I was the teacher I wanted for my own children. Awakened by the political games they used to drive wedges between parents and teachers, I refused to operate against parents. I was determined to give my students their best fourth-grade experience. I became an investigative reporter and documented everything to expose the truth about our schools. I was confident I would make this not ready for prime time issue public someday.

I met with the superintendent about the principal's harassment. I discovered he does not care what she is doing to me. It doesn't matter that I'm a popular, effective teacher. He says, "Any trouble' from you, I will make your life miserable." Unlike his promise to care about children, he keeps this promise.

As part of her plan to harass and trash me, the principal moved me from fourth to fifth grade and assigned me to teach two sections of lab science, aware that I was a certified reading specialist and had not taken a science course in thirty years. To her dismay, more than half of the parents requested that their students remain in my class.

When it became public knowledge that this harassment was happening, sixty parents signed a petition urging the Board to support me. I had no intention of filing a lawsuit. I refrained from speaking to anyone about the ruthless educrats, despite a shocking incident where the principal put my health at risk by ordering me to deal with a vindictive parent to use the episode against me. I have to fight these brutes somehow, but I think it will be via a book, not a legal path.

Before psychologically assaulting me, the principal had disposed of two experienced teachers. I had suspected one was about to get the axe since the principal harassed her all year and scheduled a meeting with her after our staff meeting, the Friday before spring vacation.

These are vivid memories. They rise from deep within as I write and bring me back. During the staff meeting, feeling angst for this gentle soul, I noted that the principal was mocking that teacher's habit of carrying large amounts of work home in a shopping cart. Could she really be planning to fire her a few minutes after making her the brunt of a joke?

Granted, the allusion to a bag lady is funny, but when one is taking away a person's livelihood and opening the door to precisely that, it is sadistic.

I then recall the one time in my business career when I managed a sales and marketing operation in the film industry and had to fire someone. Although deficient at her job, to me, she was a person; it disturbed me. I went out for lunch to have a drink so I could cope. I hardly drank liquor, never at lunch! It is unthinkable that this principal could relish inflicting pain on her.

I stop in the outer office, hoping I'm wrong. I see the giddy principal in her office, which used to be separated by a wall to the outer office, speaking with this teacher, tears streaming down reddened cheeks. I feel unsettled seeing into her office, recalling when this principal began her reign, the first thing she did was replace the wall of her office with a window. I found it strange that she wanted to have others see in.

Now, the reason is apparent. I see the principal close to her victim, the victim's face in clear view of the outside office, where I was, the principal's back to me. I shudder. This principal wants to hurt this teacher. Terminating her doesn't satisfy her thirst for power; she needs to put her victim on display, like a prized animal! That she enjoyed others' misery was clear. She wants to hurt this teacher. The reason for that window still haunts me.

The tipping point occurred soon after. Although that episode convinced me that something beyond business was happening, the following year, a comment converted me from focusing on the good in this principal to needing to protect myself from her. During a chat after a meeting, a new staff member mentioned how one of our previous teachers had stolen many supplies from her classroom when she left.

I approach her to inquire about the teacher's name, suspecting last year's trophy. She confirms. Now, if there was one thing I knew, the teacher was loving. I often felt she would have made a great nun if only she were Catholic. She had spent much of her salary buying supplies for her class. And even if the impossible were true, it was ghastly for the principal to impugn her integrity without a trial or an open accusation.

I stood there feeling my insides churn, thinking: What lie will the principal spread about me? From that day forward, I realize I was better off engaging in open warfare than disappearing into the sunset as that teacher had. My reputation is at stake. A soul war comes into being. I go down paths that no one should experience, much less a dedicated teacher.

Praise from parents fills my record. The principal finds one parent to speak against me, then catapults her from cafeteria cashier to head of food services. Innovative, exciting, and motivating programs overflow in my classroom. They help my students soar as they master working harmoniously with their classmates. From my creative approach to improving reading via vocabulary to my unique behavior modification programs, my students love learning despite my no-nonsense approach. I integrate skills with artistic projects, teaching geography by having them make a papier-mâché map of the US and writing by publishing a newspaper. Students learn by way of multiple intelligences. I discipline by maintaining a group of highly functioning students. I am the teacher I want for my own children.

I love teaching and love my students. I have mastered the science and art of teaching to the place our schools claim they seek to reach. Indeed, my teaching excellence is a fact that none dispute.

The school board president tells me my problem is that I am "too dedicated," a fault that may disturb educrats but never parents! Vice President Pence is too honest. I am too dedicated. The Trump way and the WCCrime way harmonize. Thoughts about our democracy's demise swirl as I relive my life as a dedicated teacher.

Embroiled in conflict with educrats who prioritize supremacy over providing children with the best teachers, I find myself isolated from anyone with the power to force right to prevail. The parents' desires hold no weight with those determined to purge me from "their" system. I appeal to the Illinois State Board of Education (ISBE), which informs me that no watchdog group exists and that affecting the school board election is the only way to clean up a corrupt board.

In the fall of 1997, I write an essay for the local newspaper, included herein soon, to expose the malfeasance to the community so the public would know the political ploys used to rig the upcoming school board election. I soon discover the local newspaper is an arm for propaganda for the school. They refuse my essay, claiming that exposing a rubber stamping board has nothing to do with a board election. They print only what the educrats want; the public can't distinguish good guys from bad guys and will reelect the sycophants. A parent posts my essay online, and a guerrilla war ensues.

Urged by concerned citizens, I asked to speak directly with the school board, something I, along with many other teachers, was made to think a teacher could not do. I made a presentation on January 19, 1998. In a month, I received a reply. It said it did not investigate and ordered me to get along with the vicious educrats, which it refused to judge as anything but exemplary. The Board develops a plan to dispose of me. It orders me to participate in a contrived conflict resolution process with the culpable superintendent in charge.

Meanwhile, a group of older teachers, also discriminated against by the principal, sought advice from an attorney. I worked with that attorney to find a way to expose the misconduct and then file an EEOC age discrimination charge alone since the others were afraid. I attribute the Board's lack of concern about the law to the affluence and smallness of the district, with no idea it is a widespread phenomenon.

My trek with attorneys became almost as abusive as my experience with the district. That abuse includes my encounters with attorneys at the IEA, an affiliate of the National Education Association. On April 23, 1999, after deceitfully setting me up in every way possible, the Board fired me on sham charges.

The Board's most cunning tactic was to order me to undergo a fitness-for-duty exam by "District Psychiatrist" Dr. Peter Fink, who's a Chicago forensic psychiatrist infamous for testifying that a cognitively challenged 9-year old boy read his Miranda rights in the middle of the night, no adults present, understood his rights. He's the hired gun for their law firm and has efficiently rid the Board of at least one other teacher before me. State law says that an unbiased physician must perform a medical exam. I request a choice of three psychiatrists. The vote was 4 to 3, forcing me to be interrogated by their official tool. Three board members either have a conscience or fear complicity in an unethical and illegal act.

After all, using an invasive medical order to run a teacher out is a pretty severe affront to constitutionally guaranteed privacy when you know if you are actually using it to determine fitness for duty, any certified psychiatrist would suffice. I must provide my entire medical file and discuss my sex life for the Board to enjoy.

EPILOGUE: COURT-ASSISTED, END OF A TEACHER STORY

The loyal players figure that forcing me to see a known teacher cleanser might get me to resign. Instead, I signed a release saying Fink must issue that report simultaneously to me and the Board.

Soon after my two-hour plus Fink grilling in July, the Board offered a generous financial settlement, an amount it would take me six years to earn. It requires my resignation. The district's attorney reminded me that Fink had not issued a report but that my career would be over once he did. It is the last power play that this law firm uses on me since when I do not bite, the attorney suddenly switches law firms and takes the case with her. Their regular law firm is washing their hands of the filth.

My political sense is that I took them beyond their arsenal of customary dirty tricks, and they are not about to keep a case that surpasses their "expertise" for disposing of teachers. The district continues to use its original law firm, except for my case, which substantiates my belief. A law firm would not let go of a million-dollar case unless the case has uncomfortable, political ramifications. Business is money. This is an aggressive district, willing to use two law firms to have their way.

Since my goal is to expose wrongdoing in schools. I intend to remain on that course. Based on this alleged "fitness for duty" declaration, I am waiting for an all-clear to return to my position. No report. I begin teaching. My attorney advises me to let them hang themselves for allowing me back with no report, as it proves the exam is retaliatory. In October, I file a federal lawsuit, listing this retaliatory doctor visit and other proof of vindictive treatment. They evaded my privacy and ordered me to reveal my most personal information on the premises they had to protect the children. But, they never found out if I was fit for duty—unless Fink violated my terms of the release.

Soon, I learned that the dirty tricks leach into the medical field. Fink testified that he broke my release and issued a report only to the Board. He said that so I cannot prove that the Board had ordered an illegal, retaliatory exam. I could only prove Fink was named appropriately. He probably told the truth because a cover for the Board that made him look like a rat fink was included in his price.

Karma happens later when a local certified public accountant, who had used Fink as her psychiatrist, does a Google search and learns what he did. Go to EndTeacherAbuse.org. Search Fink on the Home page. I haven't ruined that search by calling other administrators "finks." I celebrate his fitting name and save it just for him!

Changed my mind. I'll make it easy to find the page with money rolling on it for the past twenty years http://www.endteacherabuse.org/fink.html and where I wrote in 2002:

> It is time teachers saw these people for the ethical midgets that they truly are and stood up to them. Only then will this stop. We would like to be able to forgive these people, but we can't as long as they are hurting our children. We need to maintain our anger so we can stop them. Someone has to, and so far not one public official shows any promise of taking these scoundrels on.

That CPA phones me, expressing disgust. She says she did Google searches to check people and was glad she discovered what scum he was before spending more time with him. She shares that at her last visit, she confronted him, and he wormed out, saying he couldn't talk about it. She is adamant. She cannot deal with anyone with a lack of integrity.

Good thing she isn't a teacher, as that is a basic requirement! I picture Dr. Fink walking in circles before he testified. He looked like an expectant father outside a delivery room when men weren't allowed in. It was clear that his conscience was pounding him. However, I prefer consciences that stop people from evil acts rather than consciences that drown guilty people in fear. Fink knew how to maintain his salary and "acted accordingly." Fink's violation of the Hippocratic Oath, a promise to do no harm, places him outside the doctor role, which, if judged honestly, would have deemed him biased and unqualified for the job.

I have had all "Excellent" evaluations the entire time I have been employed. Sixty parents sign a petition asking the Board to support me and investigate the administrators. The Board refuses to investigate, saying, "That is not what they do." The board president testified at the tenure hearing that I am an excellent teacher but must be terminated due to unprofessionalism. Yet, my evaluations for all my years of employment before filing a legal complaint indicate that I was an excellent professional. Evaluations are legal documents mandated by law to be accurate. Either my evaluations or the termination is unlawful.

To humiliate me, the principal and her henchmen hand me fifty nasty letters from October 1998 through March 1999, ordering me to put my hand out to receive them in front of parents, colleagues, and children. She encourages teachers to turn against me, a fact many teachers admit to me privately. And when disagreements occur, she fans the flames rather than helps mend things and makes it evident that teachers will earn brownie points by taking stands against me.

Without ever speaking with me, the union president called me unprofessional in a newspaper article and claimed the school always treats teachers professionally if they are professional. She knows this is false based on what they did to the librarian. A parent contacted me, shocked to read that a union leader went against a member.

To create chaos, the principal loads my class with children whose records state, "Don't put him with him." She puts him with him. Educrats monitor my class and spread heinous accusations about me. She, backed by the superintendent and Board who support whatever, accuses me of child abuse based on causing a student to cry when it was an issue of his adjustment, which his mother's testimony later confirms. She uses this inflammatory label to inflict more psychological pain, as evidenced by her failure to report it to the authorities, a mandatory requirement for actual child abuse and engages the special education director and special needs resource teacher to sabotage my efforts with exceptional students. I endure the abuse to force them to fire me to have a record for future use.

I, and one of the other older harassed teachers, plead to a board member for protection. He agrees to meet at my home. My colleague parks her car inside my garage to avoid being spotted at my house. He is well aware of our fear and assures her that he will do whatever he can to protect her. He turned to me and said that since I filed a lawsuit, he has a fiduciary responsibility to the district. His admittance that he focuses his responsibility on money and not on what is right begins my unraveling of why our schools could have sunken to the depths that they have.

If a lawsuit about educrat wrongs is simply a money issue, who is protecting the moral issues? The answer is no one since those rare principled citizens in administration or on boards are usually outvoted. Recognizing that law is codified morality, dodging the law to save money is special interest immorality. Besides, spending hundreds of thousands of dollars to win a case against me rather than admitting the truth and correcting the wrongs in this district, which would have cost far less, is not financially responsible.

This hollow man, who had a fiduciary responsibility to address my appeal to the Board to stop the age discrimination before I filed a lawsuit, only allowed that responsibility to kick in after I filed a lawsuit. And fiduciary means a trusted financial relationship. A tax-sponsored cover-up is not that.

Another board member, with whom I met because she had been a principal and would understand that allowing educrats to harass dedicated, veteran teachers would cause harm to children, proves to be more morally vacant. She meets with me alone, listens to my concerns, and encourages me to present them to the Board, which I do. At the termination hearing, she perjures herself, denying having told me to give my concerns to the Board. Not only were these board members never going to take my concerns seriously, but they also pretended I had no right to have them. The board member who perjures herself votes to terminate me; the other, with whom I met, abstains as if taking no stand preserves absent integrity.

The disillusionment continues; my attorneys are as disappointing as the board members. My first two attorneys, who knew my sole purpose was hearing this in court, took my money and told me to settle or they would abandon me. I found a new attorney who assured me he could get this in court based on a parallel case he had won.

He points out how easy it will be to prove the truth about my district with the documentation I had after seeing my colleagues shrink into a fetal position during their depositions, proving they are holding back terror. He's confident that would convince a jury. I lose on summary judgment. I have no day in court. The federal judge ruled there were no First Amendment issues or age discrimination since the district had hired many teachers over forty.

I don't blame the judge. The Board submitted briefs falsely stating that my principal had hired several over forty full-time teachers when she had hired none. My attorney, who months later tells me someone had "stolen" the precious "principal caught lying" audio tape, proves his untrustworthiness. He failed to dispute or adequately explain that the age complaint was against my principal, not other administrators who had complied with the law. The Board's misleading statistics fool the judge and deprive me of my day in court.

Concerning my being fired over speech, the state held the termination decision for 19 months, well past my chance to use it to appeal my federal case. They rigged it, so I can't prove that I had been fired over speech.

Then, regarding my state case, this union attorney insists that getting my decision is hopeless and that I need a new hearing or a new officer to go over the record if we could retrieve the record from the hearing officer, which she says is debatable. I think it's fishy that she and the ISBE are saying they have no way of getting my record back when it's a public record, and it would be a felony to keep it. That gives you an idea of how stupid they think teachers are. They lie to you, and you figure it must be valid since why would your union lie? That doesn't work for me. He cannot steal a public record, but I'll have a record of him stealing it if he did.

I told her I would have to sue her if she didn't write a letter asking the union to sue the state to demand my record. The union assigns me a new attorney, replacing the semi-retired lawyer who charged them $85 an hour with a big gun who probably tripled the charge. While in California, in March, the ISBE attorney phones. I don't call back. I don't want to ruin my vacation.

Back in Chicago, I go downtown to a swanky law firm to meet my new, more powerful, replaced union attorney. It's April, 2002. My decision was mandated to be at the end of 2000. We meet for four hours. He tries everything you can imagine to get me to give up on obtaining that decision and hold a new trial. He tells me I'm ridiculous since the district has what they want with me going nowhere and that the hearing officer will never rule. I explain that I have two altered documents in the record and am determined to have this exposed in a higher court. He insists I can enter them in a new record. I know that's untrue.

I had tried to submit a medical record showing my blocked artery and need for a heart procedure, and the hearing officer denied it as irrelevant. It was very relevant. So I know this lawyer is wrong.

My hunch is correct. In the later acquired decision, Hearing Officer Rubin accuses me of feigning a medical condition, which he couldn't have done had my document verifying the condition been in the record. I now suspect hiding documents that rise to criminality was another motive for holding the record; they only needed to hide it for three months to put a dagger in my federal case, not the nineteen months they kept it. A new trial would disappear the wildly illegal, altered documents.

I tell him I want that original record and will accept nothing less. He tells me that many teachers wanted to expose what was happening, but none could ever get anywhere and that I am a fool to think I can. He told me not to call the ISBE attorney, who had phoned me while I was on vacation, insisting he would. I point out that he has refused to represent me in court to force the decision or to find the process unconstitutional, so I need to handle the ISBE myself.

I called the ISBE attorney the following week. Guess what? He tells me that he had called me in March to say that due to some "miracle," he finally found Rubin, the hearing officer, who promised "in blood" to rule on July 1, 2002. I asked if he had it in writing. He sent me a fax from Rubin promising a decision in a letter dated before the meeting with the replacement union attorney.

One of two WCCrime acts happened. Either the state failed to inform my union attorney that a decision was forthcoming, which is against state law, which states that all correspondence must be sent to the teacher's attorney or the union attorney knew this decision was coming down and was manipulating me to gain control over the documents. Now that I know the state was in cahoots with the union, I become more determined to take my case to the highest court.

I bet the union knew the decision was coming down. Why else would they pay an attorney, charging way more than $85 per hour, to talk me out of something for four hours? Why would they care if I just sat on it forever if they were correct that he would never rule? They were anxious that I might be able to expose WCCrime with that record. Moreover, I judge the union's duplicity based on its track record, which, according to the majority of NAPTA members, ranges from disappointing to deceitful. The district, state, and union cleverly collaborated to deny me my day in federal and state court.

The only opportunity to expose the truth was via the state tenure termination hearing. That's why that record was so important. Tenure guarantees an unbiased hearing. According to the Constitution, a state cannot take a citizen's property without due process; the right to teach is property. Therefore, hanging in there until they terminated me provided me a guaranteed day in court. Federal court is not assured. A deficient record, in my case, a tax-subsidized-manipulated-deficient record, ended that opportunity.

However, this day in court is in front of a hearing officer, not a jury of peers as the federal case would have been. The ISBE provided a list of hearing officers that are to be unbiased. He didn't belong on that list. What I endured to get a decision was unconscionable. Since hearing officers work for the state, what happened reflected a state interested in silencing a citizen. It was a staged hearing process that did to due process what rigged elections do to democracies, destroy institutions and ideals while pretending to honor them! As pointed out, in addition to denying me an unbiased hearing officer, the state helped my district get my federal case thrown out. Their design to break me down, as does every aspect of teacher abuse, added expense well beyond attorney fees.

With so many working in tandem to keep WCCrime covert, nothing about the legal journey dealt with what the district did. The Board simply used its money and power to silence me. The procedure should have addressed whether they did anything wrong. It held that what they might have done was irrelevant to the termination procedure. No one has investigated their wrongdoing yet, and no one will, as long as those in power choose to silence the rare educators brave enough to speak of it. Thus, although WCCrime is more than teacher abuse, teacher abuse fuels it and, hence, needs to be extinguished, not just for teachers' sake.

HOW THE STATE WOULD SILENCE A TEACHER IF IT DID IT

They held my tenure hearing in the summer of 2000. Hearing Officer Rubin's decision was due that October. As mentioned, it was not forthcoming. The ISBE's incredible, arrogant untruths suggested it believed it could ignore a law requiring it to render a decision in 30 days. It treated the record as if it was not a legal document and as if there were no laws to charge Rubin with obstruction of justice for playing games with a public record. It thought we had the power to do whatever we wanted. It did!

Even though the right to a speedy trial is a cornerstone of our judicial system, and depriving me of my decision for well over a year was not compatible with that right, the state union, IEA, refused to file a lawsuit against their unconstitutional withholding of the decision, so I represented myself.

The attorney general's office said they could not help me despite their alleged concern about teachers. The ACLU said they do not have the money to support this, yet they find the money to support terrorists. Illinois Senator Peter Fitzgerald was the only faint light in the tunnel of abuse. He acknowledged my letter to him and forwarded it to the Justice Department, which did nothing. The rest ignored me or gave me a runaround. I was in limbo until a hearing officer felt like deciding.

I knew it was unwise to demand the decision and incite Rubin's wrath, but the ISBE left me with no choice. I needed to move from limbo to a "real" court that followed the law. After writing hundreds of public officials and imploring a reporter from *The Chicago Tribun* to phone the ISBE, she forced the ISBE's hand. Yet, she did absolutely no follow-up about their wrongdoing.

Rubin decided that my termination stood. In his mean-spirited decision, a 67 single-spaced-paged diatribe that served his personal need to retaliate against me for refusing to settle, he said that I all but called my administrators liars and used terms such as psychological rapists and that this was insubordinate and cause for termination.

My attorney protested his opinion that calling administrators untruthful was insubordinate by asking: What if they were liars? Rubin acknowledged that he did not answer this question. To this day, no one has. Not one legal authority has cared what these administrators did. They were free to do whatever they wanted, leaving the children and me victims of their whims, illegal ones included. Even more outrageous, he terminated me due to my oral and written speech, when a year earlier, the federal court had ruled that I was not terminated over speech and denied me my day in court over this. How fruitful it was to unlawfully hold the decision until my federal case had expired!

To add to the disgusting litany of subterfuge, Rubin stated in his decision that it was good that the Board had not terminated me due to my "Internet Article." Since then, he would have had to do a First Amendment analysis on speech, admitting he didn't do one. They absolutely did fire me over it, which I will show later. And what about terminating me because I spoke of the administrators' untruthfulness? Didn't that also warrant an analysis that could not have been made since no testimony about what they did to me was allowed? He judged my speech in a vacuum, when no citizen can lose their property rights over unexamined speech was the law.

I kept my case moving up through the courts to see if more courts would rubber stamp the outrageous decision and, if so, expose that teachers do not have the right to protected speech about their employers' misconduct. My case revealed that the ISBE, a government body, obstructed my right to a fair trial when they allowed Rubin to hold his decision so he could foil my federal case.

Rubin's statement that the Board had not terminated me due to the "Internet Article" did not reflect the record. I can document three statements where board members stated it was part of their decision to remove me and their attorney's testimony that it was part of their decision. The highlight is that I can show a statement on the record where Rubin himself said it was part of the charges for cause for termination.

If influential people continue to fabricate and manipulate the truth, those affected eventually give up. That is usually true, but not in my case. My plan was to take their false statements, now under oath, to the first authority who would apply the law. I found no court that would. My case is over, but the WCCrime woven throughout remains, and I can end WCCrime with this data once investigated, which is my goal.

Rubin had stated on the record that he did not care if the administrators were picking on me since they were not on trial.

He refused testimony to prove I was retaliated against. Still, despite this obstruction, Rubin stated in his decision that I did not prove retaliation. He did not find that a physician who violated a patient's release was biased. Rubin's position that board members had no business being privy to a tape that showed a team sabotaging a student's progress should outrage anyone who knows that by this opinion, Rubin was severing a special education student's rights and helping a district carry on WCCrime.

It must be that the district's decision-making authorities are entitled to know everything occurring in that district. But immersed in a pack of lies and spins, what chance did I have of getting this scrutinized? Rubin's decision was seething with contradictions to the record and the law; it forced me to defend myself against a corrupted record so I would give up. Their plan.

Meanwhile, the former union president, who gave false testimony at the tenure hearing, secured a job at another school. The targeted librarian earned a job in special education after she falsely signed an affidavit helping the district deny me my day in federal court. As my substitute, who knew I was being railroaded, she promised to testify about my having had lesson plans contrary to the principal's false accusations but let me down.

A year after I was gone, another teacher filed an age discrimination charge against my previous district because the same principal struck again. More tax dollars were squandered, with nothing learned; nothing needs to be understood when the law does not apply to educrats. I began writing this book to tell the public how to save our schools, figuring that we had a court system asleep at the wheel; I now know we have a court system driving us over a cliff. We need to stand tall and unite to grab the wheel.

The Paper Trail, Also Known As Memo Wars

Words are a teacher's only weapon. I use them. I took on the tedious task of creating a paper trail to show WCCrime so that the institutions that ignored it would leave their fingerprints behind. To better describe the journey, I include some of what I wrote along the way, seeking justice for the profession that had called me.

I spent over $300,000 on attorneys. I remember thinking that spending that money was worth more to me than buying a retirement home in a warm state, something Chicago weather makes you crave. There wasn't much else I wanted but didn't have. Soon after, we were able to buy that home. I've always believed that the universe cares for those who respect it. That's why money has never owned my soul. The winter home confirmed my belief.

All the legal documents are still available, including a motion I concocted to hold my Board in criminal contempt of the law in chancery court. That court, where I appealed the termination decision, rubber-stamped everything, including their putting altered documents into the record. So, I made it as obvious as I could.

The motion to hold them criminally responsible was a highlight, if you could call anything light on that journey. It was when my mind gave birth to WCCrime. I enjoyed watching the judge squirm as he labeled it out of his jurisdiction. I had had a different judge for months before submitting that motion. I wonder if the original judge wanted out of my case and passed it on to the new judge the way we used to play hot potato at birthday parties.

I dug up every criminal charge I could find at the law library in downtown Chicago. It became my strange new home for that period. My self-taught legal training may have been lacking, but based on the acts of many current politicians with Harvard and Yale law degrees, I'm not sure I don't know more than them.

My favorite charge was an archaic law finding an attorney violating the law for representing a knowingly false case. Of course, the altered documents, as illegal as they were, gave the motion most of its substance. These documents, you can see for yourself in this book, remain like landmines that have held danger for years. But that only happens if someone ventures to the site. That's my hope. Ronan Farrow comes to mind when I hope.

EPILOGUE: COURT-ASSISTED, END OF A TEACHER STORY

There was other proof of WCCrime. My district's state reading scores declined significantly during my principal's regime. Whereas nearby districts remained mainly in the 90 percentiles at that time, we had a third-grade reading score of 73%, unprecedented in a community of highly educated professionals.

This book only includes my local termination hearing and my appeal to the Chancery Court in Chicago. The rest of my legal journey, which ended at the US Supreme Court, is in the enhanced ebook. It includes the whistle that started all this—the essay I wrote about my school that appeals to public officials for help, which a parent put online.

http://www.endteacherabuse.org/PetitionIntro.html has more about my US Supreme Court saga.

A POEM

TRYING EVERYTHING
TO BE HEARD

By Karen Graver Horwitz,
An idealistic teacher who won't give up

I am a teacher.
They can keep me from teaching children,
But not from teaching
What they are doing to our children.
They cannot terrorize me enough to stop
Teaching the truth,
Because I am a teacher.

I am a teacher,
No longer of children.
Now, I teach teachers all about the power
Given to them because they are teachers.
Chosen to make a difference,
In a world where others are too busy
Acquiring things,
Rather than pursuing ideals
As do teachers.
Most people are survivors—material warriors,
Not teachers.
This was a perfect plan.

A GRAVER DANGER

I am a teacher,
No longer of children.
Now, I teach the public
All about the lies.
How our schools are,
Treasure chests for the greedy,
Who have been allowed
To steal our schools,
Because we have trusted survivors,
And ruined that perfect plan.

I am a teacher,
Replaced by a survivor who is
Slowly edging this world
Toward Materialism,
Away from ideals.
So, I must keep teaching,
Using millions of words,
To bombard the propaganda,
To keep the American dream alive.
Who else will?
Certainly not those who tolerate
White Chalk Crime.™

I am a teacher
Teachers help children grow
So they won't need to spend their lives
Groveling before bullies—
Those obsessed with power
I am a teacher.
Barred from the classroom
I have created my own.
Who will come to my class?
Will those who think only of survival,
Realize that they need to learn this?
Or will they learn this too late because
They foolishly think we're all the same?

A POEM: TRYING EVERYTHING TO BE HEARD

Children need teachers, not survivors.
Yet teachers no longer fit in our schools.
Our schools have become mean,
Self-serving, political, hollow.
I must keep teaching this.

I am a teacher.
In a classroom without walls,
But with plenty of tears.
Yet, I will continue to teach.
I am a teacher

I am a teacher,
Not a survivor.
I am focused on ideals and principles.
God had to make some of us this way
Or there'd be no balance.
Our nation would become all about power,
Competition and greed,
A world of anything goes,
Whatever anyone could finagle.
Including those posing as teachers.
Sadly, it already has.

I am still a teacher.
But can anyone hear me now that survival
Not common purpose has taken the lead?
With the utmost survivors in control:
Corporate warriors with deep pockets for
Propaganda and no respect for ideals?
Yet, not being heard never stopped me.
I am a teacher.
Teachers find a way to teach,
Even when the student resists.
Even when the student is you!

CONCLUSION

Given my age and what I've been through, you'll find this hard to believe, but I swear this is true. I had finished this book, and last night, I had one of my recurring dreams a couple of times a year when I am happily back in the classroom teaching. I struggle because I can't find the teachers' manuals and have no lesson plans. I worry the principal will discover me, but I am so happy to be back.

When recess happens, I feel relief that I'm alone in the room so I can gather needed books. I go into the teacher's closet and discover this was my former classroom, and a lot has stayed the same in that closet. I see my handwriting on things. Then I see a folder with "A graver danger" written in several places and think, "They're going to find out." At the same time, I'm surprised I had written that phrase so many years ago and now find it in my materials. I begin to worry they'll be after me. I decide no, they won't figure out that phrase. They don't know my maiden name. I then woke up.

I'm sure you're amazed that I still have those dreams of joy I'm teaching again—and fear I'm teaching again. Even people close to me have no idea. You may never truly understand what it feels like to be called to teach, but now you know why our children are not safe and why our country has fallen apart. Rest assured, many people like me have been miserable because it wasn't supposed to be like this. I don't have to ask my fellow thrust-from-the-profession teachers whether they have these dreams to know that they do. And, unlike this book, some things in life never conclude. When you're called to teach, the calling never stops. It's not rational. It's spiritual.

I'm not an organized religion fan, but I believe a higher power has a plan. We've messed that up by handing our schools to shysters with no interest in expertise, and we're all paying a high price. I gave you all the necessary information to end the deep state. But more than that, I shared my calling with you, so it will call you as it has called me, and you'll join our group of teachers devoted to a profession that's not a profession. Instead, it's a shame.

Further proof I needed to share my calling is the US Supreme Court's July 1, 2024, decision that reverses our founding fathers' pledge that America will always share power with its people and will never have a king. It created new law that leaves the option of being a king open from now on.

Fortunately, it ruled before it was too late to add to this book. In addition to validating my warnings that Trump will be a king who makes all of us miserable, including the people who support him because that is what kings do, this ruling created a line in the sand that made this book essential reading so people could evaluate their choices. They can cross the Rubicon with this Court and accept a king. Or they can read this book and learn how we got here and how to return to America without a king that so many of us hold sacred.

Our not-so-supreme Supreme Court handed our country what it gave me years ago—a colossal betrayal of our most sacred beliefs. I partly feel like my book revealing what our schools did to us is more critical while thinking, why bother? Then, I remind myself that I must work harder to get this read since I know how democracy has declined. Most do not.

This book is a blueprint that a decent president can use to awaken people's hope, so they'll vote for a candidate who will safeguard our democracy, not the one who asked this Court to remove its crucial guardrails. What happened to me as a teacher has now happened to all citizens of our country—the US Supreme Court telling us we don't have a democracy.

The Court paved the way for a second Trump term, with the presidency having almost limitless powers. You don't have to just take it from me. In her dissent, Justice Sonia Sotomayor wrote, "The Republican appointed-majority in this opinion has … opened the door to a President exercising wide dictatorial powers without any ultimate legal accountability for his actions."

Chief Justice Roberts mocked her and the other two female dissenters for pointing out the dangers of this decision as if they were teachers. It's come full circle. The guardrails are off for everyone, not just teachers. The Court created an upside-down world, making it harder for us to climb out. Education used to ensure they could not do that; WCCrime changed that for education and now for every American. Now, everyone knows what I went through and exactly how I felt when I discovered that my profession was a hoax.

Whereas the Court may have been clueless about education years ago, they saw Trump and his desire to kill his political enemies clearly. They found destroying the rule of law acceptable. They have transformed the rule of law into rule by the lawless. Because our people have been undereducated for decades, they have anointed a king in a country founded on the we-will-have-no-king promise. The crown is in clear site, and although its weight might challenge Trump's royal combover, he will eagerly seek dictatorial power.

The entire premise of this nation was to never have a king, and the whole premise of education was that the people would make sure a king never happened. WCCrime altered our schools and brains enough for this Court to feel safe violating this sacred promise, undoing the law.

This decision has devastated everyone who believes in democracy, as it has devastated teachers for years. However, you are in that place holding this book, a map of how to return to a real democracy.

This book can help change the minds of those who think we need an autocrat to change this nation. One of those leaning toward not voting said she'd feel like voting "If either one [candidate] had a coherent plan like your kid won't get shot in school." This book has that plan. It would thrill voters. Get it to our president ASAP so he will free our schools before a king ensures this book never sees the light of day.

Meanwhile, the more people understand the actual deep state, the more they, like me, will forgive our presidents for not figuring education out. It is simply too complicated and too ignored, and combined with the Harvey Weinstein factor—better to just put up with bullies—it stood little chance of being known. This book shows what it took me to get nowhere for almost thirty years. Even when I succeed, it will still qualify as a winning-the-lottery endeavor. (I decided not to use "if" because Trump is on our doorstep, and I am more determined!)

Pundits wonder how to educate the public. They must help people learn the lessons of this book, including the need to get it to our president. The media owes teachers to support this book after years of failing us. I forgive them for the reasons I cited about how hard WCCrime is to detect. If they continue to fall for the powerful in education when our country needs the media's help to avoid losing our democracy, it is unforgivable. Where's our investigative reporter?

There isn't a better book to get citizens started on a path to save democracy. It explains how we lost it and has a plan for getting it back, which includes moving some voters from Trump to the person who does this for America. We need that to happen before a fatal election.

Having excellent schools would have been a better path for avoiding an authoritarian takeover. Learning why this happened is our only choice now.

Other recent Supreme Court decisions began dismantling the administrative state in line with Project 2025. This decision just removed our country's soul. The rest of us must use this book to restore it. Despair and fatalism are the tools of authoritarianism. Hope is the antidote. You have now been inoculated.

I've introduced you to the people who've made school reform impossible and why they block reform by design. It's time to exile

CONCLUSION

them so reform can begin. Almost everyone has taken education for granted, and that is its fatal flaw. A handful of scholarly, dedicated types care about what's wrong with education. Still, our work doesn't go viral for reasons explained in this book. Here's hoping this book becomes a springboard for change. For the sake of this country, it must.

"Never in the history of our Republic has a President had reason to believe that he would be immune from criminal prosecution if he used the trappings of his office to violate the criminal law. Moving forward, however, all former Presidents will be cloaked in such immunity … With fear for our democracy, I dissent." Supreme Court Justice Sotomayor said about the Supreme Court's most impactful decision to help free our president from criminal prosecution for things like starting an insurrection or murdering a political enemy.

With fear for our democracy, I offer this book.

TAKE ACTION FOR DEMOCRACY & THANK YOU

It's time that NAPTA members, who, after eighteen years, took the time to participate in a podcast to help others understand the truth about education, became influencers and celebrities for democracy. Go to https://soundcloud.com/ karen-horwitz/howwegottrumped?ref=clipboard &p=i&c=1 Listen to the wisdom of the teacher harassed for trying to stop another Columbine.

Please do your part to save our democracy. Share this book on social media! Help shine a light on the good people who will give us good government and authentic reporting. We will know them when we see them do the work to hear and support dedicated teachers. Once citizens see them doing this work and apologize for not doing it, they will replace the toxic rage with hope, which has gone missing for understandable reasons.

Learn more at http://www.endteacherabuse.org/ background.html#twenty. Read testimony from hundreds of dedicated teachers.

Our country has a history of dodging controversial issues. The sinister corruption in our schools is virtually unknown, so not dealing with it will remain its destiny unless this book goes viral. Only movements with large numbers force those in power to deal with change. There is little anyone can do about this alone. The minute I tried to make a difference, I was deemed an outsider and left to give up on the world I loved. After trying everything possible for three decades, no one knows this better than I do. Only a movement will change this.

Your children are right to be afraid and disappointed in adults letting this happen. Active shooter drills are a disgrace we've accepted. Teachers with guns will make matters even worse. Until we create a grassroots movement to turn our counterfeit schools into legitimate schools, sending children to our schools is playing Russian roulette with their lives.

We need your support. http://www.endteach-erabuse.org/MemForm/MembershipForm.html Membership is free.

Ending school shootings is but one goal of this book. Real schools will save democracy. This book has a chapter with solutions that, once known, will allow education to lead us from the chaos we are experiencing to a far more perfect union. These solutions must be studied, improved, and employed!

This is about our schools. Our political solutions for this nation might differ, but we all agree that our schools are not okay. We must unite over our schools, not politics, to expose corruption and force change. Don't let anything weaken our power to make our schools what they should be.

NAPTA has never been partisan. We blame the unions, the courts, the media, the ACLU, and political leaders from both parties for the shameful practices in our schools. Both parties need to listen to us. Our solution lies in the hearts of people who care about education, creating a movement that will be heard. We cannot let politics steal our solution for authentic schools. Instead, let politics untangle from its currently dreadful state once we have schools that support a democracy—something that's been missing for decades.

Help force our counterfeit schools to become legitimate schools. When you join, you can request a PDF of QuickNotes, a quick overview explaining WCCrime. Or sign up with a short statement about what you learned from this book in the comment box and request a PDF of the enhanced ebook.

Tell your friends to sign up, too! When signing up, they can ask for a free PDF of CHAPTER 10 of this book: "FINALLY the Why Behind School Shootings—WCCrime's Miserable Curse" and/or a PDF of QuickNotes.

Thank you for wanting to be wise about the sacred foundation of our democracy. Join and help us earn our investigative reporter, who will verify the truth about our schools and compel authentic reform for our children and our democracy. http://www.endteacherabuse.org/MemForm/ MembershipForm.html. Membership is free. Not joining will cost us all more misery.

We promise anonymity for all who need it—working teachers! Thank you for reading this book!!!!!

Dedicated to the children, I remain,

Miss Karen Graver, Mrs. Karen Adrian, Mrs. Karen Horwitz,

—My three names when I taught, mainly in Illinois (1968-69 in Phoenix, Arizona) between 1966 and 1999, in case any of my students read this book and want to contact me. Because I knew them, it was much easier to do this work.

I won't give up as long as we have a democracy. Look for me teaching about WCCrime and that includes Tic Tok or wherever I need to go to make the theft of our schools known!

Meet the teacher determined to teach you: what happened to America?

ENDNOTES

1   https://www.npr.org/2024/06/17/1198912663/social-media-warning-label-surgeon-general-youth-mental-health-crisis-lawsuit

2   https://www.theatlantic.com/magazine/archive/2023/09/us-culture-moral-education-formation/674765/

3   "Jesse Watters' Fawning Over Trump Mug Shot Street Art Goes Seriously Sideways" https://www.huffpost.com/ entry/street-art-mugshot-donald-trump_n_64edca2be4b 03845723dbf3a?ncid= APPLENEWS00001

4   https://www.kpbs.org/news/2009/sep/22/richard-dreyfuss-fights-civics-american-education/

5   https://gadflyonthewallblog.com/2023/08/07/teach-for- america-promised-to-fix-the-teacher-exodus-before- anyone-even-noticed-there-was-one-now-its-choking-on-its- own-failure/

6   http://www.endteacherabuse.org/dreamer.html

7   http://www.endteacherabuse.org/Kimball.html

8   https://www.chalkbeat.org/2023/7/25/23806247/parents-schools-covid-anger-polling-satisfaction

9   Rudy Crew's WCCrime history; OPPORTUNITIES LOST: How Personnel At August Martin High School Mishandled A Breach Of Security And The Rape Of A Student In Classroom 324 SEE EXTENDED ENDNOTES- https://www.whitechalk-crime.com/references/

10 http://www.endteacherabuse.org/DownLoadWCC/JohnSam.pdf

11 https://www.nbcnews.com/news/us-news/investigation-georgia-teen-found-dead-gym-mat-closed-charges-rcna13868#

12 https://www.nbcnews.com/news/us-news/parents-teen-found-dead-rolled-gym-mat-meet-officials-plead-flna8c11493315

13 https://www.laprogressive.com/education-reform/civic-education-foundational-to-democracy

14 https://www.thedreyfussinitiative.org/about-us/

15 https://thehill.com/capital-living/cover-stories/113632-qa-with-richard-dreyfuss/

16 http://www.endteacherabuse.org/testing.html

17 https://nncwa.com/special-grand-jury-concludes-its-investigation-and-report-on-the-shooting-at-richneck-elementary-school/

18 https://apnews.com/article/abby-zwerner-teacher-shot-6yearold-virginia-newport-news-richneck-118dd583e32c04b72b5f8f793ffbfb2b

19 https://abcnews.go.com/US/US/virginia-assistant-principal-charged-year-after-6-year/story? id = 109084407

20 After this teacher retired he allowed us to add his name: See his You Tube at: endteacherabuse.org/AnonUSA3.html

21 Published by: The Baltimore Sun, by Ira Chaleff, February 14, 2008

22 http://www.endteacherabuse.org/AnonUSA3.html

23 https://www.laprogressive.com/education-reform/civic-education-foundational-to-democracy

24 https://robertreich.substack.com/p/the-common-good-chapter-10-civic

25 https://reason.com/2014/08/27/la-schools-1-billion-ipad-fiasco-ends-af/

26 https://tultican.com/2020/07/29/infamous-john-deasy-resigned-under-suspicious-circumstances-again/

ENDNOTES

27 https://www.homelandsecuritynewswire.com/dr20150617-violence-and-corruption-scandal-at-cbp-fbi-clean-up-or-cover-up-pt-6?page=0,1

28 https://www.youtube.com/watch?v=DM1KYW5cPN8

29 https://www.theatlantic.com/politics/archive/2020/09/trump-americans-who-died-at-war-are-losers-and-suckers/615997/

30 https://christiancountytrumpet.com/ozark-teacher-waiting-for-axe-to-fall-part-1/

31 https://dailysoundandfury.com/the-trump-voters-who-just-want-to-watch-the-world-burn-and-2all-of-us-along-with-it/

32 https://edsource.org/2023/when-we-fail-education-we-fail-democracy/699281

33 https://www.ky3.com/2024/01/22/missouri-legislation-aims-tie-superintendent-salaries-that-starting-teachers/

34 By D. Dowd Muska, posted in the Journal Inquirer, January 17, 2008

Printed in Great Britain
by Amazon

59535685R00218